Marketing Communication Management

Otto Ottesen

MARKETING COMMUNICATION MANAGEMENT

Copenhagen Business School Press
HANDELSHØJSKOLENS FORLAG

Marketing Communication Management

© *Copenhagen Business School Press*, 2001
Cover designed by Kontrapunkt
Book designed by Jørn Ekstrøm
Set in Plantin and printed by Nørhaven, Viborg, Denmark
1. edition 2001
ISBN 87-16-13335-8

The preparation of the manuscript in English
has been supported financially by
The Rogaland Foundation for Higher Education
and Research in Business Administration
and Pro&Contra Marketing

Distribution:

Scandinavia
Munksgaard/DBK, Siljangade 2-8, P.O. Box 1731
DK-2300 Copenhagen S, Denmark
phone: +45 3269 7788, fax: +45 3269 7789

North America
Copenhagen Business School Press
Books International Inc.
P.O. Box 605
Herndon, VA 20172-0605, USA
phone: +1 703 661 1500, fax: +1 703 661 1501

Rest of the World
Marston Book Services, P.O. Box 269
Abingdon, Oxfordshire, OX14 4YN, UK
phone: +44 (0) 1235 465500, fax: +44 (0) 1235 465555
E-mail Direct Customers: direct.order@marston.co.uk
E-mail Booksellers: trade.order@marston.co.uk

All rights reserved. No part of this publication may be reproduced or used in any form or by any means
– graphic, electronic or mechanical including photocopying, recording, taping or information storage or
retrieval systems – without permission in writing from Copenhagen Business School Press, Solbjergvej 3,
DK 2000 Copenhagen F, Denmark.

Preface

This book is intended for students of marketing at university level and practitioners who wish to develop their competence in strategic marketing communication planning and management.

The presented holistic approach to strategic marketing communication management is a result of many years of research, teaching, and practice. I first put forward the need for a more holistic view of marketing communication in an article published in 1964*. The present text is based on my most recent book on marketing communication management: *Markedskommunikasjon – Strategisk helhetsplanlegging for økt lønnsomhet* ("Marketing communication – Strategic holistic planning for increased profitability", Copenhagen 1997.)

My work on developing a holistic approach has been inspired and supported by a number of colleagues and practitioners. In particular I would like to thank professors Ole Hagh and John Ibsen Kjeldsen at the Aarhus School of Business and Hans-Øyvind Sagen, managing director of Pro&Contra Marketing, for interesting discussions on concepts and hypotheses, and for their willingness to try out relevant ideas in teaching and practice. I would also like to thank my former students at Stavanger University College, The Norwegian School of Management, the Copenhagen Business School and the Aarhus School of Business. Their perceptive questions, comments, and suggestions have been of great assistance to me in developing the concept of a holistic approach.

* See list of references.

I am especially indebted to my colleague and friend, professor Brian Oliver, for his competent, patient and accurate support in preparing the manuscript in English. I would also like to express my gratitude to the Rogaland Foundation for Higher Education and Research in Business Administration, Stavanger, and Pro&Contra Marketing, Sandnes, for their financial support.

Last, but not least, I would like to thank my dear wife, Turid, for her untiring inspiration and patient support.

Stavanger, Norway, in September 2000

Otto Ottesen

Contents

Preface 5

Part I: Introduction 15

**1. Purpose, underlying assumptions
   and outline of contents** 17
   Purpose 17
   Underlying assumptions 23
   On buyer behavior 23
   On company goals 24
   On planning, implementation and management 24
   Outline of contents 26
   The concepts of "marketing tool" and "product" 27

**Part II: Outline of a holistic view of marketing
           communication** 29

**2. Marketing communication: Concept and
   functions. Marketing communication tools** 31
   Types of marketing tools. The distinction between
      offering and communication tools 31
   The marketing offering 31
   Marketing communication 35
   Buyer and seller initiative 36
   Standardized and customized offerings. Standard and
      (competence) transformation communication 39
   On the interplay between marketing offering and
      marketing communication 41
   Four main types of marketing communication 43

  Marketing communication tools: Media and
    communication symbols 43
  Marketing communication costs: Media and
    content symbolization costs 48
  Summing up 48
  The concepts of "receipt", "handling" and "follow-up"
    of orders and inquiries 51

**3. Marketing communication strategy as part
of a company's total business strategy** 53
  A strategy model. Marketing communication strategy
    as one of six sub-strategies 54
  Implications for marketing communication planning . . . 59
  Summing up the elements of a marketing
    communication strategy 61

**Part III: Further elaboration of a holistic
    approach to marketing communication:
    The marketing offering and the tasks of
    marketing communication** 67

4. Describing the marketing offering 69
  Identifying the appropriate elements in an offering . . . 69
  Identifying elements in an offering via
    "the buyer's route" 69
  Stimulating the identification process. Examples of
    elements in offerings and relevant buyer experiences 73
  At what conceptual level should the elements in an
    offering be identified? 76
  Describing the marketing offering 79
  Describing an offering on the basis of its elements . . . 79
  Describing a marketing offering on the basis of
    buyers' relevance criteria and buyer value 80
  On buyers, users, consumers, buying units and
    relevance criteria segments 84
  Summing up 87

5. Transformation communication. Conveying the marketing offering in transformation markets .. 91
Vendor roles and customization processes in transformation markets.......................... 91
The buying process and the task of conveying the offering in transformation markets. The relevance of supplier criteria 94
Summing up. Describing the marketing offering in transformation markets...................... 97
Marketing offering, marketing communication and buyer-seller relationships 100

6. Developing buyer competence. Summing up the tasks of marketing communication......... 103
The development task of marketing communication.. 103
Summing up the tasks of marketing communication . 106

7. How communication tasks are determined by degree of market penetration of a product, an offering or company reputation 109
The relationship between communication tasks and degree of market penetration of a product 109
Degree of product penetration 109
Product penetration and development tasks 111
Market development versus market utilization 112
Non-durable products: The relationship between communication tasks and the degree of market penetration of an offering 112
The degree of penetration of an offering 112
The degree of market penetration of an offering and the nature and extent of communication tasks . 115
Durable products: The relationship between communication tasks and company reputation 116
Transformation markets........................ 118
Strategic implications.......................... 119
Changes in the nature and number of communication tasks 119
Changes in the extent of buyer initiative........... 120
Summing up. A communication task matrix 124

8. Marketing offering and communication effect .. 129
Can marketing communication have a function that is unrelated to the inherent properties of an offering? . 130
Do buyers have to take some properties of an offering on trust? 130
Some properties cannot be experienced until after purchase 132
Buyers may not be sufficiently competent 134
Added value may be created through association ... 135
Does the offering have to be competitive? 138
Summing up 139

Part IV: Holistic strategic marketing communication planning 141

9. Strategic, holistic marketing communication planning: Process, tasks, and premises 143
Planning process and planning tasks 143
Analyzing and describing the planning premises 153

10. Carrying out the task analysis: Surveying and describing the communication tasks 163
The task analysis: Purpose and procedure 163
Estimating the overall demand, turnover and contribution potential 166
Assessing the competitive strength of the offering and organizational basis 169
Diagnosing the extent and nature of the communication tasks 170
Outlining the task structure: The Market Map 170
Describing the specific communication tasks 175
Assessing the extent and nature of buyer initiative .. 177
An example 181

11. Developing a target group strategy: Prioritizing buyer segments and selecting target groups 189
Viability and profitability criteria. Target groups 189

Segmenting and prioritizing: The procedure 191
On profitability criteria 194
Two possible search procedures 194
Criteria based search 195
Contribution and cost based search 197
The Prioritization Path: A search and
   prioritization model 201
The course of the Prioritization Path 203
Using the Prioritization Path as a planning tool 205
Coordinating the selection of end-buyer and
   dealer target groups 205

12. Developing a content strategy 209
Impact of content strategy on symbolization
   and media strategy 209
A communication model and the concept of
   "content" 210
Outline of the strategy development process 215
Identifying, prioritizing and clarifying content
   elements 215
The content platform: Concept and functions 217
Clarifying, prioritizing and selecting core content . . . 220
Clarifying core content 220
Prioritizing core content 223
Facilitative communication content 225
Various kinds of facilitative content 225
Prioritizing facilitative content 227
Selecting communication content in the context
   of low involvement. Three hypotheses 228
Clarifying, prioritizing and selecting content
   in transformation communication 230
Summing up 231

13. Developing a media strategy:
Task, media and media characteristics 233
The media 234
Buyer and seller initiative media 234
Controllable and uncontrollable media 235

The elements of a media strategy. Action planning
   and preparatory planning 236
The elements of a buyer initiative media strategy . . . 236
The elements of a seller initiative media strategy 239
Relevant media characteristics 241
Exposure capacity 243
Communication capacity 248
"Intrusiveness" 252
Competing stimuli 252
Media attitudes and behavior 253
Closeness to point of purchase 254
Timing flexibility 254
Cost characteristics 254
Summing up 258

14. Developing a media strategy: The process 259
The media strategy development process 259
Aspects of buyer initiative media strategy
   development 265
Expected buyer initiative as a starting point
   for strategy development 265
Preliminary media evaluation and strategy search . . . 270
Aspects of seller initiative media strategy
   development 271
The seller initiative gap as a starting point for
   strategy development 271
Preliminary media evaluation and strategy search . . . 278
Determining frequency and extent of media use.
   A theory of response functions 280
Timing exposures and media use 289
Summing up 291
Low-involvement, response and media use 293
Media strategy development in transformation
   markets 294
Media strategy development in markets with
   intermediaries 296

15. Developing a symbolization strategy 301
   Symbolization as a communication tool 301
   The scope and elements of a symbolization strategy . 303

16. Holistic strategic marketing communication planning: Some further issues 307
   Setting aside five simplifying assumptions 307
   Vendor company is newly formed 307
   Heterogeneous relevance/supplier criteria 308
   Decision units have more than one member 308
   The company offers a range of offerings: "Cross-communication", "separate communication" and "co-communication" 309
   Planning cross-communication and co-communication. The concept of a "locomotive offering" . . . 312
   Adapting communication strategy to changed planning premises 316
   Some comments on pre- and post-control 318
   Information sources and information use 321

17. Summing up a holistic approach to strategic marketing communication planning 329
   A holistic approach to strategic marketing communication planning: A summary 329
   A framework for describing, monitoring and developing a company's marketing communication strategy 331
   Comments on long-term effects and long-range planning 337
   Introducing holistic strategic planning in an organization 340

References 345

Subject index 348

Notes 353

Part I

Introduction

1. Purpose, underlying assumptions and outline of contents

Purpose

This book is intended for students of marketing at university level, as well as practitioners who wish to develop their competence in marketing communication planning and management. Its purpose is to introduce a view of marketing communication and an approach to marketing communication planning which differ in several respects from those prevalent in contemporary marketing literature and practice.

In this book:

1. "Marketing communication" refers to *every kind of communication between a company and buyers about what it has to offer.*

The term covers *absolutely all kinds of communication media,* i.e. one-way as well as two-way processes, mass and individual as well as personal and impersonal communication. Advertising media are relevant, as are all kinds of personal meetings and conferences between two or more persons, ordinary sales calls, stationary and mobile telephones, video and telephone conferences, order phones, hot-lines, facsimile transmitters, letters, and e-mail. The term encompasses not only communication activities, which are typically planned and implemented by a sales- and/or marketing department. It also embraces every communicative episode occurring between buyers and any of the company's employees, e.g. between an industrial buyer and a production manager or product developer, between a guest and a hotel receptionist or between a customer of a consulting firm and a switchboard operator. The aim of marketing communication planning is to develop an integrated plan covering all these communication processes.

In marketing literature, as well as in marketing practice, the term "marketing communication" is generally used in a much narrower sense than that indicated above. It typically covers advertising, some elements of sales promotion, such as point of purchase activities, and personal selling.[1] The more recent, and seemingly wider, concept, "*integrated* marketing communications", includes activities such as public relations (PR), direct marketing and event marketing.[2] Other kinds of communication are "personal selling", "sponsoring", "telephone selling" (or "telemarketing"), "correspondence", "personal communication", "dialogue marketing", "negotiating", and "Internet/ interactive marketing".[3]

This means that the field of marketing communication is divided into a number of separate, relatively narrow and isolated disciplines. Textbooks and research publications typically deal with either advertising or personal selling or sponsoring etc. Planning tools offered in the form of concepts, models and methods are partial and designed to optimize such things as the advertising budget, the advertising media mix, salesmen's traveling routes and the sub-division of a market into sales districts. Of course, such tools lead to sub-optimization. The same narrow focus is true of courses offered in university marketing programs as well as of practical planning procedures and decision-making.

2. The suggested concepts, models and planning procedures are general.

This means that they can be used as a basis for marketing communication planning, whether the company is large or small, whether or not it operates in a consumer or industrial market and whether or not it offers physical products such as machines or services such as consulting assistance.

In contrast to this, each type of market and product constitutes a separate (sub-) field with its own textbooks, articles and courses in the existing marketing literature and educational programs. For example, some textbooks, articles and courses deal with consumer advertising, while others deal with industrial advertising. Implicitly or explicitly, much of the literature deals with large companies operating in consumer markets.[4]

3. Marketing communication planning is discussed at a strategic level.

Concepts, models and methods found in the existing literature, in university courses and in practical use, are heavily oriented towards tactical decisions. Typical issues are selection of advertising media, methods of advertising budgeting and procedures for dividing a market into optimal sales districts.

The aim of this book is to discuss how to develop a *coherent* marketing communication strategy. In this context, the term *"strategy"* means *the general pattern of a company's communication activities, e.g. of its use of relevant communication channels.* A procedure for strategy development will be suggested which emphasizes the interdependence of marketing communication activities and other elements of a company's strategy. These other elements include the "pattern" of the markets in which the company operates and its organization and relations with the business environment. In this connection special importance is attached to the competitiveness of the company's marketing offering, i.e. its product, price, guarantee etc.

4. Marketing communication planning includes planning for buyer-initiated as well as seller-initiated communication processes.

It seems obvious that the sales volume a company makes may follow from initiatives taken by buyers as well as those taken by the company itself. Buyer initiatives may follow from such things as previous experience of the company's product(s) and favorable word-of-mouth communications. Buyer-initiated communication may actually account for a major part of a company's sales. Despite this, writers and researchers have paid scant attention to the relevance of buyer initiative for marketing strategy and tactics. According to the prevailing view, the term "marketing communication" includes seller initiative only.

In this book, however, great importance is attached to the extent and nature of buyer initiative. Estimation of the sales (volume) potential arising from buyer initiatives, as well as access and dialogue in the form of handling and follow-up of buyer-initiated orders and inquiries, are among the topics that will be considered closely here. Depending on the type of market in question, as well as other circumstances, such dialogues may take the shape of inquiring and responding to inquiries about the attributes of a specific offering, or discussions and talks leading, when successful, to the development of a customized offering.

5. Strategy development is based on a task analysis that indicates the marketing communication tasks for a forthcoming planning period.

The extent and nature of communication tasks in one period of time depends, among other things, on the effect of communication activities in previous periods. For example, the larger the number of buyers who are aware of a company's offerings and have relevant knowledge about them, the fewer the number of communication tasks. However, when a company changes its offering, new and more extensive communication tasks arise in order to inform buyers in the market place.

Keeping track of a company's communication tasks is vital if it is to be able to make realistic decisions as to the amount of resources to be spent on communication and how these resources should be allocated to various activities. Task analyses help to keep strategy development dynamic. Surprisingly little attention has been paid to this topic in marketing research and literature.

6. Profitability is in sharp focus.

One main goal of a company is to make money. Strategic communication planning cannot be carried out without considering the effects on sales volume, turnover, contribution margin, costs and profit. The planning procedure and models proposed here focus on the impact of alternative solutions upon such things as contribution margins, the marketing communication cost budget and the operating budget. The *"marketing communication cost budget"*, of course, should embrace costs incurred by all kinds of communication.

Contemporary marketing literature is too fragmented to offer appropriate tools for communication strategy development that is directed towards profitability. In general, scant attention is paid to sales volume, turnover and costs. A typical example is advertising management literature, which places very little emphasis on sales volume and cost budgeting and profitability. Models and procedures proposed in the literature within the various sub-fields can at best be used for sub-optimization purposes.

This book sets out to

1. introduce a *holistic view of marketing communication.*

2. suggest *a procedure for holistic strategic marketing communication planning* to be followed in order to develop a coherent marketing communication strategy.

3. suggest *concepts, models etc. to be used in order to solve the various planning tasks* in the strategy development process.

The view and planning procedure suggested here rests on the belief that increased insights and the development of useful practical tools for planning and management call for a more holistic approach. The partial approaches, which have hitherto been predominant in scientific work, have unquestionably produced a vast amount of useful knowledge. However, the limits of partial approaches to both theoretical and empirical research are widely recognized among researchers. These violate the widely accepted maxim that "the whole is more than the sum of its parts". For example, marketing researchers have paid little attention to the interplay between various kinds of marketing communication, such as advertising and the handling of orders and inquiries, which is itself essential for effective communication. Moreover, partial approaches often overlook relevant phenomena. The importance of buyer initiative for communication planning, mentioned earlier, is a case in point. The emergence of fields such as "system theory", "total quality management" and "strategic planning and management" indicate a growing recognition of the need for holistic approaches in business administration research. The approach introduced here should be seen in the light of that need.

Of course, no approach, model or procedure can be truly "holistic" in the sense that it captures every aspect of "reality". The word should be interpreted in a relative sense when applied to an approach or to strategic planning. Like any other phenomenon in the real world, marketing communication may – and should – be viewed, explored and modeled in numerous more or less holistic ways. In this field, as elsewhere, the advance of knowledge depends on variety in theoretical and methodological approach. So the intention here is to propose a more holistic approach to marketing communication than the prevailing one and, based on this, a more holistic and strategic marketing communication planning procedure.

The suggestions offered here are made in the belief that they will prove fruitful in practice and that they will lead to increased company profitability. In educational programs they may serve as a basis for developing a wider, more general competence in marketing communication planning and management. Hopefully, they might also inspire researchers to evolve a more basic and general theory of marketing communication. Our existing knowledge about marketing communication activities such as advertising and personal selling may then be fitted into the theory as sub-fields of specialization.

In the following discussion, several new concepts, models etc. are introduced in order to develop a holistic view of marketing communication and its associated procedures for strategic marketing communication planning. The work of other writers will be extensively drawn upon. This book aims broadly at a holistic "structuring" of what is, in the author's view, a field of marketing communication. It does not set out to summarize or assess existing knowledge in the various sub-disciplines or attempt to go into them in any depth. However, some writers will be referred to in connection with specific, important issues. Concepts that have become common property within the field of marketing will consistently be used without reference. Examples are concepts such as "consumer", "segmentation" and "habitual behavior". Suggestions and opinions presented here are also heavily influenced by the author's own practical experience within the field of marketing, strategy development and organization. It is hoped that the reader will accept that a number of opinions are presented rather bluntly in order to make a point.

Underlying assumptions

This text is based on the following implicit assumptions.

On buyer behavior

Buyer behavior is assumed to be goal-oriented. Behavior is driven by needs or motives and governed by cognitive processes and dispositions. Examples of cognitive processes are awareness, interpretation, thinking and remembering. Such processes are also referred to as "information processing". An example of a cognitive disposition would be a person's tendency to perceive elements in the environment, such as particular product brands.

Changes in buyer behavior may take place through various modes of learning, i.e. through insight (information processing), trial and error (instrumental conditioning) and association (classical conditioning). Buyers generally learn to make decisions and act in a way that most fully satisfies their needs. Consequently, they generally tend to choose the product or the supplier that seems to offer the greatest satisfaction at the least cost. This *difference between satisfaction and cost* is referred to here as *"buyer value"*.[5]

Buyer value reflects the buyer's *subjective* perception rather than any objective assessment. The buyer is assumed to be (subjectively) rational. Rationality is, however, limited by the individual's cognitive capacity. Buyers inevitably fail to cope with a complex and ever changing environment. For instance, habits formed on the basis of rational assessment cease to be rational when individuals ignore subsequently improved offerings. The amount of relevant information may be too large for a buyer to cope with. Information processing may also take place on the basis of insufficient knowledge.

These assumptions are widely accepted in contemporary literature on buyer behavior and will be familiar to many readers.[6]

On company goals

The main assumption made here relating to company goals is that the primary goal of a company is to earn money. This is not to say that a company may not have other legitimate goals. However, this book focuses upon profitability, albeit not without reservation. While the nature of truth may often be contentious, the discussion that follows rests on the axiom that one should consistently aim at telling what one believes to be the truth about a company's offering when planning marketing communication. The author regards attitudes to honesty in marketing as very important and, for this reason, certain concepts, hypotheses and models are not included in the following discussion. One example is a rather well-known hypothesis regarding the effect of one-sided as opposed to two-sided argumentation.[7] This hypothesis implies the following decision rule: If a buyer is "incompetent" in the sense that he is unaware of certain negative features of a product, then choose to convey a one-sided message, i.e. a message that conveys only the advantages of the product. If, on the other hand, the buyer in question already knows about the drawbacks, a two-sided message should be chosen, telling about pros as well as cons. Hypotheses of this kind are not considered acceptable as a basis for discussing choice of communication content.

On planning, implementation and management

The main assumption relating to planning, made here, is that the goal to be reached is a certain budgeted operating profit.

While it makes obvious sense to call such things as advertisements "marketing tools", it may, at first sight, seem contradictory to use that term to apply to a feature of the product itself. However, insofar as a company can control such factors as the quality or price of a product, these too can be considered as *tools* in the marketing process because the seller is able to *use* them to achieve the desired goal. The relationship between such marketing tools and operating profit depends on the nature of the business environment i.e. the characteristics of buyers, competition, and various societal and natural conditions. A planner's task, then, is to lay down guidelines regarding the use of marketing tools in ways that are appropriate to his company's goal and the nature of the business environment. In *"operative planning"*, guidelines are detailed. In *"strategic planning"* guidelines take the form of overall patterns. (See Figure 2.1.)

A planner can merely aim at developing a *satisfactory* – not an *optimal* – plan.[8] Marketing planning is a complex process of problem solving. The pace of change in the business environment is increasing and becoming ever more complex. Among other things, new marketing communication channels, such as the Internet, are constantly emerging. Strategic planning requires analytical capacity as well as creativity and sound intuition. Planners have to cope with considerable complexity and uncertainty. They can never be aware of all possible options, and consequently, their judgments are bound to rest partly on expectations regarding future developments and partly on presumed means-end relationships. Given these conditions, in the real world, optimal solutions will always be elusive.

In the light of this, marketing theory may be of use to a planner and serve to enhance competence by offering various perspectives, concepts, hypotheses, models, methods and other tools. The suggestions in this book relating to these have a holistic perspective, a procedure for holistic strategic marketing communication planning and a number of concepts, hypotheses and models that may be used in order to carry through such a procedure. Among other things, the hypotheses concern relevant characteristics of the business environment, such as buyer characteristics, the interplay between various marketing tools, and the relationship between these tools, the environment and sales, costs and operating profit.

"*Strategic management*" consists of strategic planning (strategy development) and strategy implementation. Holistic strategic marketing communication management should not be understood as a straightforward two-step process. It is not just a matter of first making a comprehensive written strategic plan to be followed up and implemented. Nor should the term "*planner*" (used extensively below) be understood to mean merely a specialist developing a company's marketing communication strategy. In most cases, a large proportion of a company's staff – employees as well as managers, will and should be involved in the development and implementation of a marketing communication strategy. How much of a plan should be put down in writing, depends on the circumstances. In an ever changing and complex environment, a written plan tends to date rather quickly. While strategy development and strategy implementation may take place in two consecutive distinct events, more often than not they are interwoven activities and must take place piecemeal, in small steps, as a continual process of incremental learning.

It should be noted that in the following, the terms "strategic planning" and "strategy development" are used interchangeably.

Outline of contents

The four remaining parts of this book have the following contents. Part II sets out to give a rough outline of a holistic approach to marketing communication. In Part III a number of important aspects of a holistic approach are elaborated. Part IV discusses how strategic, holistic planning of marketing communication can be carried through. An outline of the planning process is given, and the various planning tasks that have to be solved in order to develop a coherent marketing communication strategy are discussed. Part IV also contains a discussion of issues connected with information sources and use. Other issues touched on are the adoption and implementation of a holistic approach and holistic strategic planning in a company and ways in which a holistic approach may serve as a framework for describing, monitoring, developing and implementing changes in a company's marketing communication strategy.

The concepts of "marketing tool" and "product"

It has been pointed out that such things as the quality or price of a product can be considered as *tools* in the marketing process because the seller is able to *use* them to achieve an operating profit. In the following discussion, the term *"marketing tool"* is used to refer to *any element affecting sales volume and/or costs that can be controlled by a company*. A marketing tool may have several sub-elements, aspects, components, dimensions or properties. The product itself is a marketing tool with several elements, dimensions or properties. Product properties or dimensions of a car model include its design, color, driving characteristics and the number and types of its safety features. The *use* of a marketing tool, such as the specific design or price of a car model, is determined by organizational processes connected to such matters as planning, decision-making, organizational development and management.

It should be noted that in this book the term *"product"* is used in two different senses. The first of these is in the *generic* sense of the word, referring to *product categories* such as cars, buildings, hairdressing, and charter trips. Generic products may be tangible products (e.g. physical products such as cars and beer) or intangible products (i.e. services such as consulting assistance and training courses). Where there might be uncertainty as what is meant the term "physical product" will be used to refer to a tangible product. The second sense refers to *the specific form that the product takes as part of a company's offering*. For example the specific design, engine power, and performance of a car model as distinct from other elements such as guarantee, price, terms of delivery etc.

Part II

Outline of a holistic view of marketing communication

The second part of this book sets out to introduce some concepts, hypotheses and models underlying a holistic view of marketing communication. The main issues dealt with in Chapter 2 are the concept of "marketing communication", the tasks of marketing communication in marketing, the relevance of buyer initiative for marketing communication planning, marketing tools and costs of marketing communication.

Chapter 3 discusses marketing communication strategy as part of a company's total business strategy.

2. Marketing communication: Concept and functions. Marketing communication tools

Types of marketing tools. The distinction between offering and communication tools

All conceivable marketing tools can be grouped into two main categories. These are:

1. *"marketing offering tools"* (use of properties of the marketing offering itself), and
2. *"marketing communication tools"*.

The specific ways in which features of an offering are used determine the company's marketing offering. Similarly, the ways in which marketing communication tools are used determine the company's marketing communication.

This means that marketing consists of

1. delivering an offering, and
2. communicating about that offering.

The marketing offering

The term *"marketing offering"* covers *everything relevant to the buyer in connection with preparing to buy, carrying through the purchase of, using and consuming a company's product.* In other words, an offering has several elements and includes everything that contributes to the "buyer's *total experience"* in the form of *"sacrifices and rewards"* – i.e. the experienced or perceived (net-) buyer value

– of obtaining and using or consuming a company's product. This value may be measured in terms of pleasure, displeasure, effort, cost or gain.

Obviously, the product in question is an important part of an offering. Product features such as appearance, function and packaging may be experienced as favorable or unfavorable, rewarding or involving some kind of sacrifice on the part of the buyer. Elements in an offering may include various kinds of promotion such as premiums and coupons, sponsorship of sports or the arts. Other elements are price, service, guarantees, terms of payment, treatment of complaints, and terms and observance of delivery. Friendly attention in the course of making a purchase or obtaining a service would be counted among the rewards or benefits. The price, time and effort spent carrying out a purchase and late delivery would be counted among the sacrifices.

Figure 2.2. illustrates the fact that in markets where a product is distributed through one or more distribution channels, the company is in complete control only of the marketing offering and communication directed at the dealers and of its own marketing communication directed at the end-buyers. The company *cannot determine* a dealer's offering and communication directed at end-buyers. Obviously, end-buyers will experience physical products like cars and personal computers as designed and produced by the producer. The dealer will himself make decisions about most aspects of his offering, such as price, terms of payment, service and in-store availability.

However, it is obvious that producers may *influence* decisions made by dealers. Through its offering and communication a company may seek to affect the dealer's

a. offering
for instance, by offering to train the dealer's staff in order to enhance service competence, to provide service support or to pay for a favorable in-store placement. The producer may also offer such things as credit or other kinds of financial support.

b. communication
for example, by being willing to pay part of the dealer's advertising costs, to train his staff in order to secure sufficient product knowledge or to provide brochures, posters and other advertising material.

The question of the degree to which and the means by which producers should try to influence dealers' marketing offering and communication is an important issue in holistic strategic marketing communication planning. The same holds good for considerations regarding whether, to what degree and how to direct communication directly at the end-buyers.

In should be emphasized that a buyer's experience of an offering, is itself determined by some kind of contribution on the part of that buyer. Optimal use and consumption of any product requires some effort and some kind of competence on the part of the buyer. Products differ with regard required "*buyer competence*". It is relatively easy to eat a sausage or to prepare and eat a meal of corn flakes. It is correspondingly difficult to operate a production robot, a whole production system or a personal computer. Acquiring and having the necessary competence, and making the necessary effort may be perceived both as a reward and a sacrifice.

Figure 2.1. Main elements in marketing planning

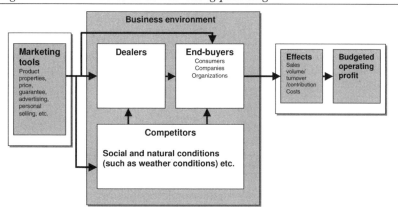

34 *Marketing communication: Concept and function*

The buyer's competence and the effort required of him determine how far the potential buyer value of an offering can be realized. Buyers who lack the necessary competence are unable to fill the requisite purchasing or user/consumer role, and will thus be prevented from realizing the full potential value of an offering.

For example, a knife, a production machine, a tractor or a brand of cake mix must be used correctly in order to function optimally. Lack of user competence may result in injury, defective articles, erratic furrows, and a flat cake respectively. In order to obtain full value from a personal computer, one has to spend time and money learning to master software programs. Likewise, dealers must possess the necessary marketing competence in order to obtain a satisfactory sales volume of a company's offering.

In the light of the above considerations, deciding on a company's marketing offering may be viewed as making decisions about

Figure 2.2. Vendor company's influence as regards own and dealers' marketing offering and marketing communication

```
┌─────────────────┐      ┌─────────┐                              ┌─────────┐
│ Marketing       │      │         │                              │         │
│ offering        │─────▶│ Dealers │                              │  End-   │
│ of vendor company│     │         │                              │ buyers  │
└─────────────────┘      │         │ ⋯⋯ Marketing offering ⋯⋯▷    │         │
                         │         │                              │         │
┌─────────────────┐      │         │ ⋯⋯ Marketing communication ▷ │         │
│ Marketing       │      │         │                              │         │
│ communication   │─────▶│         │                              │         │
│ of vendor company│     │         │                              │         │
└─────────────────┘      └─────────┘                              └─────────┘
        │                                                              ▲
        └──────────────────────────────────────────────────────────────┘
```

──────────▶ Controlled completely by the company

⋯⋯⋯⋯⋯▷ Indirectly influenced by the company

the contribution to be made by the company and the buyer (user, consumer) respectively. The relationship between the seller's and the buyer's contribution will tend to be inverse. Convenience products, for example, require little effort and competence on the part of the consumer. Similarly, the use of product components bought from a supplier may replace the competence and effort otherwise required of an industrial customer.

Marketing communication

As emphasized already, the term "marketing communication" covers every kind of communication between company and buyer about a company's offering(s). In other words, the holistic concept of marketing communication embraces every marketing tool that can be used by the seller or the buyer to communicate about a company's offering.

Marketing communication takes place in a number of ways. Communication may take the form of one-way and two-way processes (dialogue).

A great variety of media may be used. Communication may take place between a buyer and a company's switchboard operator or a shop assistant, by post, e-mail or facsimile, in buyers' telephone conversations with employees in order, production or marketing departments, in the course of meetings and demonstrations, in advertisements, etc.

The tasks of marketing communication are:

1. To convey the value of marketing offerings, i.e. to inform about needs they will meet, about relevant properties of an offering, about how to use the products (buyer's contribution), etc.

2. To "show the way" to offerings, i.e. to inform about how, where and when they can be purchased. For example, indicating which dealers carry a brand, which phone number to call, and who to ask for.

3. To remind buyers of the existence of the offering, as well as where, when and how it can be purchased.

Buyer and seller initiative

In a given planning period, both sellers (vendor companies) and buyers may initiate marketing communication processes.[9]

On the one hand, *the seller may decide to establish "initial contacts"* through advertising media such as TV, radio, magazines, newspapers or direct mail, or by telephone, facsimile transmitter, mail or by personal approach. Such decisions and their implementation are referred to here as *"seller initiatives"*. The term *"buyer initiatives"*, on the other hand, refers to *approaches made by buyers to sellers* by telephone, facsimile transmitter, mail, personal appearance etc. *where the former are not influenced by communication from the latter.*

Buyer initiatives may manifest themselves in two different ways, namely as:

1. *"Orders"*, i.e. the buyer knows exactly what he wants from the outset.

2. *"Inquiries"*, i.e. the buyer wishes to obtain further information about an offering he has heard of.

Selecting a certain brand of toothpaste from a supermarket shelf or ordering a favorite meal in a restaurant are both examples of orders in consumer markets. Examples in industrial markets would be when a supermarket's purchasing department calls a supplier's order department requesting a specific delivery or a hardware dealer asks a wholesaler to send him a number of particular spare parts. Examples of inquiries would be when a potential consumer actively seeks information from a car dealer's representative or when a company's marketing manager sends a fax to a hotel asking about its conference facilities.

A number of factors may be presumed to determine the extent and nature of the buyer initiative directed towards a particular offering in a forthcoming planning period:

The extent, nature and timing of seller initiative in previous periods of time:
Successful contacts initiated by the seller in a given period make potential buyers aware of offerings leading to purchases, which may in turn form a basis for future buyer initiatives. In a dynamic perspective, all buyer initiatives occurring during a particular period may be assumed to be some function of one or more seller initiatives in previous periods. All other things being equal, relatively intensive seller initiative early in a company's lifetime should lead to relatively larger buyer initiative sales potentials in later periods.

Buyer experience with company offerings:
The extent to which seller initiatives in previous periods of time lead to buyer initiatives in subsequent periods is likely to be depend on a buyer's experiences with the company and its offerings before and after a sale.

A buyer's experience of an offering, and his consequent perception of its value, is probably an important source of future buyer initiative. For example, favorable post-purchase experience with such offerings as a bottle of hair shampoo of brand X, a specific suite in a hotel or a specific brand of printer paper from a dealer in office supplies may dispose the buyer to buy again on later occasions in the same or later periods. Also, a buyer's experience with one offering may induce trust, reduce perceived risk and raise value expectations in relation to other offerings. In other words, experience with one of a company's offerings "rubs off" on other offerings in the same or later periods. Satisfied car owners who are in the market for a new car typically start off their buying process by contacting a dealer in their present make.

Experience with handling and follow-up of orders and inquiries:
The above assumptions refer to one aspect of buyers' post-purchase experiences with a company's market performance,

i.e. its offerings. The way in which orders and inquiries are dealt with is another important factor in market performance. Inaccessibility, lack of sufficient handling capacity or competence or lack of follow-up will tend to make future buyer initiatives less likely.

Difficult access may take the form of unserviceable opening hours, occupied phone or facsimile lines, phone calls or e-mails not being answered promptly or at all, or difficulty in contacting some person within an organization.

Buyer-seller relationship:
Close, co-operative relationships between buyers and suppliers involving social, structural, economic and/or legal bonds are frequently found in industrial markets. Such relationships, in which switching costs reduce the buyer's flexibility as to choice of supplier, are in themselves likely to be important determinants of buyer initiative. For instance, contracts for supply may produce orders in several successive planning periods.

External forces:
We may also assume that external forces on which a company exerts no influence may affect the extent and nature of buyer initiative. One such factor is the market performance of competitors. Enhanced competitiveness on the part of other operators in the market will tend to reduce the extent of buyer initiative. Other factors are the product life cycle stage of the product in question and various economic forces influencing overall demand.

The extent of buyer initiative is also likely to depend on specific market characteristics. For example, in some markets, buyer behavior is characterized by relatively extensive problem solving involving active information seeking. This may itself be a source of buyer initiative. Examples of especially active and goal-oriented buyer initiatives may be found in industrial markets where companies practice active purchasing strategies. Also, markets differ as to the level of intensity of word-of-mouth communication, depending on, among other things, the extent of perceived risk on the part of the buyer and the social visibility of the product in question. Buyers may pass on their experiences, positive as well as negative, to other potential buyers, thus enhancing or reducing the effect of the company's marketing activities. Favorable word-of-mouth may even produce buyer initiative on the part of new, potential customers in a forthcoming planning period. For this reason, buyer initiative may come from new, potential customers as well as from existing and former customers.

Owing to the existence of buyer initiative, holistic strategic marketing communication planning requires decisions concerning:

1. a company's accessibility and preparedness with regard to handling and following up buyer initiative – and

2. the extent and nature of seller initiative.

Consequently, a marketing communication strategy includes a buyer initiative strategy and a seller initiative strategy.

Standardized and customized offerings. Standard and (competence) transformation communication

So far, the discussion has focused on standardized offerings. A *"standardized offering"* may be defined as *an offering, which cannot be influenced by the buyer, whose options are merely to buy or not to buy.* Most offerings in consumer markets are standardized. Obvious examples of *"standard markets"* are markets for food, chocolate, detergents, washing machines and refrigerators. Standardized offerings are, however, also common in industrial markets. Examples are markets for mass produced office and production equipment, and postal services.

However, in many markets, only some part of an offering is decided upon in advance. *The core of the offering, including the product in question, is customized to the specific needs of each buyer. The capacity and competence of the company is,* so to say, *trans-*

formed into a *"customized offering"*. Such competence transformation processes are to some degree found in consumer markets, but are widespread in industrial markets, especially in markets consisting of relatively few, large buyers with different needs, varying from one point in time to another. Examples of typical *"transformation markets"* are markets for products such as offshore installations, production plants, buildings, ICT-software, market analyses, and consulting services. In recent years it has become increasingly common for suppliers to retail chains to deliver customized offerings. These may involve such things as negotiating prices and discounts, providing advertising support, agreeing terms of in-shop placement, and even delivery of own-label brands.

In such transformation markets a marketing offering is made up of two parts:

1. a customized offering.

2. a standardized offering, which is not adapted to the individual buyer, for instance as regards certain product characteristics, terms of payment, billing routines, and guidelines regarding complaints.

Consequently, the function of communicating about a marketing offering is more comprehensive and complex in transformation markets than in standard markets.

In transformation markets, marketing communication includes:

a. *"Standard communication"*, i.e. *communicating about the standardized part of a customized offering.* This function may also include *conveying information about organizational characteristics, which indicate the company's ability to develop and deliver competitive customized offerings.*

b. *Transformation communication, i.e.* conducting a dialogue with the buyer in order to develop a competitive customized offering.

On the interplay between marketing offering and marketing communication

It is assumed here that *the viability and sound development of a company is fundamentally dependent on competitive offerings.* Companies exchange products for buyers' money and effort. The offering determines the buyers' perception of the terms of exchange, which in turn determines future sales. Whether or not he will tend to make repeat purchases, is a function of the buyer's total experience of the offering. For example, whether or not a trial purchase of a coffee brand results in preference, indifference or rejection depends on the properties of the offering. Similarly, the marketing offering determines whether or not a first visit to a restaurant will be followed by additional visits, whether or not an industrial buyer will become loyal to a supplier of semi-products etc. Post-purchase experiences with an offering also affect whether or not word-of-mouth processes will be favorable or unfavorable. This will, in turn, affect the extent and nature of future buyer initiatives on the part of new, potential customers.

Figure 2.3. sums up why *the sales effect of marketing communication is fundamentally dependent on the properties of the offering.* One reason for this is that these properties determine which *relevant content* (messages) can possibly be communicated to buyers in the market place. Another reason is that while communication may lead to (trial) purchases, *further effects* in the form of repeat purchases, favorable word-of-mouth communication, buyer initiatives, etc. depend on *pre- and post-purchase experience* of the offering (i.e. perceived buyer value).

The likely interplay between offering and communication may be illustrated as follows:

Sales effect of marketing effort =
marketing offering * marketing communication

This "equation" should not be taken too literally. It serves merely to underline that a holistic approach to marketing communication and the suggested strategic planning procedure are both based on the assumption that the sales (volume) effect of mar-

42 Marketing communication: Concept and function

keting communication ultimately depends on the offering. Marketing communication based on an uncompetitive offering will have little impact. However, in order to contribute to a company's sales, buyers in the market place must be made aware of a competitive offering.

Implicit in the above assumption is the hypothesis that marketing communication alone cannot affect the perceived value of an offering. This rather controversial view will be further discussed in Chapter 8.

Figure 2.3. Properties of the offering determines communication effect

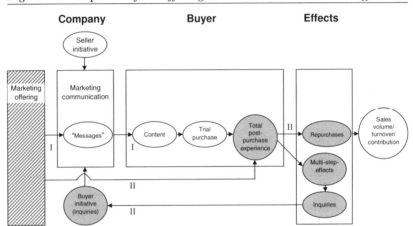

The figure illustrates two hypotheses underlying the contention that the sales effect of marketing communication depends on properties of the marketing offering:

I. The offering constitutes the basis for what "messages" the company has to tell buyers. The more competitive the offering, the more "interesting" the "messages" (communication content = interpreted messages), and the higher the probability of purchase.

II. The properties of the marketing offering determine buyers' total post-purchase experience of perceived net buyer value. Favorable post-purchase experience increases the extent of re-purchases (i.e. buyer initiatives in the form of orders) as well as the extent of favorable multi-step communication, for example in the form of favorable word-of-mouth. Favorable word-of-mouth, again, is positively related to the extent of buyer-initiated inquiries.

Four main types of marketing communication

All conceivable types of communication that can occur between company and buyers may be grouped into one of four main categories:

1. *impersonal mass* communication,
2. *personal mass* communication,
3. *impersonal individual* communication, and
4. *personal individual* communication.

The term *"mass communication"* covers *communicative episodes in which more than one person,* typically a mass audience, *is exposed to the same communication symbols,* such as pictures and spoken or printed words. Examples of mass communication media are newspapers, TV and various kinds of conference, such as meetings with dealers. Conversely, in *"individual communication"* processes, *only one person is exposed and the choice of communication symbols can be adapted to each individual buyer.* Examples of this occur in letters, face-to-face discussion between salespersons and potential customers and telephone conversations between employees in order departments and buyers making inquiries.

The term *"personal communication"* covers *communicative episodes that give room for dialogue.* The communication symbols are "produced" by one or more persons at the very moment of communication and it is possible for the buyer to respond immediately. Typical examples of such episodes are meetings, face-to-face talks, and telephone conversations. In *"impersonal communication",* of the kind that occurs in television commercials and newspaper advertisements, *immediate feedback is not possible.*

Marketing communication tools: Media and communication symbols

Box 2.4. contains an overview of the four main types of marketing communication. The figure also illustrates how communication tools can be subdivided into two main categories, namely:

1. *media*
and
2. *communication symbols*.

The term *"media"* signifies *any channel which buyers and/or sellers may use to expose the other part to communication symbols* in order to initiate a marketing communication process. Examples of such *"exposure"*, i.e. *opportunity to see or hear communication symbols*, are when a newspaper reader turns over to the page containing the seller's advertisement, when a salesman addresses a buyer in his office or when a buyer's phone call to an order department or a restaurant is answered.

Further distinctions may be drawn between:

1. *impersonal* and *personal mass media*
and:
2. *impersonal* and *personal individual media*.

In order to develop a *media strategy* a company must decide:

a. *What types* of media should be used in order to:

  - take seller initiatives and
  - receive, handle and follow-up buyer initiatives.

b. To *what extent* the selected media should be used.

The term "extent" concerns such matters as staffing capacity or technical capacity. These include the number of telephone and facsimile lines, the number of newspapers and advertisement insertions to be used, the number of buyers to be approached personally by salesmen and the number of dealers to be invited to a conference.

c. In *what order* and *when* the media should be used.

For example:

- When newspaper advertisements are to be inserted.
- At what points in time during the year, week or day the company is to have sufficient capacity to receive, handle and follow-up orders and inquiries.
- How great this capacity must be.
- How sales calls are to be timed in relation to the insertion of newspaper advertisements and the running of TV-commercials.

Conceptions of and possible feelings connected to the offering are conveyed to buyers through the use of *"communication symbols"*.[10] Typical examples are pictures and spoken or printed words. *"Content symbolization"* involves making decisions regarding specific symbol structures in the form of such things as advertisements, letters, films and spoken messages. The term *"symbol structure"* is used here to refer to *a specific, mutually independent set of symbols that are related to each other in a unique way in time and/or space*. The specific content (meaning and/or emotions) that is conveyed by a specific symbol structure depends on interpretation on the part of the buyer. Different buyers may interpret the same symbol structure differently. (See Figure 2.5.)

The term *communication capacity* is used to refer to among other things *"symbolization capacity"*. That capacity refers to the kinds and combinations of symbols that can be conveyed by any medium. Symbolization capacity varies from one medium to another. Newspapers and magazines, for instance, can carry visual symbols only, and radio solely auditory symbols. Film, TV and personal computers are audio-visual media. An advertising film has the capacity to convey a course of events visually, while in magazines visual symbolization is limited to static graphic images such as drawings or photographs. In a meeting, a person can use spoken words (auditory symbols) together with visual symbols on a flip-over or an overhead transparency or auditory and visual symbols in a video presentation or any combination of these. The implication of these differences in symbolization

Box 2.4. Main types of media and marketing communication tools

Main types of media and marketing communication tools:			
Mass communication		**Individual communication**	
Personal	*Impersonal*	*Personal*	*Impersonal*
Meeting (1) (face-to-face)	Newspapers Magazines Trade press Periodicals …….	Meeting (4) (face-to-face) Telephone conversation (5)	Mailing service (6) (letters etc.) Facsimile (7)
	Sponsoring media in connection with sporting and cultural events etc.		
Telephone conference (7)	Telephone directories/ yellow pages	Interactive use of the Internet (7)	E-mail (7)
	Cinema commercials Cinema slides		
Video conference	Television commercials Radio commercials		
	In-store-media (3)		
	Billboards		
	The Internet		
	Addressed and unaddressed direct mail		
	Etc…… (2)		

Marketing communication tools 47

Main types of marketing communication tools:
1. Media   Developing a media strategy involves deciding: a) Which media to use, b) to what extent, c) in which order, and d) when.   **2. Content symbolization**   Developing a content symbolization strategy involves making decisions regarding choice of *symbol structures* (see definition in text) to use in the various media in order to convey the selected communication content elements effectively.   Notes: (1) At the seller's or the buyer's premises in the form of such events as ordinary meetings, demonstrations, seminars or conferences.   (2) For example leaflets, commercials in rented videos, illuminated advertising media such as neon signs, and commercial gifts.   (3) For example brochures handed out at a store or a bank.   (4) At the seller's or buyer's premises, e.g. in an office, a conference room, in the shop premises or in a hotel room.   (5) Including stationary and mobile telephones, direct lines, answering machines, automatic order telephones, bleepers, and services such as green numbers (which a buyer can use free of charge in order to contact the company).   (6) Letters, brochures etc.   (7) Where the facilities required are available.

Figure 2.5. Examples of visual content symbolizations

capacity is that decisions regarding content symbolization must be made with due regard to media options, and vice versa.

Marketing communication costs: Media and content symbolization costs

The ways in which companies exploit available channels of marketing communication affect costs as well as sales volume. When developing marketing communication strategies, planners must accordingly weigh turnover and contribution against communication costs in order to assess the impact of strategic options on operating profits.

Marketing communication costs consist of

1. symbolization costs, and
2. media costs.

Symbolization costs are the costs of preparing such things as Internet homepages and advertisement or brochure layouts and texts. Media costs are costs of media use such as those incurred by inserting advertisements in magazines, running spots on TV and distributing brochures through mail services. Media costs also include such items as travel expenses incurred by sales and other personnel, mailing expenses, and telephone and facsimile charges as well as depreciation of facilities such as showrooms and conference facilities and telephonic, ICT and video equipment. Handling and follow-up activities may also involve such costs as those connected with individual distribution of brochures, use of telephones, facsimile transmitters, postal services and e-mail. Other media costs include wages to managers, sales personnel and other employees who deal with buyers.

Summing up

The main issues discussed in this chapter have been the concepts of the marketing offering and marketing communication.

Summing up   49

The marketing offering comprises everything relevant to the buyer in connection with preparing to buy, carrying through the purchase of, and using and consuming a company's product. The term marketing communication includes every kind of communication between company and buyer about a company's offering(s).

The tasks of marketing communication are:

1. Standard and transformation communication, i.e. communicating about standard and customized offerings, including organizational characteristics that indicate the company's ability to develop and deliver competitive customized offerings.
2. "Showing the way" to standard and customized offerings, i.e. communicating about how, where and when standard offerings can be purchased and customized offerings negotiated.
3. Maintaining buyers' awareness of standard offerings or relevant organizational characteristics.

Buyers as well as sellers may initiate marketing communication processes.

Since both buyers and sellers may initiate communication processes, the extent and nature of expected buyer initiative in a forthcoming period are of fundamental importance for marketing communication planning. Four main types of marketing communication have been described, namely, impersonal mass communication, personal mass communication, impersonal individual communication, and personal individual communication. The main tools used in marketing communication are media and communication symbols. Using these incurs two types of communication costs, namely, symbolization and media costs.

Together, the concepts, hypotheses and models that have been introduced here constitute a basis for working holistically and strategically with a company's marketing communication strategy. The above discussion implies that a holistic marketing communication strategy includes the following main elements:

1. *Guidelines for using marketing communication tools,* i.e.

- media use and
- content symbolization

related to

- seller initiative and
- buyer initiative,

directed at

- dealers as well as
- end-buyers.

2. A *"marketing communication budget"* containing estimates of

- media costs and
- symbolization costs

incurred in relation to

- buyer initiatives and
- seller initiatives,

directed at

- end-buyers as well as
- dealers,

together with

- estimates of the resulting sales volume, contribution, costs and operating profit.

The concepts of "receipt", "handling" and "follow-up" of orders and inquiries

The terms *"receipt"*, *"handling"* and *"follow-up"* of orders and inquiries are used extensively below. These terms are used here in the following senses:

"Receipt" has to do with accessibility. It concerns such things as:

- whether or not attempts to contact the company and a competent person succeed at all.
- efforts, time, money, irritation, pleasure etc. connected to getting in contact with a competent person.
- the number of "rings" that occur before a telephone is answered.
- the number of days a buyer has to wait before a letter, an e-mail or a facsimile is answered.
- the "tone" of the switchboard operator.
- whether or not the operator shows efficiency in referring the buyer to a competent person. For example, even though the person is inaccessible at the moment the operator knows where he is or where he can be reached, or offers to take a message and ask him call back.

"Handling" refers to the extent to which a buyer's wishes are recognized, his information needs are understood and whether these are met appropriately. It also refers to effort, time, money, irritation, pleasure etc. connected to responses to the buyer's approach. The term covers such things as being attentive, listening, understanding, asking relevant questions, being able to give correct answers or showing friendliness and being polite.

"Follow-up" has to do with whether or not a buyer who does not make an immediate decision to purchase is contacted by the seller at a later point in time. It also refers to when the contact takes place and how it is handled.

3. Marketing communication strategy as part of a company's total business strategy

This chapter introduces a concept and a model of a total business strategy, takes a closer look at the interplay between a marketing communication strategy and other strategic elements, and discusses relevant implications for marketing communication planning.

Marketing communication strategy constitutes only part of a company's total business strategy. A holistic view of marketing communication is founded on the assumption that marketing communication interacts closely with other strategic elements. For this reason, a company's marketing communication strategy must be developed with due regard its total strategy. The importance of a competitive offering for the sales effect of marketing communication has already been emphasized.

As indicated in Chapter 1, *"strategy"* is defined here as the *"pattern"* of such things as the company's marketing communication activities, the markets in which it operates, its organizational structure, and its relations to suppliers, financial institutions, local and regional authorities and other relevant organizations and institutions in the business environment. Of course, any such "pattern" reflects a specific point or period of time. The term may refer to an intended state of affairs in the future (a plan) or to an existing state of affairs (i.e. to reality). That means that every company *has* a strategy in the sense "an existing pattern" of markets, communication activities, organization etc. Of course, it does not necessarily follow that managers and employees have a complete overview or understanding of their company's existing strategy or that they carry out deliberate work in order to monitor, evaluate and develop that strategy.

A strategy model. Marketing communication strategy as one of six sub-strategies

Figure 3.1. contains a model suggesting that a total business strategy may be viewed as consisting of six elements or sub-strategies.

In order of priority these sub-strategies are a company's

1. purpose,
i.e. beliefs and ideas held by employees, managers, owners etc. as to why their organization exists (its "mission"), where it should be going and what has to be done in order to get there. Different interest groups within a company may, of course, have divergent ideas.

2. goals,
i.e. concrete beliefs about what results must be achieved within a given future period of time in order to satisfy the company's purpose.

3. operating profit.
Of course, purposes and goals do not have to be concerned with profit alone. The number of jobs offered or environmental issues are examples of other concerns. However, as has been mentioned, the following discussion focuses upon profitability, i.e. upon a planned and achieved operating profit that is sufficient to secure the company's future existence and sound development. Obviously, such an operating profit will include a reasonable return on investment to owners.

4. product/market strategy,
i.e. the "pattern" determining which products are offered in which markets.

This is illustrated in Figure 3.1, which shows a product/market matrix consisting of 24 possible combinations of 6 products (a-f) and 4 sub-markets (1-4), i.e. 24 *business areas.* Arrows indicate a product/market strategy including 10 business areas. If, for example, a company offers 3 different PC-models A, B and C in 4 different sub-markets, e.g. elementary schools, high-schools, colleges and universities, and small and medium-sized manufacturing firms, its product/market strategy includes 12 business areas.

In cases where a product is marketed through a distribution chain with one or more intermediate "links", a product/market sub-strategy exists in relation to each link in the chain. If, for example, a company markets a range of food products to consumers through dealers, its product/market strategy will include two sets of business areas, one with reference to dealers, the other to end-buyers.

A company's choice of product/market strategy will determine the market conditions under which it has to operate. Business areas differ depending on factors such as the size and development of demand, the number of links in the distribution chain, the number of buyers, and the number of competitors and their strengths and weaknesses. Furthermore, developments relating to factors such as technology, national and international business cycles and economic policy, and developments within distributive trades usually affect business areas differently.

5. *marketing strategy,* including

a. an *offering strategy* and
b. a *marketing communication* strategy.

As previously emphasized, a company is in complete control of its own communication activities directed at any link in a distribution chain. Consequently, in markets where a product is marketed through a distribution chain with one or more intermediate links, a marketing strategy includes one offering strategy related to the nearest following link, and two or more marketing communication strategies, i.e. one for each link and one related to end-buyers.

6. *strategy* relating to *organizational basis.*
A company's *"organizational basis"* is defined here as *its organization in the* widest sense. This comprises:

a. The *"internal organization"*, including employees, managers and owners, their areas and levels of competence, their attitudes towards the company, towards their work and towards other members of the staff. The internal organization also includes formal and informal distribution of tasks, responsibilities and power, production technology etc.

b. The *"external organization"*, i.e. the company's relations to the business environment, including suppliers, finance companies, labor market, local authorities, governmental institutions etc. This means that a company's organizational basis includes its external network as well as its position within this network. Relations to other network members may be more or less close. Examples of very close relationships are strategic partnerships and alliances.

The lines in part 6 of Figure 3.1. connecting the various elements of the organizational basis indicate the importance of interaction. Relevant examples are the interaction between product development, purchasing, production and marketing, and the significance of relevant operating competence on the part of managers and employees where technological equipment is concerned. Other examples are the interaction between a production department and suppliers or between a product development department and an R&D institution.

The vertical arrows in Figure 3.1. indicate ways in which the six sub-strategies seem to relate to each other:

1. The organizational basis "produces" offerings and marketing communication in relevant business areas.

2. Offerings deliver buyer value in the relevant business areas. Marketing communication informs, "shows the way to " and reminds buyers of offerings. Thus, in a total business strategy, marketing communication serves as a link between marketing offerings and buyers in business areas.

3. The "production" of offerings for business areas – and mar-

keting communication directed towards them – will be reflected in sales volume and costs. Sales volume, turnover and costs are determined by various properties of a company's organizational basis and business areas. For example, a factory's production costs are a function of such factors as its adopted production technology, the specific competencies of its workers and the dependability of its suppliers as regards quality and ability to deliver. A company's choice of product/market strategy affects sales volume and costs because it determines the market conditions under which it has to operate. The sales volumes and costs connected to alternative offerings and marketing communication strategies are largely determined by buyer and competitor characteristics. For example, strong competition usually causes higher marketing costs. The requirements that offerings have to meet in order to be sufficiently competitive in the various business areas are largely determined by such factors as buyers' needs and the strength of competitors.

4. Turnover minus costs equals operating profit. The size of the operating profit determines the degree of goal achievement and fulfillment of purpose.

The elements of a business strategy interact. Sales volumes achieved and costs incurred are a function of this interaction. The hallmark of a viable business strategy is a good match between sub-strategies. A company will achieve a sufficient operating profit, provided it has an organizational basis that is able to produce competitive offerings and marketing communication in sound business areas with respect to such things as size and development of demand and strength and development of competition.

Elements of sub-strategies relate to each other in a variety of ways that may or may not match. For example, in transformation markets, the competitiveness of customized offerings (= offering strategy) depends on the negotiation skills of managers and employees (= property of organizational basis). The effect of mass communication activities (= element in marketing communication strategy) depends on the capacity

58 *Marketing communication strategy*

Figure 3.1. A strategy model

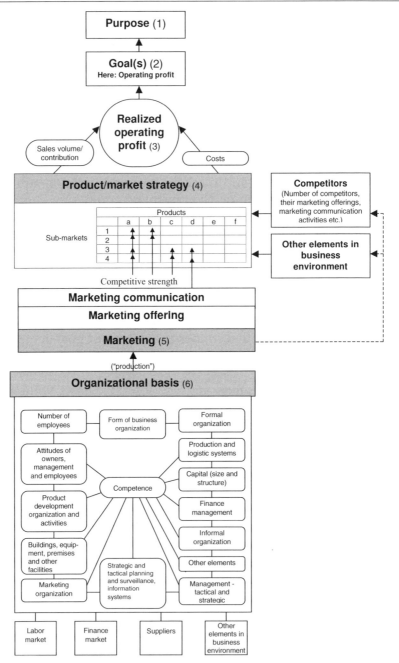

to receive, handle and follow-up resulting orders and inquiries (= property of organizational basis). The company's ICT equipment (= property of organizational basis) affects which media are at the planner's disposal (= marketing communication strategy). Sets of business areas relating to the various links in a distribution chain are mutually dependent. For instance, when developing a product/market strategy relating to retailers in a consumer market, one will need to consider which consumers use which distribution channels.

The viability of a strategy may deteriorate in a number of ways and for a number of reasons having to do with developments within business areas, offerings, marketing communication, and organizational basis. Demand may decrease in business areas. Competition may become stronger due to the entrance of new competitors and successful product development on the part of existing competitors. Buyer needs may change. The organizational basis may become less effective as a result of such things as bad management, organizational inflexibility or failure to invest in competence development and new technology. If nothing is done, sooner or later such developments undermine profitability. The purpose of strategic planning and management is to monitor strategy, bring to light existing and potential problems and opportunities, find and make plans for – and implement – appropriate changes in strategy in order to restore viability.

Implications for marketing communication planning

The fact that various strategic elements interact with each other means that marketing communication strategy cannot be developed without taking other sub-strategies into account. In holistic strategic marketing communication planning, these must be taken into consideration either as

- factors that are *given*, or as

- factors that have to be *changed* in order to develop a basis for a sufficiently profitable communication strategy.

In some cases, the existing or planned goal, product/market strategy, offering etc, form a sufficient basis for the development of an acceptably profitable marketing communication strategy. Buyer segments at which to direct marketing communication activities can then be found within previously selected business areas.[11] Communication content can be formulated on the basis of the existing or planned offering. Media strategy can be developed on the basis of the management and employee competencies, organizational culture, ICT-equipment etc. that are actually in place.

There will, however, also be cases where a strategic marketing communication planner finds that a sufficiently profitable marketing communication strategy cannot be developed unless changes are made in one or more of the other sub-strategies. A planner may, for instance, conclude that the competitiveness of an offering needs to be improved: Unless certain properties of the offering are altered, effective communication content cannot be formulated. Alternatively, he may discover weaknesses in the company's organizational basis relating to its capacity to receive, handle and follow-up orders and inquiries, and he may conclude that these weaknesses make it impossible to develop an effective media strategy. In such cases the planner will suggest that the necessary changes are made, and make his continued work with the company's marketing communication strategy conditional on those changes being carried out. Examples of appropriate measures might be investments in telephone and ICT equipment, reinforcement of the sales organization and implementation of programs designed to enhance staff competence.

The reasons above lead us to conclude that a critical analysis of the other sub-strategies is an integral part of holistic strategic marketing communication planning. In instances where an analysis indicates that changes need to be made in one or more of these sub-strategies, marketing communication planning may – and should – initiate problem solving processes that improve the match between the sub-strategies, and thereby the viability of the total business strategy. A fruitful interplay between marketing communication planning and the development of other sub-strategies is more likely to be realized in a company that practices deliberate and systematic strategic planning and management than in one which does not. This subject will be further discussed in Chapter 17.

Summing up the elements of a marketing communication strategy

Chapter 2 concluded that a holistic marketing communication strategy includes the following main elements:

1. guidelines with regard to the use of marketing communication tools.

2. a marketing communication budget.

The above discussion implies that, in addition, a holistic marketing communication strategy comprises

3. a description of changes in business areas, offering and/or organizational basis that are considered necessary before a proposed use of marketing communication tools can be implemented and a profit goal can be achieved.

It should be obvious to the reader that the view of marketing taken in this book amounts to far more than is normally seen as the province of marketing, advertising or sales departments. Indeed, the terms used in this book and elsewhere in the literature to refer to various marketing tools are viewed here as simply denoting *various kinds of interaction or* points of *contact* between buyers and a company's organizational in affected business areas.

These contribute to one of two things:

- the perceived value of dealing with the company.

- conveying information about or reminding of the offering/company or "showing the way" to the offering/company.

In the first case, they constitute the company's offering, in the second case, they constitute the company's marketing communication.

"*Soft contacts*" take place between people, as when a buyer and a shop assistant interact in a store, where the latter may render various kinds of service (part of the offering) and/or communicate about the shop's offerings. "*Hard contacts*" take place between buyers and objects such as tangible products, invoices and brochures. Use or consumption of a product influences the perceived buyer value of the offering, as does the clarity and correctness of an invoice. When a buyer reads a brochure, communication is taking place.

Contact episodes involving communication processes or influencing the perceived value of an offering may take place on the premises of the company. Such *"in-contacts"* may take place for example in a conference room, in a shop or in a bank office. Contacts may also take place outside the company, i.e. in the market place, as when an industrial buyer meets a salesman in his own office or reads a fax or letter from the company. Other examples of such *"out-contacts"* are when a service engineer carries out work in the home of a customer, when a consumer is exposed to an advertisement or uses a tube of toothpaste.

Seen from the perspective of contact or interaction, the significance of a company's staff for its marketing efforts becomes quite evident. Every single manager or employee who interacts with buyers acts *front stage* and directly influences its marketing strategy. Indeed, the ways in which they behave during contacts *constitute* part of the company's offerings or marketing communication – or both. While interacting with a customer, a staff member can deliver value (i.e. rewards and/or sacrifices) as well as communicate about an offering. An example of this is when a waiter serves a course and at the same time informs about various dessert options. Company staff who *do not* interact with buyers act *back stage* and influence its offerings, its marketing communication or both *indirectly*. The quality of the company-buyer interactions depends to a large degree on the interplay between front stage and back stage actors.

The proportion of a company's managers and employees who interact with buyers, varies from one type of market to another. It tends to be large in service companies such as hotels, banks, restaurants and consulting firms, and trade companies such as retail chains. The same is true of companies operating in transformation markets. For example, marketing/sales people and engineers, middle and even top managers in building contract companies, frequently take part in dialogues leading to customized offerings. By way of contrast, relatively few employees of companies that mass-produce consumer products, interact with buyers.

The view taken here is that a company's marketing strategy, i.e. its offerings and marketing communication, is equal to *all contacts between the organizational basis and buyers in the business areas*. As contended above, marketing is far more than what is normally regarded as the province of departments of marketing, advertising or sales.

In the last 50 years, most marketing research and literature has had a much narrower focus on relatively few marketing tools. The 4P-paradigm has been especially predominant. This paradigm in which the Ps stand for "price", "product", "place" (distribution) and "promotion" (advertising, sales promotion), fails to reflect the variety of marketing tools. Admittedly, the last few years have seen the emergence of somewhat wider approaches, which are more in keeping with that taken in this book. It is, however, a fact that these have taken several decades to evolve. One may wonder why it has taken half a century to discover the multiplicity of marketing tools, despite the fact that companies have been using most of them for the best part of two centuries. It may, for instance, be assumed that the popularity of a restaurant has at all times depended on its choice of courses, the quality of its food and the manners of its waiters.

If we are to account for the tenacity of the narrow approach, it may be worth looking at how marketing theory and research have developed over the years. Until the mid 1960s, marketing theory, empirical research and literature dealt mainly with mass produced branded consumer products such as beverages, detergents, and toothpaste, marketed to consumer mass markets through wholesale dealers and retailers. Marketing was conceived from the point of view of the marketing, advertising and sales departments of a large mass producer. Pricing, product development, gaining distribution and carrying through sales promotion and consumer advertising campaigns are the main tasks of such departments. From such a "distant" perspective, the price, the product, the distribution and promotion may easily seem to be *the* only marketing tools. The 4P-paradigm was the natural outcome of that perspective and, perhaps, not surprisingly, marketing tools that have to do with contacts between buyers and people inside an organization were virtually ignored.

In the late 1960s and 1970s marketing researchers gradually began to show increasing interest in other types of products and markets. Greater attention was paid to markets for services, industrial or business-to-business markets, and even to trade markets. In such markets, products are typically marketed directly to end-buyers and a relatively large proportion of staff interact with buyers. These researchers came to see marketing in a "closer" perspective and gradually discovered the relevance of several kinds of contacts between buyers and managers/employees. One result of this research is the concept of "the augmented product", which, in an industrial market, may include the actual (core) product and its additional attributes such as design and packaging, installation services, guarantee, and financing.[12]

However, even though wider and more realistic views of a company's marketing tools are emerging, there seems to be a long way to go before a real breakthrough takes place in the literature. Textbooks, articles in academic journals and other writing in the field are still characterized by relatively narrow perspectives. Books on consumer marketing, industrial marketing, service marketing etc. adopt different approaches to the question of identifying the marketing tools that are at a company's disposal. Introductory textbooks on marketing are still particularly heavily oriented towards markets for mass produced consumer products. The 4P paradigm, which became extremely popular as far back as the 1950s, still underlies many texts. In several respects, this paradigm has functioned as a straitjacket. Admittedly, two more Ps have been added, the fifth being "personnel" and the sixth, "power". However, this does not solve the problem: Not all relevant marketing tools begin with a P! In the books referred to here, very little weight is put on exploring, conceptualizing and structuring the marketing tools of a company, on illustrating their full variety, or on developing methods which can be used to identify appropriate marketing tools in a specific planning situation. This is particularly true of the literature on marketing communication.[13]

Part III

Further elaboration of a holistic approach to marketing communication: The marketing offering and the tasks of marketing communication

Part III of this book goes on to elaborate on a number of important aspects of a holistic approach to marketing communication.

The significance of the marketing offering in a holistic approach to strategic planning of marketing communication has been emphasized above. Chapter 4 discusses how relevant elements in an offering can be identified and how a standardized marketing offering can be described.

So far, the tasks of marketing communication have been merely touched upon. Chapter 5 explores the tasks of marketing communication in transformation markets. Chapter 6 deals in some depth with the particular task of developing buyer competence and sums up the tasks of marketing communication. Chapter 7 discusses how the communication tasks vary with the extent of market penetration of the product type in question and the degree to which the company's offering is established in the market.

In Chapter 2 it was contended that marketing communication has no independent function. i.e. that the effect of marketing communication is fundamentally dependent on the properties of the offering. Chapter 8 discusses the relationship between offering and communication in more detail.

4. Describing the marketing offering

In order to gain necessary insight into an offering in any given planning situation, planners must:

1. identify all relevant elements in an offering – and
2. describe the uses of these elements.

Identifying the appropriate elements in an offering

Planners who look to marketing literature as a source of ideas and examples to help with identifying appropriate elements in an offering will find that scant attention has hitherto been paid to exploring, conceptualizing and structuring marketing tools. There has been correspondingly little effort to develop methods for determining whether particular marketing tools are appropriate to given planning situations. For example, the literature does not contain anything approaching complete lists of tools at a company's disposal in different kinds of markets. A planner who wishes to gain a sufficiently complete overview will get little help there.

Some possible procedures for identifying relevant elements in an offering will now be outlined and illustrated.

Identifying elements in an offering via "the buyer's route"

A search for relevant elements in an offering may take as its basis the very concept of offering. The term "marketing offering" was defined above as "… everything relevant to the buyer in connection with preparing to buy, carrying through the purchase of, and using and consuming a company's product".

That is, an offering includes

"... everything that contributes the buyer's total experience in the form of sacrifices and rewards – i.e. the experienced or perceived (net-) buyer value – of obtaining and using or consuming a company's product."[14]

By dividing the *total process of buying and using/consuming* a product into relevant *phases*, we can undertake a systematic search for those points of contact between buyers and the company's organizational basis that influence a buyer's total experience. We can then evaluate each possible contact we find in such a search process in terms of sacrifices and rewards.

A company marketing washing machines, refrigerators etc. might, for example, operate with the following phases:

1. preparing to purchase,
2. making the purchase,
3. making preparations for using the product, and
4. using the product.

In a search within the first phase, i.e. preparing to purchase, the question of the buyer's costs in the form of time, money, effort and possible sources of annoyance might come easily to mind. Thinking about this question might give a lead to elements in an offering such as location, accessibility via telephone and opening hours. The greater the distance the buyer has to travel in order to get to the shop, the greater the sacrifice in the form of time, effort and – possibly – money paid for transportation (gasoline, bus fare etc). Inconvenient opening hours may be associated with stress.

In the second phase, i.e. making the purchase, it should be asked what kinds of rewards and sacrifices buyers might experience in the process of arriving at, entering and being in the store. Will they feel satisfaction at being dealt with pleasantly and competently? Will they be able to enjoy nice, tidy premises and fresh air? Or will the process generate annoyance at not

Identifying the appropriate elements in an offering 71

being noticed or at being kept waiting, and irritation at disorderly premises and impolite or slovenly shop assistants? Answers to these questions might throw light on various facets of the elements in an offering such as staff dress codes, appearance and behavior, treatment of customers, shop-fitting and interior design, use of color, tidiness and so on.

An analysis of the third phase, i.e. preparing to use the product, would probably lead to identification of elements in the offering such as distribution, pre-purchase service and product properties. Does the shop offer a delivery service or not? If it does: When will delivery take place? Will delivery be free or will a charge be made? Does the product need to be partly assembled by the buyer? Does the company provide assistance with preparing the product for use?

A search within the fourth phase, i.e. using the product, might easily lead to identification of elements in the offering such as product properties, post-purchase service, guarantee, and guidelines for and manner of handling complaints.

The phases indicated above may be seen as a rough description of a "route" along which the buyer moves in the total process of buying and using/consuming. Similarly, the procedure outlined may be regarded as *a search for elements in an offering along "the buyer's route"*. The planner "travels" along "the buyer's route" looking for contacts with the company's organizational basis that may influence the buyer's perceived (net-) value of obtaining and using or consuming the product. The actual route will, of course, vary from one product or market or buyer to another. It is the task of the planner to find and describe the route that applies to each particular planning situation.[15]

In some cases, such as that of a consumer purchasing groceries in a supermarket, it might suffice to work with the following three phases:

1. preparing to purchase,
2. making the purchase, and
3. consuming the product.

However, in a company marketing a durable product to consumers through dealers, it might be necessary to operate with the following four phases:

1. preparing to purchase,
2. making the purchase,
3. reselling the product, and
4. after-selling.

A search within the reselling phase would probably quickly indicate rewards and sacrifices for the dealer, such as probable sales volume and storage expenses. This again might give a clue to product properties likely to influence demand, the amount of space needed for storage, and whether or not the product is easily handled. A search along "the buyer's route" within the after-selling phase would be likely to draw attention to such matters as the probable number and nature of complaints and after-sale services that a dealer will have to handle. This, in turn, would identify durability as a relevant product property, as well as elements in the offering such as terms of guarantee and complaint handling, and training programs for dealer employees in performing relevant after-sale services.

In many cases, more than one route leads to purchase and consumption or use. For instance, a buyer may approach the organizational basis in person or by phone, facsimile or letter. Consequently, the planner must investigate all possible buyer's routes in order to take account of all relevant contacts and elements in the offering.

In a search along a "buyer's route", the elements in an offering that are *commonly used* are, of course, most easily identified. However, it is often wise to conduct a *creative search for new, potential kinds of contact and elements in an offering*, since these may well constitute the best – and in some cases the only – basis for developing competitive strength. In recent years, airlines, among others, have discovered a number of such new elements. One example is the airport businessmen's lounge, where travelers can wait for their flights in comfortable surroundings, with a drink and a journal or newspaper to read.

Stimulating the identification process.
Examples of elements in offerings and relevant buyer experiences

A search and identification process may be stimulated in several ways.

One technique involves *systematically pairing opposing concepts*, thereby encouraging divergent thinking. For example, in connection with each of the phases in a "buyer's route" the concepts "in-contacts" and "out-contacts", might prompt the following questions:

1. What kinds of contacts may possibly take place on the premises of the company? In trying to answer, one's attention might be drawn to such things as the appearance of buildings, frontages and entrances, to parking lot properties, to tidiness, decor and general appearance of reception and meeting rooms, and to the ways in which they are furnished and equipped.

2. What sorts of contacts may possibly take place outside the premises of the company? The search for an answer, would be likely to focus attention on such things as the product, the packaging, the invoice, service engineers, and salesmen handling orders and rendering services.

Another possibility is to think of soft contacts, i.e. contacts between people, as opposed to hard contacts, i.e. contacts between buyers and physical objects. Thinking about soft contacts might make one aware of interactions such as those between buyers and shop assistants, switchboard operators, service engineers and staff in the order department. Thinking about hard contacts might lead to awareness of the physical product itself, the intelligibility and accuracy of invoices and the color and general appearance of counters and walls.

Yet another opposing pair are *sacrifices and rewards* that a buyer may experience. Everyday speech is rich in words referring to various sacrifices and rewards, each relating to one or more of our five senses. Inspiration may also be drawn from concepts, hypotheses and models offered by the literature on buyer behavior, which contains numerous concepts and hypotheses relating to sacrifices and rewards. The prevailing view is that experiences connected to income and to costs in the form of money, time and effort are the most important ones in industrial (business-to-business) markets, since purchasing is based on business motives. In consumer markets, on the other hand, experiences directly or indirectly connected to the gratification of "private" human needs or motives such as hunger, thirst, sex, security, and social acceptance are the most important.

The following are some examples of types of sacrifices and rewards, that may be useful to have in mind when searching for elements in an offering along a "buyer's route".

Sacrifices and rewards may be connected to:

1. The nature and degree of *product performance*. This may concern basic need-satisfying functions, social relations or design. People visit a theatre or a cinema in order to learn, to laugh, to cry, to experience suspense and so on. A company buys a production robot with the purpose of reducing production costs, improving quality, and/or reducing time of delivery. Children's car seats are purchased in order reduce the likelihood of severe injury in the event of a collision. Consultants are hired in order to improve organizational structures and processes, and – ultimately – profitability. Consumer products are bought in order to signal membership of a social group or identify oneself with an idol.

2. The nature and amount of *financial* contribution and yield in the form of such things as price, terms of payment, operating expenses incurred by using a car or a machine, and the rate per hour to be paid for repair services. Further examples are the turnover a dealer may expect as a result of dealing in the company's product, or the amount of money a consumer can save by assembling a piece of furniture himself.

Identifying the appropriate elements in an offering 75

3. The nature and amount of *effort* connected with purchasing and using or consuming a particular product. Is it possible to park one's car near a shop, or does one have to walk a long way with heavy shopping bags? How heavy is a power saw to work with? How easy is it to open a can?

4. The amount of *time* that has to be used in connection with such things as making the necessary preparations to purchase and making the actual purchase. How time-consuming are the activities necessary to have the product taken home and to learn to use the product properly?

5. The nature and amount of *annoyance and satisfaction*. Annoyance will often be experienced when things like cars, washing machines or copying machines need repair or service. Satisfaction may be derived from shopping in a store, working together with a consultant or using a particular kind of flour to bake bread.

When searching for relevant experiences it may also be worth considering the fact that experiences can be *direct* as well as *derived*. Derived experiences are sacrifices and rewards deriving from other people's reactions to a marketing offering, whereas direct experiences are independent of other people's reactions. For example, buying and using consumer products such as jeans or cars may result in both positive and negative expressions of praise or disapproval. Buyers' reactions will largely determine a dealer's sales volume of a product, as well as his expenditure of money and effort in honoring guarantees and handling complaints. The taste of a hamburger is experienced directly by the consumer. Similarly, a dealer's costs in connection with transport and storage represent direct experiences.

Finally, when analyzing phases of "the buyer's route" involving consumption, use, reselling and after-selling, it can pay to make a systematic effort to determine how much *buyer competence* is required at each stage. In this way attention is directed to those aspects of the marketing offering that affect sacrifices and rewards on the part of the buyer in respect of:

76   *Describing the marketing offering*

- developing necessary buyer competence, and

- filling a necessary purchasing or user/consumer role, which may require willingness to learn new skills, expend effort and time and so on.

Of course, the actual sacrifices and rewards that are most decisive will vary from one company, product and market to another. Consequently, ideas must be selected and elaborated by the planner in accordance with the characteristics of the specific planning situation.

Box 4.1. and Box 4.2. contains a number of examples of various elements in an offering.

At what conceptual level should the elements in an offering be identified?

Identification of the elements in an offering may take place on different conceptual levels. Some of the ideas emerging in an identification process may concern relatively concrete matters, such as "price". However, some apparently obvious concepts may actually have several components, each of which may be viewed as a separate element in an offering. We may, for example, say that the expression "terms of payment" indicates an element in an offering. Alternatively, we may think of it as comprising three different elements, namely "period of credit", "cash discount", and "interest on overdue payments". Similarly, we may feel that "complaint handling" includes both "guidelines for" and "ways of handling" complaints.

The concept of "service" has several sub-dimensions, relating to such things as:

- Various kinds of pre- and post-purchase services (installation, clearing, repairs etc.)
- How services can be ordered: Over the Internet or by telephone, facsimile etc?
- The service ordering process. How promptly are telephone,

Identifying the appropriate elements in an offering 77

e-mail or facsimile answered? How long does it take to get through to the responsible department and employee? How politely and competently does the person in question respond?
- How soon a service can be carried out.
- Whether or not a service is carried out at the time agreed.
- Whether the buyer is informed in the event of a delay in carrying out the service.
- Whether a defective product can be repaired at the purchaser's premises or whether it has to be transported for repair.
- The quality of an executed service.
- The behavior of service personnel.
- The cost of a service.

When attempting to form a picture of the important elements in an offering, planners must make deliberate choices as to conceptual level. A marketing offering encompasses the qualities of each of its elements, so that the purpose of identifying these elements is to establish a proper basis for describing the marketing offering itself.

The conceptual level chosen must correspond to the objectives for which the marketing offering is to be described:

1. The first of these objectives is to form a basis for comparing the company's marketing offering with competing offerings, in order to evaluate its competitive strength, and – if necessary – to make changes which will improve that strength.

    A relevant description must be fairly concrete in order to uncover specific strengths and weaknesses, and offer unambiguous guidance as to what changes to make. A term like "service" is likely to prove too vague in most contexts. Simply to state that an offering lacks competitive strength as regards service is to invite the question: "With regard to what?" Clearly, nothing can be done without knowing more about the exact sources of the problem. Are service telephones not being answered in time? Are promises regarding service delivery at an agreed hour not being kept? Is the waiting time for service too long?

Box 4.1. Examples of relevant elements in an offering directed at dealers

Examples of relevant elements in an offering

Product:
Durability
Functional properties
Design

Price

Discounts:
Cash discounts (size)
Quantity discounts (quantity limits, size)

Terms of payment
Period of credit
Rate of interest

Rate of interest on overdue payments

Invoices

Comprehensibility
Correctness

Terms of freight
Freight paid
Freight charges

Guarantees
Terms (period, on which parts)
Implementation
(processing time, treatment of customers)

Treatment of complaints
Terms
Implementation
(processing time, treatment of customers)

Terms and observance of delivery
Time of delivery (promised)
Ability to deliver as required
(quality, quantity, price etc. on time)
Handling of delays

Donations
(art, sports etc.)

Service
Type of pre- and post purchase services offered, e.g. clearing, instruction materials (service/user handbook), training of dealer's staff and repair services.

Service quality (technical, customer handling)
Time of (service) delivery
Financial terms of service delivery

Marketing support
Training of dealer's staff
Marketing planning support
Advertising material and support
Financial terms of support

Marketing communication directed at end-buyers
Type (e.g. advertising campaigns)
Extent
When
Etc.

Note:
The above examples refer to a producer of farming machines such as plows and harrows. The producer markets his products to farmers (end-buyers) through dealers, i.e. the offering is directed at dealers. However, most of the elements would be relevant in relation to any dealer-directed offering based on a durable product.

he above elements are described at a certain conceptual level. Several, such as ervice quality and not the least the product itself, might, of course, be viewed as aving *several sub-dimensions*, each of which may be viewed as a separate element in an offering. For example, each functional or design property of the product ight be viewed as offering elements.

2. The second of the above objectives is to form a basis for formulating and selecting relevant and precise communication contents.

   If this objective is to be achieved, the elements in the offering must be identified at a relatively concrete conceptual level. Precise messages could probably not be formulated on the basis of a term such as "guarantee". A message like "We offer you the best guarantee on the market!" is unlikely to convey much information to the buyer. More precise messages would have to identify such things as the product parts and functions that were covered by the guarantee and specify for how long it was valid.

In conclusion, the relevant elements in an offering should be identified on a concrete and detailed conceptual level. However, the optimal level will vary from one planning situation to another.

Describing the marketing offering

Describing an offering on the basis of its elements

It has already been argued that a marketing offering is the sum of all the uses of each element in that offering. Consequently, once the planner has identified the relevant elements in an offering, he must go on to describe the *intended* use of each of these elements if he is to gain sufficient insight into the marketing offering itself.

The following examples should illustrate the above point. An extract from a description of an offering for a plow, marketed through dealers, might read as follows:

- Price (to dealer): $ 6 000
- Terms of payment: 30 days – 3%
- Time of delivery: 7 days
- Ability to deliver on time: 90%
- Guarantee: 3 years on all parts

- Marketing support: 1 000 brochures free of charge. Producer pays 50% of advertising costs in local media limited to 5% of gross purchase value (on a yearly basis). 2 weeks service course for one employee. Free of charge. All costs, including traveling expenses and hotel bill, paid by producer.
- Etc.

An extract from a description of a branch bank might read as follows:

- Saving with tax reduction: 6% rate of interest
- Adjacent parking for 30 cars
- Coffee and cakes served on the premises
- Local newspapers available
- 10 comfortable chairs
- Etc.

Whether or not an element in an offering can be described quantitatively or qualitatively depends on the nature of the element in question. An element such as "time of deliver" obviously lends itself to a quantitative description, for example, "7 days". The same applies to such things as weight, size and so on. Conversely, elements such as "product design", "treatment of customers", "staff clothing and general appearance" can only be described qualitatively – verbally and or visually.

Describing a marketing offering on the basis of buyers' relevance criteria and buyer value

Describing a marketing offering usually involves more than just describing specific uses of each of its elements. A buyer may not be able to recognize whether a particular element in the offering will involve rewards or sacrifices on the basis of that description alone.[16]

Diverging experience, language background and perceptions of the marketing offering itself may act as barriers between planner and buyer. Social learning processes, as well as direct pre- and post-purchase product experiences, lead buyers to associate

Box 4.2. Examples of relevant elements of an offering: A clothes shop

Opening hours
Location

Parking facility
Number of spaces
Distance to shop

Shop appearance – outside
Materials, design, colors,
tidiness, cleanliness, hygiene etc. (X)

Shop appearance – inside
Layout, materials, design, colors,
lightning etc.(walls, ceiling, floor)
Plants (X)
Fitting room
Tidiness/ cleanliness/ hygiene (X)

Product accessibility
Arrangement and exposure
On-the-spot information
(e.g. signs referring to product
categories) (X)

Staff
Appearance (X)
Clothing (X)
Name badges (X)

Capacity – waiting time
Staff
Cash desks

Customer handling (in general)
Attentiveness (X)
Friendliness (X)
Recognition of former customers (X)
Handling of customers waiting on line (X)
(fairness, "reassuring tone" etc.)

Order handling
Attentiveness, interest, understanding (X)
of customer's requests etc.
Effective and friendly execution (X)
Giving advice regarding use,
maintenance etc. (X)
Dealing with inability to deliver immediately(promise to deliver at a later point
in time etc.) (X)

Products
Range
Functional properties
Design
Social properties (fashionable)
Finish

Prices
Level
Special offers and discount prices

Ability to deliver and handling of delays (X)

Acceptance of return/exchange
Terms
Implementation (customer handling etc.) (X)

Guarantees
Terms
Implementation (customer handling etc.) (X)

Treatment of complaints
Terms
Implementation (customer handling etc.) (X)

(X) indicates elements in offering being directly dependent on staff's attitudes, competencies, skills and behavior.

specific offering properties with particular values, seen in terms of sacrifices and rewards. We say that buyers acquire subjective *"relevance criteria"*, which *represent potential value for themselves.* Planners, on the other hand, often tend to perceive and describe their offerings in more technical terms.

There will probably always be some conceptual and language barriers between planners and buyers. Consequently, an important task in marketing communication planning is to identify such barriers and translate descriptions of the marketing offering from "vendor language" into "buyer language". Where there is a discrepancy between vendor language and buyer language, elements in an offering must be expressed in terms of buyer relevance criteria, or, preferably, in terms of sacrifices and rewards.

The degree of correspondence between buyer and vendor language will vary, depending on the planner, the market and the marketing offering. Both parties will probably ascribe the same meaning to concepts such as "price", "period of credit", "cash discount" and "interest on overdue payments". However, in cases where the languages do not correspond, the relationship between elements in an offering and relevance criteria/values may be quite complex. For example, one particular element in an offering may be related to one or more relevance criteria. For example, the design of a car may be thought of as an element related to relevance criteria such as "acceleration", "fuel consumption", "driving characteristics", and "appearance". Conversely, one particular relevance criterion may relate to more than one element in an offering. A newspaper editor, for instance, may think of "format", "word usage" and "length of sentences" as relevant elements, whereas all of these are related to the relevance criterion "readability".

Two points should be made regarding relevance criteria:

Firstly, the development of relevance criteria depends on buyer characteristics as well as the context surrounding use of a product. For instance, a buyer's assessment of a sailing boat may be colored by the skill of the captain and crew and the weather conditions prevailing at the time he sailed in it. A diner's enjoyment of his restaurant meal may partly depend on the number of other guests present, on their appearance and behavior. In cases where the buyer has to use the same product in a number of different situations, we may suppose that relevance criteria will reflect both or all of them. An obvious example would be a farmer who has to use the same plow in both flat and hilly terrain, in soft as well as hard soil etc. However, consumers who can afford to do so will often invest in more than one product in order to satisfy their needs in different situations. One might, for example, buy a small boat with an outboard motor for short trips on the fjord, and a larger motorboat for longer excursions.

Secondly, only a buyer with perfect knowledge could have a complete set of relevance criteria in relation to any particular product. A buyer may not know which of a product's properties are reliable indicators of sacrifices and rewards because he has not learned this from others or because he has not used the type of product or service in question. For example, a young couple buying a baby carriage for the first time may overlook the importance of durability or stability, or not have considered how easily the carriage can be cleaned. When making purchasing decisions, buyers with insufficient experience may also attach importance to product properties that they *believe* are relevant, but which are, in fact, irrelevant. For instance, they may, quite wrongly, believe that the size of the pores in the peel of an orange indicates its sweetness. This means that, depending on a buyer's (product) competence, his *"choice criteria"*, i.e. the criteria on which he actually bases his decision-making in relation to a product, may not entirely match his relevance criteria. Consequently, in situations where buyers are expected to be less than competent, we cannot identify relevance criteria solely on knowledge of their choice criteria. A planner has to draw on other sources of information and, in some cases, on pure deduction.

The task of describing a marketing offering in the form of relevance criteria and sacrifices and rewards can be quite demanding. This will be facilitated to the extent that buyers and planners have shared concepts and language to communicate about them, as well as by the level of buyer competence. However, this task has to be carried out in order to create a sufficient basis for evaluating the competitive strength of an offering and for formulating and selecting precise and relevant communication contents.

Figure 4.3. and Figure 4.4. illustrate the task of describing a marketing offering. These figures also illustrate the relationship between elements in an offering, relevance criteria and sacrifices/rewards.

On buyers, users, consumers, buying units and relevance criteria segments

So far, the terms: "buyer", "user" and "consumer" have been used as if these generally referred to one and the same person. Further, it has been implicitly assumed that all buyers in a market develop identical relevance criteria in relation to a product and attach the same importance to the various criteria. In most cases, none of these assumptions hold true.

Firstly, it is obvious that relevance criteria will usually vary from buyer to buyer and that buyers attach varying importance to different criteria. For instance, the opportunity to chat to a bank clerk or shop assistant probably means more to older people than to younger ones. One buyer of a durable consumer product may view period of delivery as most important, while another may consider price as crucial.

Secondly, in many – if not most – cases, more than one person influences the purchasing decision. For example, both parents and their children may influence the decision process leading to the purchase of a car. The acquisition of a series of production robots may involve the company's CEO and all its managers in charge of production, product development, marketing and purchasing.

The individuals who influence a buying decision constitute a *"decision unit"*, whose *members* may have different *roles*. These roles may involve doing such things as introducing relevance criteria, providing information regarding various marketing offerings, discussing the pros and cons of offerings, and making the final decision. Also, members of a decision unit may have different relevance criteria and attach different levels of importance to criteria they have in common. While horsepower and acceleration may be crucial to the husband, the wife may be more concerned with the functionality and design of the car they are planning to buy. The purchasing manager of a company may attach more importance to the price of new personal computers than the staff who will use them, while the latter may more interested in such features as screen size and keyboard design.

Thirdly, a product may be used or consumed by more than one individual. Numerous products are used or consumed by two or more family members. This is true in the case of a house, furniture, a car, or a packet of corn flakes. The entire staff of an office will often make use of products such as electric coffeepots and copying machines.

Finally, users of a product need not necessarily be members of the decision unit. Parents, for instance, make a lot of decisions on behalf of their younger children. Department managers may make decisions about such items as new computing equipment without consulting the users.

In cases where buyers in a business area have differing relevance criteria and priorities, planners should consider grouping them into more homogeneous segments. They should then make a description of the marketing offering in relation to the criteria relevant to each segment. The competitive strength of a marketing offering and the resulting basis for profitable marketing communication is likely to vary considerably from one segment to another.

In situations where the decision unit consists of two or more persons, there are usually good reasons to form relevance criteria segments. In such cases we can expect a variety of relevance criteria and buyer values as well as different priorities as far as sacrifices and rewards are concerned. For example, in a company selling production machines one might operate with seg-

86 *Describing the marketing offering*

ments such as "users/operators", "buyers (purchasing managers/ assistant buyers)", "production managers", and "top managers". This is because, in general, different members of a decision unit are involved in different types of contact with the company's organizational basis. For example, staff who use personal computers in their work may be involved in "soft" and/or "hard" contacts related to preparing to use and using a new computer product themselves, while staff from the purchasing department may be involved in "soft" and/or "hard" contacts related to preparing to buy and buying it. In addition we can expect to find great diversity of personal motives and preferences, job content and position held in the company and perceived role in the buying process. In such cases, in order to identify relevant segments, the "buyer's route" must be viewed as a process involving all members of the decision unit. That is, in his work on identifying elements in an offering and corresponding relevance

Figure 4.3. Describing the offering

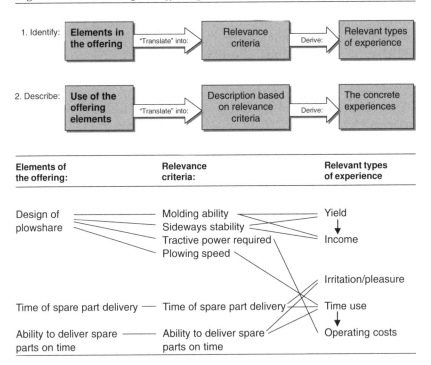

criteria and sacrifices/rewards along the "buyer's route", the planner must consider all relevant contacts between *all* members of the decision unit concerned and the company's organizational basis.

Summing up

Roughly, the tasks that planners have to perform in order to gain the necessary insight into a marketing offering may be summed up as follows:

1. To acquire sufficient insight into

   - relevant areas of use,
   - decision units (members, distribution of roles), and
   - buyers' levels of competence relating to purchasing and using/consuming the product in question.

2. To identify and define all relevant elements in an offering at an adequate conceptual level.

3. To identify and define relevance criteria and sacrifices/rewards connected to the various elements in an offering. Depending on the degree of heterogeneity among buyers, to consider the need for working with relevance criterion segments.

4. Based on the results of the work with task 1 – 3:

To describe the marketing offering of the company and competing offerings preferably in terms of relevance criteria and sacrifices/rewards (buyer values), and to use this description as a basis for

   - evaluating the competitive strength of the company's marketing offering.
   - selecting and formulating relevant and precise communication contents.

88 *Describing the marketing offering*

It may be necessary to make one description in relation to each of two or more different areas of use and/or relevance criteria segments. In cases where buyers lack the competence required to fill the various buyer roles, it may be advisable to formulate contents aimed at developing buyer competence.

In order to avoid confusion about the concepts "marketing offering" and "marketing communication", it should be emphasized that communication processes as such may be an integral part of marketing offerings. For instance, communication processes are fundamental ingredients of elements in an offering such as post-purchase services and complaint handling. However, such communication processes are *not* considered here to be *marketing* communication processes, since they do not aim at

- conveying the properties/value of a marketing offering or relevant vendor characteristics,
- "showing the way" to an offering/a vendor or
- reminding buyers of the existence of or of the "way to" an offering/a vendor.

On the contrary, they are a necessary part of what the buyer *pays* for, directly influencing buyer value. In a *perfectly informed market*, i.e. a market where all buyers knew everything about an offering and "the way" to that offering, a company would have *no marketing communication tasks*, and consequently would not spend any resources on marketing communication activities. Still, many kinds of communication processes would take place in connection with such tasks as guarantee handling and various kinds of pre- and post-purchase services. Sales, however, would be based totally on buyer initiative in the form of orders.

Figure 4.4. A model for identifying offering elements, relevance criteria and relevant types of experience (buyer value)

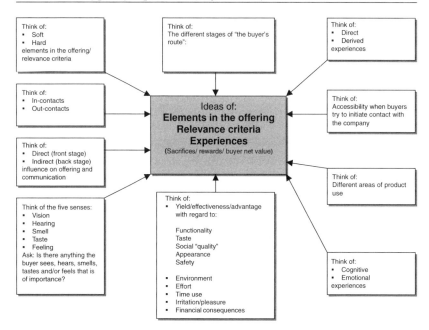

5. Transformation communication. Conveying the marketing offering in transformation markets

Chapter 4 discussed the issue of how a standardized offering can be described. In Chapter 2, it was pointed out that offerings in many markets are only partly standardized, in the sense of being decided upon "in advance", whereas the core of the offering, including the physical product or service in question, is customized to the specific needs of each buyer. One might say that the resources and capabilities of the vendor company are transformed into a customized competitive offering. Examples of typical transformation markets are markets for such things as offshore installations, office buildings, production plants, buildings, ICT-software, market analyses, and consulting services. This chapter will elaborate the task of conveying the marketing offering in transformation markets.

Vendor roles and customization processes in transformation markets

As emphasized already the task of conveying the marketing offering is more comprehensive and complex in transformation markets than in standard markets. In transformation markets, performing this task includes:

1. Standard communication, i.e. conveying the standardized part of the offering.

   This function may also include conveying information about relevant organizational characteristics indicating the company's ability to deliver competitive customized offerings.

2. Transformation communication, i.e. carrying through a dialogue with the buyer in order to develop a competitive customized offering.

The difference between standard and transformation communication is illustrated in Figure 5.1.

Depending on the degree of involvement on the part of the potential suppliers in the development of the customized offering, a distinction may be drawn between two different roles:

- a *tendering* role, and
- a *problem solving* role.

A buyer may specify the offering in great detail and invite tenders. In such cases, the supplier adopts a tendering role. His involvement in the development of the marketing offering is relatively modest and typically limited to elements such as price, period of delivery and terms of payment. The tendering role is typical of that adopted by such companies as sub-contractors in markets for buildings, quay structures, airports and road construction.

In other cases a buyer may not specify exactly what he wants to buy, but instead, approach the buying process more openly. His understanding of his needs and problems may be less than clear. The same may apply to opportunities to be exploited, important properties of the marketing offering and so on. For example, a company seeking consulting services may approach potential providers of those services with no more than a recognition that it is losing money and that "something has to be done". A firm that has decided to invest in a new production building may approach a contractor with no more than general ideas about size and margin of expenditure. In such cases the selected potential suppliers adopt a problem solving role, playing an active part in finding a solution in cooperation with the buyer. Possible solutions, i.e. customized offerings, are developed through dialogues between the buyer and each of the suppliers. These involve such processes as investigations, analyses and developmental work as well as negotiations regarding possible solutions. These processes lead to descriptions of alternative customized offerings which may take the form of project plans, written specifications, working drawings, models and cost estimations etc.

Some markets are characterized by *"advance transformation"*. This means that *the customized offering is specified completely before the buyer makes his choice* among the potential suppliers. This is the case with products such as offshore installations, ships, major steel constructions like large TV-antennas and electric masts, production machines and buildings. In other markets a complete advance specification of the customized offering is impossible. Research and development and consulting services

Figure 5.1. Standard vs. transformation communication

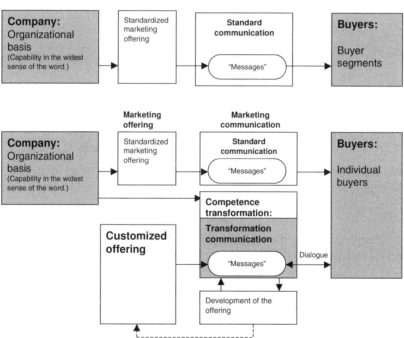

are among the most obvious examples of operators in these markets. Since customized marketing offerings of that kind involve exploration of unknown territory, they are inherently incapable of being specified completely in advance. The offering has to be customized step by step based on experience and knowledge acquired on the way. For example, consultancy assistance in connection with a strategic reorganization project often starts off with an agreement to carry through a preliminary project to explore the problems faced by the organization and uncover the need for reorganization in greater detail. A typical consultancy agreement will cover such items as the kind of services to be delivered, a budget, hourly fees and time schedules. Increasing insight into problems requiring attention, and possible solutions to them, provide a basis on which buyers and consultant can take new initiatives, discuss additional projects and implement new practices relating to marketing, production, logistics and so on. By degrees, the buyer evaluates what has been delivered and decides whether or not to continue working together with the service provider in question. Such *step-by-step competence transformation* is here termed "*process transformation*".

The buying process and the task of conveying the offering in transformation markets. The relevance of supplier criteria

In transformation markets there are five phases in a typical buying process.

The five phases are as follows:

1. The buyer specifies needs, relevance criteria, important product properties, decides how he wants to approach potential suppliers, etc.

2. The buyer decides which companies will be considered as potential suppliers and invited to offer, i.e. be included in a "bidders' list".

The buying process and the task of conveying the offering   95

3. Marketing offerings are specified and developed through a process of *"competence transformation"*, i.e. in *dialogues between the buyer and the suppliers* selected. Each dialogue results in a proposal for a partly customized and partly standardized offering. Thus, competence transformation includes *marketing communication* as well as *development of an offering*.

4. The buyer chooses a supplier and a marketing offering.

5. The selected supplier produces and delivers the marketing offering.

The relevance of the various kinds of marketing communication varies from one phase to another in the buying process:

Phases 1 and 2:
It is, of course, meaningless to talk about transformation communication as long as the buyer is in the process of making up his mind about how he wants to approach suppliers or is still deciding which companies should be given the opportunity to tender. Standard communication is appropriate to these two first phases of the buying process. This involves conveying the standardized part of the offering as well as information about the criteria which must be satisfied to show that a potential supplier is capable of developing and delivering a competitive customized offering.

Buyers in transformation markets will generally draw on experience when developing sets of such *"supplier criteria"*, defined here as *criteria indicating potential suppliers' capacity to develop, produce and deliver sufficiently competitive customized offerings to satisfy the buyer's relevance criteria*. Examples of supplier criteria are: size (sales volume, staff), references (to customers), and various characteristics of the organizational basis such as competence of key employees, ICT- and production technology, quality control system, suppliers, working capital and equity. Supplier criteria obviously constitute the main basis for selecting and formulating relevant content elements in standard communication carried through in the two first phases of the buying process. That is, to the extent that the offering is not standardized, supplier criteria are substituted for relevance criteria. The term "relevant content" refers to ways in which companies actually satisfy important supplier criteria, for instance, to specific competence possessed by key staff, to a specific quality control system that has been implemented or to specific customized offerings that have been delivered to specific customers.

Phase 3:
In the third phase of the buying process, competence transformation processes are carried through with selected potential suppliers. Marketing communication mainly takes the form of transformation communication. Members of the potential supplier's staff will study for example sketches and/or specifications produced by the buyer's organization and buyer's responses to their queries in order to understand the buyer's underlying problems, needs and wishes.

Where the vendor company has a problem solving role, a major task is to identify the buyer's relevance criteria, which constitute the principal point of departure for transforming the capabilities of the organizational basis into a competitive customized marketing offering. Relevance criteria can be revealed in a number of ways. Alternative solutions can be outlined, discussed and negotiated. In the process, the buyer may fully or partly accept suggested solutions or reject them. The competence transformation process leads to a customized offering constituting the core of the total offering to be considered by the buyer.

Various media may be used in the dialogue. More often than not, communication takes the form of personal communication in the form of face-to-face meetings and conversations over the telephone between two or more persons, supplemented by impersonal media such as letters, reports, facsimile and e-mail. The number of contacts between seller and buyer is often quite large. Transformation communication frequently concerns a relatively large part of the seller's as well as the buyer's organization. Considerable numbers of staff on each side are often involved in communication and developmental processes. These will include research and development staff, consultants, sales staff and employees working within spheres of activity such as marketing, engineering, service, production and finance.

Of course, it is also necessary to convey the standardized part of the offering during the third phase of the buying process. It may also be the most appropriate time to communicate the company's position as regards supplier criteria in order to convince the buyer that the seller is capable of fulfilling his delivery obligations.

Phases 4 and 5:
In the last two phases of the buying process, when the buyer has chosen a supplier, and the selected supplier produces and delivers the marketing offering, most contacts between seller and buyer will concern production and delivery of the customized offering. However, in process transformation markets, where marketing offerings are developed piecemeal, transformation communication processes and production and delivery processes are interwoven.

A preliminary organizational development project provides a good illustration of this, since its precise purpose is to lay the foundation for carrying through a dialogue about the next phase in the process, namely that of developing the next constituent(s) of the marketing offering.

Summing up. Describing the marketing offering in transformation markets

Figure 5.2. sums up the various kinds of transformation communication and the tasks connected to conveying the marketing offering in various phases of the buying process. The suggestions made and conclusions reached in Chapter 4 may be generalized to apply to every aspect of the task of describing the standardized component of the offering in transformation markets. However, in addition to identifying relevance criteria planners must identify relevant supplier criteria, and describe the company's concrete position regarding these criteria. Describing the customized component of a marketing offering is as integral a part of the buying process, as is the task of describing the rest of the offering.

The differences between standard and transformation markets do not mean that "the buyer's route" may not serve as useful procedure and source of inspiration. In relation to each phase in the buying process, planners may aim to identify those contacts between buyers and the company's organizational basis that may influence the (net-) value that those buyers experience in their dealings with the company. For example, in a search along the phase involving competence transformation, a plan-

Figure 5.2. Advance and process transformation

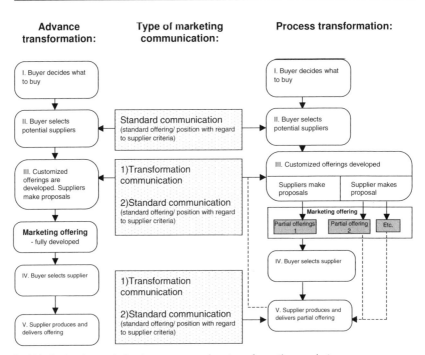

I – V indicate phases in buying processes in a transformation market.

ner might easily identify a number of significant elements in addition to relevant product characteristics. Examples of these are: "accessibility of key staff", "ability to meet agreed deadlines" and "ability to provide quick and relevant answers to questions".

The above sections have been mostly concerned with transformation communication in industrial markets. This is not meant to imply that customization of marketing offerings does not take place in consumer markets as well. Examples of consumer transformation markets are the markets for such products as private houses, gardening services, financial assistance and hairdressing. A hairdresser may ask how a customer wants his hair done while actually cutting it. As the hair cut proceeds, both sides observe and comment on the result. Finally, the hairdresser will want to know if the customer is satisfied. The customer will accept or ask for further modifications. Such a dialogue between customer and hairdresser is an example of transformation communication.

In general, buying processes can be assumed to be simpler in consumer markets than in industrial markets. This may be so, because in many consumer markets the risks perceived in connection with supplier selection are relatively low. Compared to markets for such things as advertising campaigns, ships or offshore installations where costs can run into millions of dollars, much less may be at stake and less may be won by considering two or more potential suppliers.

In consumer markets for products where financial outlay is relatively modest and/or social relevance criteria are non-existent or unimportant, consumers tend to start out trying one supplier on the basis of limited information gathering. Whether or not they will remain loyal to this supplier or try another one, depends on their experience in each case. However, if the price level is high and/or social relevance criteria are important, as in markets such as that for private houses, two or more suppliers may be involved. Thus, relatively extensive information processing and problem solving processes may equally well take place in consumer markets.[17]

Marketing offering, marketing communication and buyer-seller relationships

In Chapter 2 it was mentioned in passing that buyers and suppliers may develop fairly close relationships.[18] One reason for this may be the prospect of increased profits in cases where a strong relationship can increase the earnings of both parties to a level that would be impossible to achieve without close co-operation. Close relationships may be characterized by mutual dependence through social, structural, economic and/or legal bonds. At least in the short run, changing suppliers generally incurs *"switching costs"* in the form of such things as time lost, lower sales volume, and increased expenditure connected to reorganization, increased marketing effort and production. Changing suppliers also incurs loss of social relations with members of the former supplier's staff.

A buyer-seller relationship is primarily a function of properties of the marketing offering. Standardized as well as customized offerings may be developed with the aim of ensuring that buyers who go elsewhere incur switching costs. For instance, in the market for office accessories, the benefit from a bonus depending on the size of total annual purchase may be lost if the buyer switches supplier before the end of the year. Another example is where disloyalty to an airline which operates a frequent flyer scheme reduces the chances of going on a bonus trip.

However, it is in industrial transformation markets that strong relationships are most likely to develop. Dialogues are carried through with the purpose of developing customized offerings that may enhance the mutual benefits of co-operation. Bonds tend to strengthen to the degree that *buyer-specific* changes are implemented in the organizational bases of the two parties in the form of things like joint investments in new production technology, in the acquisition of special competencies or in new divisions of tasks and responsibilities. While such changes increase the seller's competitiveness in relation to *one* specific buyer, they may, at the same time, decrease his ability to compete for *other* buyers. The buyer will also be liable to greater switching costs, as a result, since other suppliers are unlikely to implement similar changes. More often than not, buyer-specific organizational adaptations are accordingly made within the framework of long-term supply contracts or strategic partnerships and alliances.

The implications of close buyer-seller relationships such as those discussed above are that, in transformation markets especially, strategic marketing communication planning must also take into account the strength of buyer-seller relationships that are considered desirable. The vendor company may aim to compete in ways that are more or less binding. Furthermore, it means that seller characteristics that indicate his ability and willingness to co-operate may be important supplier criteria. Examples are: attitude toward close collaboration, technology used, competencies, and financial strength.

6. Developing buyer competence. Summing up the tasks of marketing communication

It has been pointed out that buyer competence may vary from one market to another and over time in the same market. Marketing communication planners face the task of enhancing the competence of buyers when this is insufficient. By developing buyers' purchasing competence and user/consumer competence and educating them to fill requisite purchasing or user/consumer roles, companies may:

- make potential buyers more inclined to purchase their products – and
- secure optimal performance of their offerings in the market place.

This means that conveying the offering may also involve "educating" buyers or *developing their competence.* This chapter discusses this *"development task"* and sums up the other tasks involved in marketing communication.

The development task of marketing communication

Low levels of competence in a market will be reflected by a corresponding lack of awareness of the existence of the product in question. Moreover, buyers are less likely to know what a particular product can be used for or how it can be used, or to know about such things as related sacrifices and rewards, important relevance and supplier criteria and so on. Consequently, the aim of *"development communication"* may be to achieve the following five objectives:

1. Make buyers aware of the existence and relevance of a product.
2. Inform about important relevance criteria.
3. Inform about relationships between various relevance criteria and various kinds of sacrifices and rewards.
4. Inform about the relationship between relevance criteria and supplier criteria.
5. Teach the buyer how to use the product, i.e. how to make the necessary buyer contribution.

Examples of content elements related to each of these objectives are:

1. Make buyers aware of the existence and relevance of a product:
Communication contents may concern general properties of a product, areas of use, and purposes for which it can be used. Also, communication contents may deal with problems that the product may help to solve, opportunities it may help to exploit, and needs that it may satisfy, in short, with relevant sacrifices and rewards. For example, when a bank informs consumers of the existence of its *bank card*, its messages might convey the following:

- that something called a "bank card" exists,
- that their card is of a particular size, that it has a magnetic strip and a picture of the owner on it,
- that it can be used as proof of identity,
- that it can be used as a credit card in stores, restaurants etc., as a cash card in stores, and – in combination with a personal code – to draw money at cash points,
- that using a bank card reduces the probability of theft because it reduces the need for carrying checks and (large amounts of) cash
- that using the card saves time and effort – and
- that one can draw on one's account at any time.

2. Inform about important relevance criteria:
An example of this kind of information is where young parents who are about to purchase their first baby carriage might be made aware of the relevance of properties such as its stability, the reliability of its brakes, whether its colors are resistant to fading and whether it is easy to clean.

3. Inform about relationships between various relevance criteria and various kinds of sacrifices and rewards:
The young parents in the above example might be made aware of the relationship between the dependability of brakes and stability, on the one hand, and on the other hand the chance that the child might be injured. Similarly, a salmon breeder might be made aware of the importance of counting the fish regularly to ensure correct "supply of fodder" and "medicine" (relevance criteria), thereby reducing "operating costs" (sacrifice) and enhancing "water quality" (reward) in the fjord where the breeding plant is situated.

4. Inform about the relationship between relevance criteria and supplier criteria:
Communication content might, for example, deal with the relationship between the level of expert knowledge of environmental subjects possessed by an architectural or engineering firm and the probability that competence transformation processes will result in environmentally acceptable road, bridge or building projects.

5. Teach the buyer how to use the product, i.e. how to make the necessary buyer contribution:
Examples of this are where buyers have to be taught how to use PC-programs or a new, robot-based production system. Dealers may need to learn how to handle and market satellite dishes. In transformation markets development communication might aim at preparing a potential partner for entering into a closer buyer-seller relationship by suggesting and discussing new ways in which to co-operate.

106 *Developing buyer competence*

Summing up the tasks of marketing communication

In conclusion, the potential tasks of marketing communication may be summed up as follows:

1. Conveying the offering through:

a. *development communication* (i.e. developing buyer competence/ performing development tasks).

b. *standard communication,* conveying

   - the standardized (part of the) offering.
   - the company's position as to supplier criteria indicating the company's ability to develop and deliver competitive customized offerings (i.e. performing standard communication tasks.)

c. *transformation communication,* i.e. contributing to the development of customized offerings, i.e. performing transformation communication tasks as

   - advance transformation or
   - process transformation.

2. "Showing the way" to the offering, i.e. informing about how, where and when standard offerings can be purchased – and customized offerings negotiated.

3. Reminding buyers of standardized offerings or maintaining buyers' awareness of the company's position as to important supplier criteria.

Which tasks *actually exist in a specific planning situation,* depend on a number of conditions. One such factor is the nature and extent of marketing communication activities that have been implemented in previous planning periods. Tasks that existed when an offering was introduced will already have been carried out. Several factors will determine the tasks that are worth tackling from the point of view of profitability in any forthcoming planning period. One such factor is the competitiveness of the marketing offering, which is, of course, a strong determinant of sales prospects. Another relevant factor is the contribution margin per unit sold.

The next chapter discusses how a company's communication tasks depend on the degree of market penetration of a product or offering.

7. How communication tasks are determined by degree of market penetration of a product, an offering or company reputation

The relationship between communication tasks and degree of market penetration of a product

Degree of product penetration

A product that has not yet been introduced has a *degree of market penetration* equal to zero. A few decades ago, this was the case with products such as personal computers, bank cards, and production robots. After a new product has been introduced, it gradually penetrates the market until it reaches its *"saturation level"*. Not all consumers or companies in a society are potential buyers of all kinds of products. For example, some consumers will never go on the Internet and consequently never become buyers of internet-related products. Cornflakes are not consumed in every household, some families do not own a video tape recorder, and a relatively large proportion of the adult population has not taken out life insurance. A number of factors affect the saturation level of a product. Relevant determinants will include the strengths of a product when compared with alternative offerings, price levels and so on. All other things being equal, the saturation level of a product will be directly proportional to its perceived advantages and in inverse proportion to its price.

A product penetrates a market up to the saturation level at a certain *rate*. In the case of non-durable products such as soft drinks, cosmetics, hotel services, and office accessories, which last for a *shorter* period of time than a planning period, increased penetration means that *demand* increases from one planning period to another until the saturation level is reached. For durable products such as personal computers, video machines and PC programs, which normally last *longer* than a planning period, enhanced penetration means that the *stock* of the product in the market increases. That is, the number of households or businesses owning the product in question grows. We may assume that the *"penetration rate" of a product* will be increased by such factors as the number and nature of its perceived functional advantages over other products, and its social acceptability. Conversely, its penetration rate will be hampered by other factors such as price level and the nature and extent of the required buyer contribution (complexity, learning costs). Moreover, it seems reasonable to suppose that, other things being equal, the more conspicuously a product is used, the faster it will penetrate a market.

The term *"degree of product penetration"* – or just *"product penetration"* – may be defined as follows for

1. a non-durable product:

$$\frac{\text{Actual demand of a product in a given period of time} * 100}{\text{Saturation level}}$$

For instance, if the demand volume in a given period of time is 1 000 000 and the saturation level is estimated at 5 000 000, the degree of product penetration is 20 (%).

2. a durable product:

$$\frac{\text{Stock of a product at a given point in time} * 100}{\text{Saturation level}}$$

If the saturation level is estimated at e.g. 700 and the stock 350, the degree of product penetration is 50 (%).

Product penetration and development tasks

It is assumed here that buyer competence is at its lowest level when a new product is introduced to the market and that it increases as the degree of product penetration increases. This means that product penetration may be used as an indicator of the extent of development tasks facing sellers in a market. The less a new product resembles existing ones, the less buyers are able to call upon previously acquired insights and skills relating to its use. Accordingly, low product penetration means more development tasks. The newer the product, the more comprehensive and complex these are likely to be. As the degree of penetration grows, the number and complexity of development tasks decreases. Gradually buyers learn that the product exists, become aware of its relevance to their needs, of relevance criteria, associated sacrifices and rewards, and so on. When product penetration approaches 100, most – if not all – buyers will have acquired a relatively high level of competence.

Figure 7.1. shows how the degree of product penetration, actual demand and development tasks develop through time. Of course, the saturation level of a product is not necessarily a constant, as assumed in the figure. It may grow as a function of among other things an increasing number of buying households or companies, or because of gradual reductions of the price level. In recent years this has been the case in markets for products such as fax machines, personal computers and printers. However, one reason that the extent of development tasks does not grow in proportion to the saturation level, is that new, potential buyers have the opportunity to learn from experienced buyers in the market place.

Obviously, terms such as saturation level, product penetration, actual and potential demand etc. have meanings only in relation to given areas of use. In cases where one aims to develop new areas of use, new development tasks will have to be performed.

Market development versus market utilization

A number of factors determine the demand for a product in a given planning period. Among these are previous price levels and the scale and nature of the marketing communication activity of competing companies in previous periods. Furthermore, the possibility exists that, in a given planning period, a company can stimulate some latent needs and persuade otherwise potential buyers to become *actual buyers, i.e. by realizing part of a potential demand. The process of making potential buyers become actual buyers through marketing communication* is referred to here as *"market development"* as distinct from *"market utilization"*, the purpose of which is *to win a share of the total demand that would have been realized* irrespective of the company's efforts. As product penetration increases in a market, the opportunities for market utilization *increase*, while the opportunities for market development *decrease*. Of course, market development is not only relevant in connection with the introduction and penetration of new products, but also in connection with the development of new areas of use.

Non-durable products: The relationship between communication tasks and the degree of market penetration of an offering

The degree of penetration of an offering

For a non-durable, standardized offering the *"degree of (market) penetration of an offering"* is defined here as:

$$\frac{\text{The number of buyers at the beginning of a planning period who have a sufficient knowledge of the offering and of the "way" to the offering}}{\text{The number of buyers who can be expected to actually buy the product in the time period in question}} * 100$$

Non-durable products 113

Figure 7.1. Development of product penetration in a market

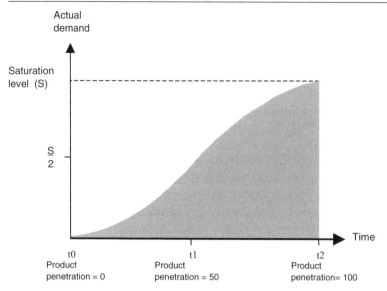

Low product penetration means:	High product penetration means:
Actual demand low Market development Buyer competence low	Actual demand high Market utilization Buyer competence high
Communication tasks: Development tasks Standard communication tasks "Showing the way" to offering Reminding of offering Transformation communication	*Communication tasks:* Standard communication tasks "Showing the way" to offering Reminding of offering Transformation communication

The degree of product penetration is defined here as:

$$\text{Degree of product penetration} = \frac{\text{Actual demand} * 100}{S}$$

S = Demand at saturation level

For instance, in t1 above, the degree of product penetration is equal to 50; i.e.: $\frac{S/2 * 100}{S}$

That is, if the number of actual buyers in a planning period is expected to be 10 000, and at the beginning of the period 5 000 of these buyers have sufficient knowledge of the offering and the "way" to the offering, the degree of penetration is 50 (%). The number of actual buyers in a planning period depends, of course, on the degree of product penetration.

As a preliminary assumption, let – for the sake of simplicity- the degree of product penetration be equal to 100. Obviously, the degree of penetration of a completely new offering is equal to zero. No buyers have sufficient knowledge of the offering or the "way" to it. Consequently, the company is faced with a large number of standard communication tasks, including those concerned with "showing the way" to the offering. Conversely, there will be no old customers to be reminded of the offering. Sales volume will depend totally on seller initiative as no basis exists for buyer-initiated orders or inquiries.

As a function of marketing communication activities on the part of the company, buyers' knowledge of the offering as well as of the "way" to the offering gradually increase through time. More and more buyers learn the "way" to the offering, make (trial) purchases and gain direct experience with the offering.

Pre- and post-purchase experience may result in

a. rejection,
b. preference or
c. indifference

on the part of the buyer. "*Indifference*" means that the buyer "*considers the offering neither better nor worse than one or more competing offerings he has tried earlier*".

As in the case of a new product, a new offering penetrates a market at a certain *rate*. The penetration rate of an offering is primarily a function of the extent and nature of the marketing communication activities carried through by the company. In some markets, multi-step communication effects enhance the rate. Such effects may take the form of word-of-mouth between two or more buyers concerning an offering and post-purchase

Non-durable products 115

experience. Or they may simply be due to product visibility. Potential customers may become aware of an offering as well as acquiring some knowledge about it simply by observing it being consumed, as, for example when someone is seen enjoying a soft drink or a hamburger.

The degree of market penetration of an offering and the nature and extent of communication tasks

Obviously, the degree of penetration of an offering may be used as an indicator of the nature and number of communication tasks facing the company. As an offering penetrates a market, the following changes occur:

1. The number of tasks connected with "showing the way" to the offering decreases. More and more buyers acquire knowledge of how, where and when the offering can be purchased.

2. The number of standard communication tasks decreases. To an ever-increasing extent buyers try the offering and react with preference or rejection. In relation to these buyers, additional communication makes no difference, i.e. there are no communication tasks.

3. The number of tasks concerned with reminding previous buyers of the offering increases to a level corresponding to the development in the number of indifferent buyers.

Also, as a competitive offering gradually penetrates a market, the amount of buyer initiative increases. To the extent that buyers learn about the offering and react with preference or indifference, a basis is created for buyer-initiated inquiries and orders. As a consequence, buyer initiative accounts for an increasing proportion of the total sales volume. However, a company can only expand "*buyer initiative sales volume*", i.e. sales volume *attributable to buyer initiative*, to the extent that its accessibility and capacity to respond to buyers' initiatives keeps pace with penetration. Needless to say, the stronger the competitiveness of an offering, the larger the buyer initiative sales potential. This is

116   How communication tasks are determined

so because competitive strength means preference and favorable word-of-mouth or at least, indifference.

The above discussion has assumed a degree of product penetration equal to 100. In cases where product penetration is lower, the number of actual buyers will increase from one planning period to another. Obviously, the degree of penetration of an offering decreases to the extent that such an enhancement in the number of buyers takes place. Accordingly, all things being equal, the effect of market growth is an increase in the number of standard communication tasks and tasks connected to "showing the way" to the offering in question.

Figure 7.2. illustrates the relationship between the degree of market penetration of a standardized offering, the nature and extent of communication tasks, and the relative importance of buyer and seller initiative.

Durable products: The relationship between communication tasks and company reputation

The concepts of "degree of market penetration of an offering", "preference", "rejection" and "indifference" are relevant only in relation to markets for non-durable products where a specific offering is purchased and consumed repeatedly in a planning period. Durable products are bought infrequently. Their lifetime covers at least one – and usually several – planning periods, during which the companies competing in a market introduce completely new offerings and/or implement changes in current offerings. For example, in the car market, new models appear every year. In innovative markets such as the markets for ICT hardware and software, products are changed continuously. This means that when a buyer enters the market in order to replace a durable product, he faces offerings quite different from those between which he chose when he bought the product he intends to replace. Consequently, it makes little sense to talk about rejection or repurchasing based on preference or indifference in relation to a specific offering.

In markets for durable products, buyers are continuously entering and leaving the market place. Some of these are first time buyers. Others enter the market to replace durable products they already own. Buyers of such items as cars or furniture may enter and leave the market in a matter of weeks or days, which means that the market is constantly being renewed. Accordingly, a specific offering cannot be said to penetrate a market in the sense that was discussed above. Since new buyers are continuously entering the market, the number of standard communication tasks and tasks connected with "showing the way" to the offering do *not* decrease as a result of communication activities carried through in any planning period. Indifferent buyers are non-existent, and so is the task of reminding buyers of the offering.

However, in the course of time, a *company reputation* develops as a spin-off effect of buyers' experiences with offerings. Some buyers purchase offerings and experience their value directly. Others may be influenced by word-of-mouth and/or product visibility. Quite obviously, a company's reputation may form a basis for buyers' perceptions of new offerings, their expectations regarding them and interest in them. For example, if a specific car model or production machine has performed entirely satisfactorily for several years, the owner is likely to show active interest in new models of the same make.

It is reasonable to assume that a company's reputation may affect the nature and number of communication tasks from one planning period to another. The emergence of a positive reputation may reduce the number of standard communication tasks and the need to "show the way" to an offering and become the source of increased buyer initiative. Beliefs and expectations based on experiences with earlier offerings may, however, be more or less correct. Therefore, in a dynamic perspective communication tasks will depend on the nature as well as on the size of changes made in subsequent offerings. Communication tasks are, of course, also a function of the degree of product penetration. When a market grows, the number of communication tasks tends to increase.

Figure 7.2. Relationship between extent and nature of communication tasks and degree of penetration of an offering

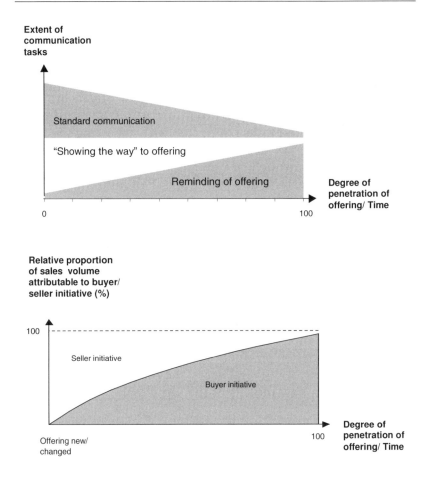

Transformation markets

Thus far the discussion has focused on markets for standardized offerings. As far as transformation markets are concerned, the main line of the above reasoning applies to standard communication tasks and tasks connected with "showing the way" to the offering. Gradually, as a result of communication activities on the part of the company, buyers learn about the standardized part of an offering and the company's position on supplier criteria. In other words, communication tasks become fewer as the degree of penetration of the standardized part of an offering and knowledge about the company's position on supplier criteria increase. However, every single customized offering requires transformation communication. Given satisfactory competitive strength in the part of a company, an *increase* in the degree of penetration will lead to an increase in the number of transformation communication tasks.

Strategic implications

Changes in the nature and number of communication tasks

The above assumptions and reasoning regarding communication tasks and buyer initiative have important strategic implications.

Low product penetration calls for development tasks to be undertaken. To develop buyer competence requires resources. Therefore, market development costs more than market utilization. Consequently, all things being equal, *the higher the degree of product penetration, the lower the communication cost per sale.*

A company which is about to introduce a new, non-durable standardized offering faces a relatively large number of tasks connected to conveying the offering and "the way" to the offering. As the degree of penetration increases, tasks will gradually be performed and the extent of buyer initiative increased. As a consequence, communication cost per sale decreases. When the degree of penetration is high, there are fewer tasks and more buyer-initiated contacts.

The same main line of reasoning holds true as regards the effects of enhanced penetration of the standardized part of an offering and/or the company's position with regard to supplier criteria in a transformation market. In markets for non-durable products the spread of a positive company reputation tends to have the same kind of effects. The better and the more widespread a product's reputation is, the larger the extent of buyer initiative and the lower the communication cost per sale.

Changes in the extent of buyer initiative

If buyer-initiated contacts can be utilized at lower costs per sale than those involved in making a corresponding turnover through seller-initiated contacts, companies can make considerable savings and show correspondingly higher profits. As a rule it will pay to adopt a communication strategy, which ensures that sufficient resources are allocated to handling and following up buyers' initiatives before resources are allocated to seller-initiated contacts. All other things being equal this means that, *as the degree of penetration of its offering or a favorable reputation increases, a company should increase its allocation of marketing communication resources to handling and following up buyer initiatives.*

The view expressed above may be supported by three main arguments:

1. Buyer initiative entails a higher probability of making a sale than does seller initiative.

2. Buyer initiative means lower communication costs.

3. Companies and their offerings tend to penetrate markets by attacking, utilizing and "draining" what they suppose to be the most profitable market segments first.

The first argument is that *a buyer initiative entails a higher probability of making a sale than does a seller initiative.* To take an illustrative example: In a planning period a buyer initiative potential exists in relation to a particular offering. Initial contacts have been established between a vendor company and a certain number of buyers. All contacts are dealt with equally competitively by the organization. All things being equal, there is a considerably greater probability of making a sale based on a buyer-initiated contact than of making a sale based on a seller-initiated contact.

For the sake of simplicity, we may compare the case of a salesman making phone calls to 100 buyers with that of 100 buyers calling the sales department of the company in question. Most importantly, all the buyers calling the sales department will be *"in the market"* for the product in question. They will feel a need for it and intend to purchase it. Not even the most able salesman could be expected to achieve such a degree of efficiency as to identifying potential customers. Campaigns employing mass media are, of course, less efficient. Only a minority of consumers exposed to a company's magazine advertisements or TV-spots will respond by trying to get access to its organization. Buyers showing initiative may be supposed to be far more interested in making a purchase. Those who want to place an order are likely to know precisely what they want, while those who wish to make inquiries are active information seekers.

Unlike potential customers who are approached by salesmen, the great majority of those buyers who initiate contacts may be presumed to have a favorable or at least neutral attitude towards the company and/or the offering in question. Otherwise, they would be unlikely to approach the seller in the first place. That is, buyers who take initiatives *are already interested* in the company's offering to some degree. This may be true of former and existing customers whose expectations are based on experience of the company and its offerings, as well as of new, potential customers who have value-expectations derived from the good reputation of the company. In short, the possibility of making a sale to a buyer who wishes to place an order should be as favorable as can be imagined, and the likelihood of selling to a favorably disposed inquirer will always be relatively strong. The second argument is that *buyer initiative means lower communication costs,* both variable, fixed and stepped costs. *"Variable costs"* are *costs directly related to the level of activity.* *"Fixed costs"* are *costs that do not vary with the level of activity* (depreciation included). *"Stepped costs"* are *fixed up to given levels of activity and "jump" as different levels are reached.*

Variable, fixed and stepped costs are connected with

- establishing initial contacts,
- handling, orders and inquiries and
- following up orders and inquiries.

Examples of variable costs involved in establishing contacts are those incurred in the creation, production and distribution of advertising messages through broadcast media, the Internet, magazines and brochures. Expenses incurred on travel, postage, telephone calls, E-mails and facsimile transmissions in connection with making initial contacts and handling and follow-up orders and inquiries are also variable costs. Typical examples of fixed/stepped costs are wages to managers, sales personnel and other employees who deal with buyers, telephone and facsimile subscription rentals and depreciation in connection with telematic, ICT and video equipment, showrooms and conference facilities.

It should be obvious that the average variable cost involved in dealing with a buyer-initiated contact will normally be lower than the average cost incurred in dealing with a seller-initiated contact. First of all it is the buyer, not the seller, who usually pays whatever it costs to make the initial approach, for instance, when he makes a call to a company's management, sales, order or production department or goes in person to a store or restaurant. In most cases, processing orders involves little effort and no follow-up activity.

As far as fixed/stepped costs are concerned, it is appropriate to compare the capacity required to deal with buyer-initiated contacts with that required to deal with seller- initiated contacts. It seems reasonable to suppose that on the average a buyer-initiated contact requires less capacity than a seller-initiated one. Relatively little capacity is required to deal with orders. Moreover, it is likely that less time and effort are needed to deal with interested buyers whose attitude towards one's own company is favorable at the outset.

The greater probability of making sales and the lower cost levels connected with buyer initiative are effects of learning processes in the market place. Buyers who take purchasing initiatives will tend to return to the company on the basis of favorable experiences with offerings and/or buyer-seller relationships. Previous transactions may provide a basis for more effective exchange processes. Some costs will be completely eliminated, while others may be reduced because handling and follow-up activities do not need to be "repeated". Sales made on the initiative of the buyer are more efficient and therefore cost less to transact than those initiated by the seller.

The third argument is that *companies and their offerings tend to penetrate markets by attacking, utilizing and "draining" what they suppose to be the most profitable market segments first.* Under normal circumstances businesses do not achieve 100% market shares. As an offering penetrates a market it becomes increasingly difficult to enhance its market share and correspondingly less likely that sales will result from seller-initiated contacts.

There is, however, little reason to believe that increased market penetration will inhibit making sales based on buyer-initiated contacts. On the contrary, competitive market performance vis-à-vis former and existing customers is likely to improve the prospects of making such sales. As an effect of learning, the cost of making a sale based on buyer initiative is likely to decrease over time, especially in cases where a closer relationship develops between seller and buyers. Close relationships are usually entered into with the intention of enhancing value for both parties. One main value-enhancing benefit of many such arrangements is higher exchange cost effectiveness. In contrast to this, the cost of making a sale based on a seller-initiated contact is likely to rise over time, as it becomes increasingly difficult to find new potential customers. Among other things advertising media functions less selectively.

The implications of such dynamic "draining" and learning effects are quite evident. The higher the degree of penetration of an offering and/or a company's position as regards supplier criteria, or the more wide-spread a favorable company reputation becomes in a market, the stronger are the grounds for adopting a marketing communication strategy which gives first priority to buyer-initiated contacts. Given these conditions, companies which adopt that strategy are more likely to make a profit.

Summing up. A communication task matrix

The matrix in Box 7.3. sums up assumptions and arguments regarding the relationship between the degree to which a product and an offering, respectively, have penetrated a market, and the nature and extent of communication tasks, the extent of buyer initiative, and the potential for profitable marketing communication. The matrix applies to markets for non-durable, standardized products.

By combining high and low degrees of penetration of product and offering four extreme and illustrative cases appear. Especially extreme are the two cases termed

"I.   Pioneering" and
"IV. Harvesting".

In the Pioneering case the potential for profitable communication is at its lowest. The degree of product penetration is low, and so is demand. The number of development tasks is considerable, i.e. market development is necessary. As the degree of penetration of the offering is also low, there are also a considerable number of standard communication tasks connected with "showing the way" to the offering. Sales volume depend totally on seller initiative. Consequently, the turnover/communication cost ratio is low.

The very opposite applies to the Harvesting case. As the product has penetrated the market, no development tasks remain to be completed. Demand for the product in question is high, and marketing communication activities can be directed solely at market utilization. The offering is well-established in the market. Consequently, the extent of buyer initiative is high. Buyer-initiated orders and inquiries account for a large proportion of the sales volume. Communication tasks are connected mainly to reminding indifferent buyers of the offering. In the Harvesting case, the ratio between turnover and communication costs is high.

Cases II and III are less extreme. Case II is characterized by a low degree of product penetration and a high degree of penetration of the offering. In other words, the offering is well-established in an immature market, consisting of actual as well as potential buyers. Some actual buyers show buyer initiative. Others may have reacted with indifference to the offering and may need to be reminded of it. In relation to first-time buyers, the company faces all kinds of communication tasks, including development tasks and standard communication tasks.

In case III, the degree of product penetration is high, while the degree of penetration of the offering is low. On the one hand, the market is mature and there are no development tasks. On the other hand, there are few, if any, buyer-initiated orders and inquiries. There are a considerable number of standard communication tasks and tasks connected with "showing the way" to a new or changed offering. Seller initiative will account for most of the sales volume. There is reason to assume that as a rule, the turnover/communication cost ratio is higher in case III than in case II, since the latter involves market development.

Box 7.3. gives a rough picture of what happens when a market matures or when new or changed offerings enter a market. *"Moving" from left to right* in the communication task matrix indicates the consequences of an increasing degree of product penetration. The number of development tasks decreases. Gradually, market utilization replaces market development. *"Moving" from top to bottom* shows the effects of an enhanced degree of penetration of an offering. For example, standard communication tasks become fewer and the extent of buyer initiative increases. Reminding indifferent buyers may become relevant. Moving from bottom to top in the matrix indicates the consequences of changes in a well-established offering or "way to" an offering. In a sense, the degree of penetration is "reversed". Depending on the nature and size of the changes, new standard communication tasks and/or tasks connected with "showing the way" to the offering arise. The greater the change, the larger the number of new communication tasks. Reminding indifferent buyers is no longer relevant. The extent of buyer initiative may tend to decrease, at least temporarily, although spin-off effects from the previous offering may work as a counteracting force.

As explained above, Box 7.3. deals with markets for non-durable, standardized products. The main lines of reasoning apply, however, to markets for standardized durable products as well as transformation markets. When using the matrix in relation to markets for standardized durable products, company reputation should usually be substituted for offering. The matrix then suggests that the emergence of a favorable company reputation may produce an increase in the extent of buyer initiative. As to transformation markets the matrix applies without reservation to the standardized part of non-durable offerings. However, further use can be made of the matrix by substituting "position with regard to supplier criteria" for "offering". When this is done, the matrix indicates that new standard communication tasks will be among the consequences of a change in the company's position on certain supplier criteria. It should be noted that the number of transformation communication tasks does not depend on the degree of penetration of a product or on supplier criteria.

This chapter has dealt with how and why the nature and extent of buyer initiative and communication tasks varies over time. Some strategic implications of these variations have also been outlined. The discussion has shown that it is clearly impossible to develop a marketing communication strategy without insight into buyer initiative and communication tasks. It is necessary to keep track of the extent of buyer initiative and the nature and number of communication tasks for two reasons. Firstly, realistic strategic decisions must be made regarding the amount of resources to be spent on communication. Secondly, strategic decisions must be made as to how these resources should be allocated to various activities. Task analysis aimed at clarifying the communication tasks and the extent of buyer initiative facing a company in a forthcoming planning period is therefore an important element in strategic holistic communication planning.[19]

Box 7.3. Communication task matrix

	Product penetration is:	
	Low Actual demand low Buyer competence low	**High** Actual demand high Buyer competence high
Degree of penetration of offering: **Low**	**I** **Pioneering** *Profit potential, i.e. turnover/cost ratio low* Seller initiative Market development Development tasks Standard communication tasks Tasks connected to "showing the way" to the offering	**III** Seller initiative Market utilization Standard communication tasks Tasks connected to "showing the way" to the offering
High	**II** Market development *and* utilization Seller *and* buyer initiative Development tasks (potential buyers only) Standard communication tasks Tasks connected to "showing the way" to the offering Tasks connected to reminding of the offering	**IV** **Harvesting** *Profit potential, i.e. turnover/cost ratio high* Market utilization Buyer initiative Tasks connected to reminding of the offering

The matrix shows how communication tasks are assumed to depend on the interplay between product penetration and degree of penetration of a non-durable standardized offering.

When reading the matrix the reader should bear in mind that the properties of the product and the offering as well as "the way" to the offering are assumed to be given (i.e. do not change over time).

8. Marketing offering and communication effect

The development of a holistic view of marketing communication has been based on two important assumptions:

1. Firstly, it has been assumed that marketing communication has no autonomous function that is unrelated to the *"inherent properties"* of an offering. Inherent properties are *properties that are*, so to say, *present in the offering from the outset*. The value of an inherent property is a function of partly personal and partly learned buyer characteristics. It becomes apparent through pre- and post-experience with the offering. The tasks of marketing communication are to convey the relevant inherent properties of an offering, "show the way to" and remind indifferent buyers of it. Buyers' perceived value of an offering cannot be affected by communication contents, for instance, simply by claiming that a product property exists. The perceived buyer value of an offering is determined solely by experiences with inherent properties. Value cannot be *added to* an offering through marketing communication.

2. Secondly, it has been supposed that the effect of marketing communication is fundamentally dependent on the competitiveness of the offering. For marketing communication to be effective, the buyer value of an offering has to be at least equal to that of competing offerings.

These assumptions constitute the main premises for contending that marketing communication strategy development should be based on the presupposition that *the effect and profitability of marketing communication is fundamentally dependent on the inherent properties of a competitive offering.*

For one thing, these properties determine which relevant content (messages) can possibly be conveyed to buyers in the market place. The more competitive the offering, the more interesting the communication content, and the more likely it is that buyers will try the product. Secondly, inherent properties determine the value experienced by the buyer. While communication may lead to trial purchases, further effects depend on post-purchase experience of the offering itself. The more competitive the offering, the more likely are repeat purchases, favorable word-of-mouth and buyer initiatives, and the more likely a company is to enhance its reputation.

The above somewhat controversial presupposition about the crucial importance of inherent offering properties constitutes a basic element in the holistic view of marketing communication presented here. This chapter aims at elaborating on the arguments in favor of and against this presupposition as well as the presupposition that a competitive offering is a precondition for profitable marketing communication.

Can marketing communication have a function that is unrelated to the inherent properties of an offering?

Do buyers have to take some properties of an offering on trust?

Recipients of a message may not be in a position to gain direct, personal experience of the realities to which that message refers. Most news stories illustrate this point. It is impossible for most readers, listeners or viewers to investigate such things as the personality of the president of the USA or the prime minister of Great Britain, incidents of war in Kashmir or hunger in Ethiopia, or to have direct experience of all the countless people, things or events reported. Images conveyed on radio, television or the Internet, in the pages of newspapers, books and magazines are nevertheless themselves *real* elements in our environment, and in that sense, part of reality. Thus, the media do not simply convey *messages about* reality: there is a sense in which they can be said to substitute one reality for another. In other words, the media offer "virtual", "artificial" or "surrogate" experience for real experience. It is not unreasonable to ask whether messages conveyed in the course of marketing communication may have a corresponding *"surrogate effect"*.

If we consider offerings bought as an effect of marketing communication, we can see that the general picture is quite the opposite of that outlined above. The act of buying and using a product is characterized by relatively frequent occasions on which the buyer gains direct experience with the offering. This is the case in consumer markets as well as in industrial ones. When preparing to make – and actually making – a purchase, and when using the product, the buyer will assess the offering in relation to his own needs. The development of a buyer-seller relationship in an industrial market normally involves numerous pre- and post-purchase contacts, i.e. occasions on which the buyer personally experiences one or more properties of the offering.

While many product properties are *perceptible*, some *are* impossible or difficult to verify through sensory experience. The beneficial or harmful effects on health or the environment of some vitamins, nutrients and other substances in food products are instances of such properties. Furthermore, some social relevance criteria relate to product properties which are imperceptible, unverifiable or difficult to verify in practice. Such criteria may be based on a desire to identify with a popular figure. Needless to say, it is impossible, in practice, to verify an advertising claim that the idol in question uses a specific product or brand. The sales effect of an advertising campaign for a particular brand is an example of an offering property that may be difficult for dealers in that brand to verify. Similarly, the efficacy of health food, medicines, and hair tonic may be far from obvious to consumers.

Whenever buyers have to decide for themselves whether or not to *believe* in claims made about imperceptible or unverifiable properties of an offering, messages about those properties conveyed in the course of marketing communication may be thought of as partial or complete substitutes for reality. However, most people are relatively well able to assess claims relating to buying, using and consuming products.[20] Moreover, the kinds of claim that can be made about partially or totally imperceptible product properties in the course of marketing communication are increasingly subject to legislation and voluntary codes of conduct. Tight regulations governing the marketing of pharmaceutical products illustrate this tendency. Other examples are regulations relating to the declaration of specified ingredients or contents in foodstuffs, health products and detergents.

The view adopted here is that what was referred to above as the "surrogate" effect of media contents can, but should not be misused in marketing communication strategy development.

Some properties cannot be experienced until after purchase

Sacrifices and rewards connected with an offering may take the form of both pre- and post-purchase experiences. Some inherent properties can be experienced only after a purchase has taken place. Examples of these are a supplier's complaint handling and after-sale service, the durability of a tool, the resistance of a car to corrosion and the operating costs of a production machine. While many supplier criteria are perceptible prior to a purchase, the ability of a supplier to deliver a competitive offering can only be demonstrated in the light of the purchaser's subsequent experience with the product. From this it may be argued that the buyer depends entirely on marketing communication messages about properties that will only become apparent after the purchase, that claims regarding *non-existent* properties can also produce sales – and that marketing communication may accordingly have an effect that is altogether unrelated the properties of the product.

However, the idea of basing communication strategy development on this kind of effect may be met with the following counter arguments:

Firstly non-durable consumer products such as gasoline, margarine, beverages, cheese, and toothpaste can be tried out on a small scale. This can be done with modest financial and social risk, and trial purchase will quickly reveal bogus claims. In industrial markets suppliers can be subjected to small scale testing for instance by embarking on an initial trial phase of a closer buyer-seller relationship.

Secondly, while some properties of durable products can be perceived and evaluated before a purchase takes place, properties having to do with durability itself are usually difficult to try out on a small scale and these can normally only be verified over time, after the purchase has been made. This is the case with properties such as the reliability of a washing machine, the corrosion resistance of a car's enamel, and the resistance of a garment's colors to fading. False claims relating to such properties as these are revealed only after the purchase has taken place. However, in the final analysis, a company's reputation depends on post-purchase experiences. Among other things, buyers remember what they perceive as broken promises. Moreover, rumors of negative experiences stemming from imprecise, exaggerated or downright misleading claims are likely to spread from experienced to new and inexperienced buyers to the detriment of a company's reputation. Consumers share anecdotes about their cars and vacuum cleaners. Farmers discuss the after-sale service rendered by dealers, and CEO's exchange views about consulting firms and advertising agencies. A company's reputation is ultimately determined by the social processes which ensure that potential customers learn from the post-purchase experience of those who have already bought its products. It has already been pointed out that a company's reputation is itself an important determinant of future buyer initiative and communication tasks. As everyone knows, "Mud sticks". Bad reputations are hard to live down.

Thirdly, when exaggerated, imprecise or downright incorrect claims are employed to arouse buyers' expectations, the latter are more likely to be disappointed and to feel more disappointment than if they had not had cause to feel misled. For example, such claims might cause a buyer who might have shown a preference for a non-durable offering to react with indifference or rejection.[21]

These three arguments support the standpoint taken here that ambiguous, exaggerated and incorrect claims about properties of an offering have no place in a marketing communication strategy. Such claims are, by definition, unethical and although marketing messages based on them may appear to have desired short-term effects, in the long run they will prove unprofitable.

Buyers may not be sufficiently competent

Several references have already been made to the importance of buyer competence. In order to realize the full potential value of an offering, a buyer has to master various purchasing and user/consumer roles. For example, if a company's managers and employees are not capable of making the necessary buyer contribution, it will not make full use of a new quality control system. It has also been contended that a company may influence the performance of an offering by enhancing buyer competence, i.e. by carrying out development tasks. In a sense this is the equivalent of viewing marketing communication as an autonomous force. Although the properties in question are inherent features of an offering, *marketing communication affects the degree to which their potential value may be realized and thereby the perceived value of the offering.*

There remains the question of whether it is more profitable to inform or "educate" incompetent buyers than to refrain from doing so. For example, the choice criteria of a young couple about to buy their first baby carriage may not be quite the same as relevance criteria when they focus on design and color to the exclusion of such criteria as the reliability of the brakes, corrosion resistance and stability. It may be asked why one should bother to make buyers aware of these latter criteria when they themselves are not concerned?

Of course, in the short run it may pay to realize "easy sales" by emphasizing design and color properties, to the exclusion of any mention of brakes, corrosion and stability. Computer hardware and software may also be sold, even though the product's properties are not consistent with users' relevance criteria. However, in the long run, a strategy based on taking advantage of buyer incompetence is likely to have a boomerang effect. Firstly, buyers are deprived of enjoying the full potential value of offerings. Secondly, through trial and error, by learning from others etc. buyers gradually enhance their competence. The result is that a company which pursues such a policy will risk losing its reputation and its customer base when the weaknesses of its products become apparent and dissatisfied customers begin to talk about them. This, in turn, will gradually undermine the company's long-term profitability.

Added value may be created through association

In Chapter 1, it was noted that changes in buyer behavior may take place through various modes of learning, i.e. through insight (information processing), trial- and-error (instrumental conditioning), and association (or classical conditioning). So far, the discussion about the tasks of marketing communication has been based on the assumption that buyers' learning is a form of information processing or instrumental conditioning. However, some theorists contend that marketing communication in the form of advertising *can* create buyer value that is not present in the product or brand from the outset. The theories in question have been applied mostly to non-durable, branded consumer products.[22]

The *association* hypothesis underlying the above theories holds that added value can be created by repeatedly exposing consumers to a combination of unconditioned and conditioned stimuli. An *unconditioned stimulus* is a stimulus that exploits prior learning processes to arouse positive emotions and responses. Examples of such emotions are feelings of joy, liberty, warmth, and a sense of belonging to a particular social group. By repeated continuous and consistent exposure to advertisements, radio- or TV-commercials the reactions associated with the unconditioned stimulus are transferred to the *conditioned stimulus*, i.e. the brand. As a result of an association process, the act of owning or consuming the brand will tend to arouse feelings and responses equivalent to those connected with the unconditioned stimulus. According to a well-known advertising textbook this kind of advertising "... involves developing associations with the brand or brand use such that the experience of using the brand is *transformed* or changed into something quite different" (author's italics).[23]

The literature on how to add value to a (non-durable) brand through advertising is comprehensive. Most of the popular advertising "philosophies" like "image building", "positioning" and "brand building" rest on the association hypothesis.[24] Probably the best known example of supposedly successful "value-transformation" deals with the advertising strategy developed by Marlboro, the cigarette brand, several years ago. According to the story that has been told in most advertising textbooks, Marlboro chose to use a cowboy and his horse against the background of a Wild West landscape as the unconditioned stimulus. It was assumed that this stimulus would arouse feelings of freedom, liberty, courage, and strength. Via repetitive advertising these feelings would be "transferred" to the brand. In this way added value would be created. The buyer would prefer Marlboro *because* of the feelings of freedom, liberty, courage, and strength aroused by smoking the cigarette.[25] To a large extent other examples referred to in the advertising literature deal with transformation of social values, i.e. emotions and perceptions associated with a specific life-style or personality. The personality may be an *idealized* portrayal of someone with desired traits – or *realistic*, reflecting the potential customer's actual self-image. The value that is added, often termed "badge value", rests on the fact that owning and using the product signals how potential customers wish to be perceived.[26]

There is no doubt that some learning does involve classical conditioning processes.[27] Association is a central mode of learning, which is well documented within the field of psychology. However, although much has been written on the subject of value adding through classical conditioning, the conditions under which association strategies can be expected to be implemented with success are still far from clear. The literature dealing with a number of important questions in this area is both fragmentary and unclear. Examples of such questions are:

- How can an effective unconditioned stimulus be identified and selected? The unconditioned stimulus must evoke exactly the right positive reactions in the buyers a company wants to attract. How can one ensure that some buyers will not react negatively to the stimulus?

- It is a generally accepted hypothesis that value adding through association requires continuous and consistent repetition. But what is really meant by "continuous"? For how long should repetition go on? With what frequency?

- It is also generally assumed that if a competitor chooses to use the same or a similar unconditioned stimulus, the result will be a weakening of the association between that stimulus and the brand of the company. For a competitor, it may be easier to imitate an unconditioned stimulus than to compete on inherent product properties. How can competitors be prevented from imitating?

- Very little is known about the nature of the interplay between inherent properties and attempts at value adding. Hardly anything is known about the effect of pre- and post-purchase experience in this connection.[28] Can added value compensate for weak inherent properties? What happens if the buyer learns from friends and colleagues that a brand does *not* yield any social value? Is added value the same regardless of field of use?

In the author's view, the notion that value can be added to offerings through classical conditioning deserves to be treated with considerable skepticism. Adding value to an offering is no easy task. Continuous and consistent repetition requires greater resources than are available to most companies. Unless all necessary conditions are fulfilled, attempts at value adding may result in a considerable waste of resources. Finally, organizations that focus their attention on added value may do so at the cost of developing competitive inherent properties.

For the reasons outlined above, the possibility of value adding through marketing communication will not be discussed further in this book. Readers interested in value adding are referred to the extensive body of literature dealing with classical conditioning, image advertising and positioning.[29] It has already been pointed out that this literature deals mainly with advertising in consumer markets. Writers on service and industrial marketing have shown little interest in value adding.

Does the offering have to be competitive?

It seems reasonable to assume that the answer to whether a competitive offering is a precondition for profitable marketing communication depends partly on

1. buyers' *ability to evaluate* the offering through their own experience, and partly on

2. their *knowledge of other, more competitive offerings*. In the light of the above discussion, buyers can generally be assumed to be capable of evaluating and comparing marketing offerings.

To the extent that buyers may not be or become aware of more competitive offerings, it is, of course, possible to communicate profitably on the basis of non-competitive offerings. However, ignoring or miscalculating the offerings and communication plans of one's competitors may have serious negative consequences. Profitable communication on the basis of a non-competitive offering becomes less feasible as the number of superior competitive offerings increases, and as competitors communicate more intensively. Also, attempts to conceal the fact that a company's offerings are inferior to those of its competitors raise obvious ethical questions.

Summing up

This chapter set out to discuss

- whether marketing communication has any autonomous function that is unrelated to an offering in the sense that it can affect the perceived value of an offering, and:

- whether a competitive offering is a precondition for profitable marketing communication.

Bearing in mind the provisos (primarily relating to development tasks and the danger of producing unrealistic expectations) discussed in the above paragraphs, we may conclude that there are good reasons for insisting that strategy development should rest on the assumption that marketing communication has no autonomous value-adding function. Its tasks are to convey the properties of, "show the way to", and remind indifferent buyers of an inherently competitive offering.

Part IV

Holistic strategic marketing communication planning

Part I and II of this book introduced a holistic view of marketing communication. Part III elaborated some important aspects of a holistic view of marketing communication. Part IV goes on to discuss how strategic, holistic planning of marketing communication can be carried through. A procedure is suggested for developing a coherent marketing communication strategy.

Chapter 9 outlines the strategic planning process. Descriptions are given of six main planning tasks that have to be undertaken in order to develop a coherent strategy. Chapters 10 – 15 deal with what five of these planning tasks involve and how they can be performed. The tools suggested in the form of concepts, models, procedures etc. are general. That is, they can be used as a basis for developing a marketing communication strategy, whether the company is large or small, whether or not it operates in a consumer or industrial market, and whether or not it offers physical products or services. Obviously, the examples used in the discussion cannot cover all conceivable combinations of kinds of products, markets, companies, etc. Readers must themselves apply the tools to contexts that reflect their needs and objectives.

The discussion in Chapters 9-15 postulates a typical going concern which intends to implement strategic, holistic planning of marketing communication for the first time. It is assumed that:

142 *Holistic strategic marketing communication planning*

- this hypothetical company markets one single variety of a product in one given market and area of use, or one type of product in a transformation market.
- the planning period for the company is relatively short, say, about one year.

The discussion thus focuses on short-term effects of communication.

Chapter 16 discusses the consequences of setting aside the above assumptions regarding the number of products marketed by the company and compares the company as a going concern as opposed to a new one. The dynamics of holistic strategic marketing communication planning are also explored with the following question in mind: How can and should a strategy be adapted through time to changing market and company conditions? Finally, the chapter discusses the need for and use of market and company information in strategic, holistic market communication planning as well as various sources of such information.

Chapter 17 rounds off Part IV and the book. It sums up holistic strategic marketing communication planning and discusses the relevance of long-term effects and long-range planning of marketing communication. Finally, it touches upon the question of how to introduce holistic strategic planning within an organization.

9. Strategic, holistic marketing communication planning: Process, tasks, and premises

Planning process and planning tasks

Carrying through a holistic strategic marketing communication planning process involves carrying out the following tasks:

1. Making a *planning premises analysis*, i.e. analyzing and describing the planning premises.
2. Making a *task analysis*.
3. Developing *a target group strategy*, i.e. prioritizing buyer segments and selecting target groups.
4. Developing a *content strategy*, i.e. identifying, prioritizing, selecting and clarifying communication content.
5. Developing a *media strategy*, i.e. selecting media and determining media use.
6. Developing a *content symbolization strategy*.
7. Forming an *overall marketing communication strategy*.

(See Figure 9.1.)

The planning tasks involved may be described as follows:

1. Making a planning premises analysis:
As emphasized in Chapter 3, a marketing communication strategy cannot be developed without taking the company's sub-strategies relating to business areas, offering and organizational basis, into account. In holistic strategic marketing communication planning, these must be taken into consideration either as factors that are given, or as factors that have to be changed in order

to develop a basis for a profitable communication strategy. In other words, the other sub-strategies constitute the premises for developing a coherent strategy.

Accordingly, the first step in a holistic, strategic planning process involves a planning premises analysis, the purpose of which is to provide the necessary insight into the premises underlying the planning process itself. The business areas (areas of use included) need to be analyzed with regard to such things as degree of product penetration, actual demand and potential for market development, degree of penetration of the offering and competition. Every important element in the offering, relevance criterion, supplier criterion, reward and sacrifice relating to the offering should be described. Planners also need information about various relevant characteristics of the organizational basis. This information may concern such matters as the organization of the marketing function (e.g. structure, capacity, and competencies) and type and capacity of ICT equipment. Financial characteristics such as working capital and liquidity may also be relevant. Communication activities affect incoming as well as out-going payments, and consequently, liquidity.

Of course, the company's operating budget drawn up for the planning period constitutes an important element in a planning premises analysis. This budget contains information about such matters as estimated costs, as well as the size of the budgeted operating profit and the sales volume to which marketing communication activities are expected to contribute. Among other things, based on the operating budget, a rough first assessment should be made of the proportion of the budgeted sales volume that can be expected to be obtained through competent handling and follow-up of buyer-initiated orders and inquiries.

The first time a company implements holistic strategic planning of marketing communication, preliminary ideas and/or plans concerning the use of marketing communication tools and resources must also be taken into consideration. One important task is to estimate the total marketing communication costs included in the budget, and to identify how these costs are allocated to various items.

2. Making a task analysis:
The second step in the planning process involves making a *communication task analysis*.

This step involves providing an overview of the nature and extent of the communication tasks facing the company in relation to dealers and end-buyers in the planning period. Which tasks exist in relation to which buyers? Are there development tasks, transformation tasks and standard communication tasks? Are there tasks connected to "showing the way" to a standardized offering and tasks reminding buyers of such an offering or of the company's position on important supplier criteria of which buyers are at present aware, but may forget. As was suggested in Chapter 6 and Chapter 7, the nature and extent of communication tasks partly depend on the number of actual and potential buyers, the size of actual demand in the planning period and the degree of penetration of the offering. Furthermore, making a task analysis involves estimating the nature and extent of buyer initiative as well as assessing the competitiveness of the offering. Most importantly, the conclusions in Chapter 8 imply that without a sufficiently competitive offering, there can be no communication tasks.

3. Developing a target group strategy. Prioritizing buyer segments and selecting target groups:
Given the outcome of an analysis of planning premises and a task analysis, the third step in the planning process involves deciding which tasks to attempt in relation to which buyers in a planning period. As a first step, buyer segments are formed and prioritized. Subsequently, the *segments that are expected to be the most profitable* are selected as *"target groups"*. In cases where a company markets its offering through dealers, the question arises of the relative importance to be attached to dealer target groups and target groups consisting of end-buyers.

The development of a target group strategy is based on three sets of considerations:

The first set concerns what is desirable and possible viewed against the background of the company's goals and sub-strategies concerning business areas, its offering and its organizational basis. More often than not, a budgeted operating profit can be realized without performing every single communication task that actually faces the company. Moreover, companies may have insufficient capacity, competence and/or financial resources to attempt some tasks.

The second set of considerations relates to how to use resources as effectively as possible. Communication tasks vary considerably as far as profitability is concerned. Resources should be allocated in such a way that the most profitable tasks are prioritized and unprofitable tasks avoided. It will be argued below that there are good grounds for giving buyers who show buyer initiative top priority among target groups.

4. Developing a content strategy:
The fourth planning task involves identifying, prioritizing, selecting, and clarifying communication content in order to formulate a content strategy. The strategy itself must take the selected target groups and planning premises into account as well as the results of the task analysis.

A distinction may be drawn between two sorts of content, i.e.

1. core content, and
2. facilitative content.

"*Core content*" refers to *the offering itself, to organizational characteristics indicating the company's ability to develop and deliver competitive customized offerings* and *to "showing the way" to the offering or the company making it.*
   Which content to select depends on such things as the nature and extent of communication tasks such as those related to:

- enhancing buyer competence,
- conveying relevant elements in the offering and relevant organizational characteristics, and
- "showing the way to" the offering or company.

In general, messages referring to competitive offering properties corresponding to important relevance criteria are typical of those to be assigned high priority.

"Facilitative content" is used to *enhance communication* and thereby make it more likely that potential purchasers will actually buy an offering. The credibility of messages may, for instance, be increased by conveying references to specific buyers who have already bought and experienced the offering or by referring to a large and growing market share. Such facilitative content does not refer to the offering itself or to relevant organizational characteristics, etc.

Potentially relevant contents have to be prioritized. Both the medium and the susceptibility of the buyer will limit how much can be conveyed in a given exposure episode. A buyer may have limited time to spend with a salesman. Obviously, advertisements have inherent limitations. Regardless of their size, they cannot convey all relevant messages. The process of prioritizing will aim at creating a basis for deciding which messages to select and emphasize within the limits determined by available time or space. What should be accentuated in an advertisement or a brochure? Which messages should be conveyed in a telephone conversation with a potential customer or in a meeting to negotiate a potential customized offering?

A content strategy is stated in a *"content platform"*, which is *a description of relevant contents and priorities in relation to each target group*. The content platform constitutes a basis for developing symbolization as well as media strategy. In order to form a useful basis for decisions concerning symbolization, prioritized contents should be clarified and formulated as precisely as possible. The content platform is important when planning media strategy because the symbolization capacity, i.e. capacity to convey different combinations and kinds of symbols, varies from one medium to another. Illustrations of this given earlier are newspapers and magazines, which can carry visual symbols only, radio which can only convey auditory symbols, and film, TV and the Internet, which are audio-visual media. The implication of these differences is that decisions about media use must be made with due regard to content strategy. Media choice must be consistent with content.

5. Developing a media strategy, i.e. selecting media and determining media use:
Carrying out the fifth planning task, i.e. developing a media strategy, involves making decisions about which media to use in order to convey relevant messages to the various target groups. Decisions also have to be taken about the extent to which different media should be used in what order of succession and when. When deciding which of the available media will be most effective, costs have to be weighed up against the properties of the media that seem most likely to enhance sales.

A strategic media plan consists of:

1. a *preparatory plan* for receipt, handling and follow-up of buyer initiative.

2. an *action plan* for seller initiative combined with a *preparatory plan* for the receipt, handling and follow-up of resulting orders and inquiries.

Thus, a media strategy is developed with the aim of

- making profitable use of opportunities for selling to buyers who initiate contact with the company or seek out its offerings on their own initiative.

- ensuring the performance of seller-initiated activities.

In this connection it is important to distinguish between *"buyer initiative media"* and *"seller initiative media"*, depending on which party has the opportunity to use the media in question. The range of media at the disposal of sellers and buyers, respectively, varies from one market to another. Typically advertising media do not function as buyer initiative media, while channels such as telephone, facsimile transmitter, ordinary mail, e-mail, and settings such as face-to-face meetings can generally – although not always – be used by both parties.

Media strategy relating to buyer initiative involves managing the organization's capacity and routines in such a way as to ensure that it responds promptly and competently to buyer initiatives. Strategy development is concerned with arranging and maintaining a state of readiness in which a company is accessible to buyers and able to communicate most efficiently with them. It involves deciding which media to select in order to make the most of buyer initiative and ways of organizing the company to ensure accessibility and efficient handling and follow-up of orders and inquiries.

Media strategy relating to the planning of seller initiative is concerned with such issues as the selection of mass media, frequency of use, and timing of mass media use (number of advertisement insertions, TV-commercials etc.). Furthermore, action planning of seller initiative involves decisions concerning such things as which buyers to call on in person or by telephone.

Since access and dialogue also determine the outcome of orders and inquiries resulting from seller-initiated contacts, the company has to ensure that it is prepared to receive, handle and follow up seller-initiated orders and inquiries.

Media costs expected to be incurred by a media strategy are set out in a *media cost budget*.

6. Developing a content symbolization strategy:
The target group strategy together with the content and media strategies form the basis for carrying through the sixth step in the planning process, which is to develop a content symbolization strategy. A symbolization strategy lays down rough guidelines for performing symbolization tasks and covers all kinds of communication, whether mass communication through advertisements, posters, TV-commercials or seminars, or personal communication in the form of telephone conversations or face-to-face meetings. Costs are set out in a *symbolization cost budget*.

The ways in which communication content is symbolized is of critical importance. Even the best task analysis, target group strategy, content strategy etc. will be wasted if buyers remain unaware of – or fail to understand – the messages a company is trying to communicate.

7. Forming an overall marketing communication strategy:
As a final step, the results of work on the six strategic planning tasks are integrated into a coherent, overall marketing communication strategy. The main elements of a holistic marketing communication strategy are:

a. Guidelines relating to the *use* of *marketing communication tools* referring to the following sub-strategies:

- A *media strategy*, and a *symbolization strategy*.

- A *seller initiative strategy*, and a *buyer initiative strategy*.

And – if relevant –

- a *dealer strategy*, and an *end-buyer strategy*.

b. A description of the *preconditions* for *implementing the proposed use of the marketing communication tools* and *for achieving the budgeted operating profit*. Such conditions may concern changes in the company's product/market strategy, in its offering or in its organizational basis. They will always involve measures aimed at ensuring that the company's communication strategy can be implemented in order to bring about the expected sales effect.

Necessary changes may become obvious as a result of the planning premises analysis. The need to make other changes may come to light in the planning process itself. For example, in order to implement the media strategy it may be necessary to hire more salesmen, reorganize the handling of orders and inquiries, enhance the competence of certain employees to deal with buyers and so on. It might also be necessary to invest in new fax machines or other communications equipment in order to improve accessibility and make it possible to communicate with buyers via the Internet and e-mail.

c. A *marketing communication* budget containing estimates of total costs incurred and costs incurred by each individual substrategy together with estimates of resulting sales volume, contribution and operating profit. The marketing communication budget is clearly related to the overall operating budget of the company, and explains how and why one can expect to achieve the budgeted operating profit.

Needless to say, the planning tasks do not necessarily have be completed one at a time in the order shown above. The process of problem solving usually leads to learning. Working with one task, a planner may acquire new insights that lead him to change or modify analyses made or conclusions drawn in previous steps of the planning process. For example, a specific target group may seem most favorable at the outset. However, as a result of his work with the media strategy the planner may come to the conclusion that the media costs incurred in communicating with the group are too high. This may in turn lead to a revision of the target group strategy that had originally been contemplated. The target group in question might, for instance, be substituted for another. Figure 9.1. outlines a holistic strategic marketing communication planning process, including the relationship between the various tasks. The "circular" search-try-and-learn character of the planning process is indicated by the dotted arrows in the left side the figure.

As emphasized in Chapter 1, a planner has to cope with a high degree of complexity and uncertainty and can only aim at finding satisfactory, as opposed to optimal solutions. The substrategies relating to profit goal, business areas, offering and organizational basis, which constitute the premises for marketing communication planning, cannot be expected to be perfect in any sense. Nor can the overall strategy resulting from a marketing communication planning process which takes these substrategies as a starting point. Holistic strategic planning is, nevertheless, likely to contribute to more profitable solutions in one or both of the following ways:

152 Strategic, holistic marketing communication planning

Figure 9.1. Phases in a holistic marketing communication strategy development process

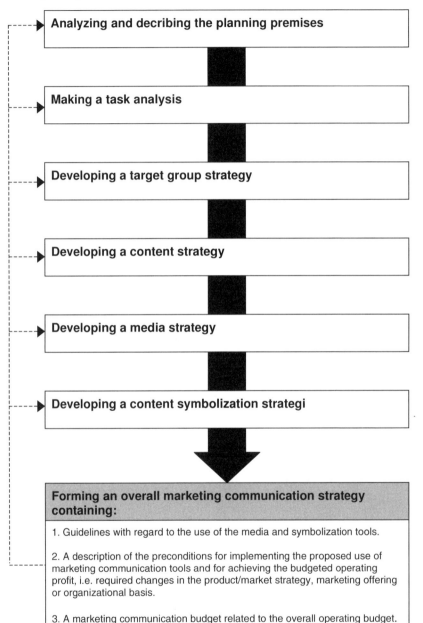

- adapting the marketing communication strategy to the other sub-strategies.

- prompting suggestions and initiatives to encourage modifications and/or more substantial changes in one or more sub-strategies.

There is, of course, no guarantee that a set profit goal can be realized, even if changes and modifications are made in relation to business areas, the offering or the company's organizational basis. Strategic, holistic marketing communication planning may lead to the conclusion that an originally budgeted overall operating profit is unlikely to be attainable and that no marketing communication strategy can produce the desired result. Thus, marketing communication planning may even lead a company to revise its estimate of overall profit in its operating budget.

Analyzing and describing the planning premises

The purpose of the planning premises analysis is to provide the necessary insight into the premises for marketing communication strategy development. The analysis can be carried out in many different ways, and be more or less extensive. General guidelines cannot be laid down. However, in most cases a premises analysis should provide information, general indications or, at least, a basis for making informed judgments regarding:

1. The sub-strategies concerning business areas (product/market strategy), offering, and organizational basis expected to be implemented in the forthcoming planning period, provided that the marketing communication planning process does not trigger any changes.

2. The marketing communication strategy implemented in the current planning period.

3. The company's operating budget, including

  - an assessment of the proportion of the budgeted sales volume that can be expected to be obtained through

    1. handling buyer initiative and
    2. seller initiative, respectively, and

  - an estimate of the marketing communication costs included in the operating budget.

A few comments will be made below on each of these issues. They are intended to apply to a company that is practicing strategic holistic planning for the first time:

1. The sub-strategies concerning business areas (product/market strategy), offering, and organizational basis:

The business areas arcas of use included – need to be analyzed with regard to such things as:

  - the number of actual and potential buyers.
  - the degree of product penetration and saturation level.
  - the size of actual and potential demand.
  - the degree of penetration of the offering.
  - the market share.
  - competitors and competitors' offerings, marketing communication activities and organizational basis.

Every material element in the offering, relevance criterion and type of sacrifice or reward relating to the offering should be described. Insight into company reputation is also needed. As far as the organizational basis is concerned, it is vital to gain insight into the company's position with regard to important supplier criteria and to the characteristics which determine its ability to implement various marketing communication strategies. Such insight helps to keep the search for strategic options on a realistic track. Consideration must be given to characteristics of such things as the organization of the marketing func-

Analyzing and describing the planning premises 155

tion, the switchboard and the order department. This will involve assessing

- the organizational structure.
- the number and type of employees and managers.
- the priority and distribution of tasks and responsibilities.
- capacity and competencies in the departments concerned.

Material characteristics may relate to such matters as type and capacity of communication and computer equipment, meeting room facilities and equipment such as overhead projectors, video machines and slide projectors. Financial characteristics such as working capital and liquidity may also be important. Communication activities affect in-going as well as out-going payments, and consequently liquidity. To the degree that sales volume grows as a result of marketing communication activities, the need for working capital will tend to reflect increases in the stock and accounts receivable.

2. Current marketing communication strategy:
Insight into the marketing communication strategy implemented in the current planning period is important in order to obtain a realistic understanding of the nature and size of the changes that have to be made to implement a new strategy. Useful information may concern the nature and priorities of target groups as well as content, media and symbolization strategy.

3. The company's operating budget. Assessment of the buyer initiative sales volume, seller initiative gap, and marketing communication costs:

In principle, an operating budget has the following form:

Turnover	(= sales volume * unit price)
- Variable costs	(= sales volume * variable unit costs)[30]
= Contribution	(= sales volume * unit contribution)
- Fixed/stepped costs	
= Operating profit	

156   Strategic, holistic marketing communication planning

The operating budget drawn up for the forthcoming planning period contains important information relating to estimated costs as well as to the size of the operating profit envisaged and the sales volume to which marketing communication activities are expected to contribute:

a. Starting from the estimated sales volume and turnover in the operating budget, a rough initial assessment should be made of the proportion of the budgeted sales volume that can be expected to be obtained through receiving, handling and following up buyer-initiated orders and inquiries and through seller initiative, respectively. This is a matter of itemizing sales volume and turnover in the following way:

Items:	*Sales volume/turnover attributable to:*
Order sales volume/turnover	Orders
+ Inquiry sales volume/turnover	Inquiries
= Buyer initiative sales volume/turnover	Buyer initiative
+ Seller initiative gap	Seller initiative
Overall sales volume/turnover	

It is important to make this assessment for two reasons. Firstly, it sheds light on the relative importance of buyer initiative. Secondly, it provides planners with an idea of the "*seller initiative gap*", i.e. *the sales volume/turnover that has to be produced through seller initiative*. As will become apparent from the discussion below, the seller initiative gap constitutes an extremely important premise for communication planning. The initial assessment will affect the search for solutions from the beginning of the planning process. More often than not the initial assessment will be subject to modifications at later stages.

b. In order to provide a basis for working out an initial marketing communication cost budget, an examination should be made of the marketing communication costs provided for in the operating budget, including how these costs are allocated to various items. As stated already, marketing communication costs include

Analyzing and describing the planning premises

- content symbolization costs, and
- media costs.

"Symbolization costs" are *costs connected to selecting, forming, combining and structuring symbols* suitable for conveying the communication contents that have been selected, prioritized and clarified. Typical examples are fees to photographers and advertising agencies connected to preparing advertisement and brochure layouts and texts, homepages or manuscripts for TV-commercials or advertising films. To these we might add costs connected with preparing contributions to seminars or meetings with dealers or end-buyers in an industrial market (speech, overhead charts, slides etc.) or with drafting correspondence.

"Media costs" are *costs incurred by media use*. A distinction may be drawn between

- production costs, and
- distribution costs.

"Media production costs" are *costs incurred in the production of the communication symbols that have been selected*. Examples are costs connected to producing TV-commercials or video materials, homepages, advertisements or poster originals, overhead charts and handouts, slides etc. as well as costs incurred in writing letters, e-mail messages or facsimiles.

"Media distribution costs" are *costs incurred in using media in order to establish contacts between the company and buyers in the market place*. Typical examples are costs incurred in inserting advertisements in magazines, in running commercials on TV, in distributing brochures through mail services, etc. Other examples are travel expenses incurred by sales and other personnel, mailing expenses, and telephone, facsimile and Internet charges. Handling and follow-up activities may involve costs connected with such things as individual distribution of brochures and the use of telephones, fax machines, ordinary mail and e-mail. Wages to managers, sales personnel and other employees dealing with buyers would also be regarded as media distribution costs.

Most marketing communication costs are running, payable costs. They may, however, also take the form of depreciation on items like salesmen's cars, communication, video and printing equipment, showrooms and conference facilities. As has been exemplified already, marketing communication costs may be fixed as well as stepped or variable.

The first time holistic strategic planning is implemented, no overall marketing communication cost budget will exist. In all probability the operating budget will be itemized in accordance with one of the commonly used charts of accounts, all of which correspond to the traditional, narrower view of marketing communication. Typically, there are separate accounts for costs incurred by advertising and personal selling activities, respectively. Communication costs incurred in using telephones, facsimiles, ICT equipment etc. are entered on various accounts together with costs incurred for example by administrative use of telephones, facsimiles, letters, e-mails, etc. This is also the case with wages and salaries to employees and managers who communicate with buyers and also contribute to delivering the offering. Typical examples are employees in an engineering department, in an order department, behind the counter in a bank or retail store. There will also be separate accounts for fixed fees and depreciation on communications, ICT and other equipment that is also used for production or administrative purposes.

Box 9.2. illustrates how an initial marketing communication cost budget can be extracted from various cost items in an operating budget. The example in question introduces the concept of *"contribution less marketing communication costs"*, defined as:

Turnover – variable (production) costs – marketing communication costs

It will be argued below that this concept provides planners with a useful budgetary item.

The marketing communication costs embedded in an operating budget may, of course, be estimated with varying degrees of accuracy. For example, an assessment of the proportion of managers and employees wages that should be attributed to marketing communication may be assessed by asking them for experience-based estimates relating to resources and time spent on marketing communication activities or by a more comprehensive and systematic work analysis. More often than not, finding the exact size of the marketing communication costs is demanding, if not problematic.

However, when searching for strategies that will contribute to realizing budgeted profits, planners normally need only rough estimates to get a sufficiently realistic picture of the total financial resources at their disposal. Of course, these resources may be reallocated as a result of strategy development. For example, should a manager need relief from some of his administrative work in order to enhance his participation in marketing communication activities, reducing the advertising budget might finance the hiring of an assistant. Similarly, a company may reallocate resources that were initially intended for advertising in order to improve its accessibility or its capacity to handle and follow up orders and inquiries.

Estimates of marketing communication costs embedded in a traditional operating budget should not be viewed as a straitjacket. On the one hand, it may not be possible to develop a communication strategy which fulfills the profit goal set in the operating budget, while keeping within the framework provided by the other sub-strategies and the budgeted marketing communication costs. Should this be the case, initiatives taken by the marketing communication planner may lead to changes in the offering, for example, in product properties and/or price. This may in turn lead to a revision of budgeted sales volume, turnover and costs – and even of the profit goal. On the other hand, in the course of his work, a planner may quite possibly arrive at a communication strategy for realizing the budgeted contribution at a lower total cost, or of making a higher contribution at the same total cost.

160 *Strategic, holistic marketing communication planning*

Box 9.2. Extracting an initial marketing communication budget from various cost items in an operating budget

Operating budget: (Figures in $ 100.)		Initial marketing communication cost budget extracted from cost items in operating budget:	
Turnover	40 000		
Variable production costs	20 000		
Contribution	20 000		
Wages warehouse/order department	1 000	300	Order department handles inquiries.
Salaries sales staff	1 200	1 200	Direct communication cost.
Salaries administrative staff	1 200	200	Administrative staff involved in handling inquiries.
Rent	1 000	100	Order, marketing and sales departments.
Heating/lighting	1 000	100	Order, marketing and sales departments.
Maintenance	200	200	Order, marketing and sales departments.
Office accessories	100	100	Sales letters, answers to inquiries etc.
Telephone	300	200	Seller initiatives, handling of inquiries.
Facsimile	400	200	Handling of inquiries.
ICT	350	200	Home page, handling of inquiries.
Postal costs	50	20	Sales letters, answers to inquiries etc.
Travel expenses/ subsistence allowances sales staff	1 000	1 000	Direct communication costs
Travel expenses/ subsistence and allowances administrative staff	300	70	Managers are involved in seller initiatives and handling of inquiries.
Travel expenses/ subsistence allowances service staff	250		
Advertising – trade journals	500	500	Direct communication costs.
Advertising – in shop	300	300	Direct communication costs.
Exhibitions	750	750	Direct communication costs.
Brochures etc.	600	600	Direct communication costs.
Patent costs	1 000		
Depreciation	3 500	460	Automobiles used by sales staff, ICT equipment etc. (pro rata shares).
Other costs	3 000	500	
Overall costs	**18 000**		
Estimated marketing communication costs		*7 000*	
Profit goal		**2 000**	
Contribution less marketing communication costs		*13 000*	

Figures are fictitious.

Analyzing and describing the planning premises 161

Carrying through strategic holistic marketing communication planning for the first time is quite a demanding process involving a good deal of learning on the part of a planner and his organization. A company that wishes to adopt holistic strategic planning, but which has not already practiced systematic strategy development, must start to do so with regard to one sub-strategy, namely marketing communication. Of course, with experience, the various planning tasks can be carried out more satisfactorily and cheaply.

For example, performing the task of analyzing and describing the planning premises for the first time means working from first principles. Planners must accept having to base their work on whatever budgetary and other information is available. However, in a company where the implementation of systematic strategy development processes is already part of the organizational working culture, a relatively good basis may exist for completing the various planning tasks. For instance, more and better information regarding such things as the business areas, the offering and the organizational basis can probably be obtained, and the operating budget is likely to be more thoroughly prepared.

The following Chapters 10 – 15 discuss each of the planning tasks. For the sake of simplicity it is supposed that

- the buyers within a business area are homogeneous as far as relevance and/or supplier criteria are concerned.

- a buyer and a decision unit is one – and the same – person.

These assumptions will be set aside in Chapter 16.

10. Carrying out the task analysis: Surveying and describing the communication tasks

The results of the analysis and description of the planning premises constitute the basis for proceeding with the next task in the planning process:

Carrying out a task analysis.

The task analysis: Purpose and procedure

As already indicated, the purpose of the task analysis is to survey and describe the communication tasks actually facing the company in a forthcoming planning period. The analysis identifies the tasks and the buyers they relate to in each business area. In other words, the task analysis clarifies the extent and nature of the communication tasks. The term *"nature"* of communication tasks refers to

- *the kind of tasks*, e.g. development tasks or standard communication tasks.
- *the specific nature* of the tasks, such as conveying the price or some specific product properties.

The term *"extent"* of communication tasks refers to *the number of buyers in relation to whom the tasks exist.*

Making a task analysis in a business area involves carrying out the following four sub-tasks:

1. Estimating the overall actual and potential demand for the product in question in the planning period together with the overall turnover and contribution potential:
These estimates are made in order to provide a realistic basis for making profitability evaluations at later stages in the planning process.

2. Assessing the competitiveness of the offering/organizational basis:
The second task involves comparing the company's offerings and relevant supplier criteria with those of its competitors. It was argued in Chapter 8 that the effect of marketing communication is heavily dependent on the competitiveness of the offering. The primary purpose of the assessment is to determine whether or not the offering or organizational basis is sufficiently competitive. If the offering or organizational basis is not sufficiently competitive, there can be *nothing to communicate*. By providing insights into the *relative* competitiveness of the company or its offering, the assessment also provides a realistic basis on which to predict how profitable it will be to allocate resources to marketing communication: The greater the competitive strength, the larger the expected return.

3. Diagnosing the extent and nature of the communication tasks:
The third task consists of surveying and describing the degree to which buyers are:

a. unaware of the offering and the company's position in respect of supplier criteria,

b. unaware of the "way to" the offering or company, or

c. need to be reminded of one or more of the above-mentioned items.

4. Assessing the extent and nature of buyer initiative:
The fourth and final task involves making a rough assessment of the extent and nature of buyer initiative to be expected from buyers. The purpose of making this assessment is to provide planners with a picture of

a. the degree to which the company's communication tasks can be performed by receiving, handling and following up buyer-initiated orders and inquiries.

b. the size of the buyer initiative

   - sales potential,
   - turnover potential, and
   - contribution potential,

respectively.

c. the seller initiative gap.

It has already been emphasized that buyer initiative may be assumed to be a function of (among other things) the proportion of buyers who know of and have bought the offering or dealt with the company as well as their experiences resulting from such transactions. Consequently, insight into the extent and nature of the communication tasks obtained as a result of carrying out the above, third sub-task forms a useful basis for estimating the extent and nature of buyer initiative.

A task analysis applying to a business area is illustrated in Figure 10.1. Most companies operate in several business areas. Accordingly, in order for a task analysis to be complete, the procedure outlined has to be carried out in relation to each of the relevant business areas. It should be noted that in cases where the product is marketed to end-buyers through dealers, buyer initiative will stem from dealers alone. Furthermore, communication tasks may exist in relation to dealers as well as end-buyers. Each of the sub-tasks within a task analysis relating to a business area will now be discussed in some detail.

Estimating the overall demand, turnover and contribution potential

The first stage of this task involves estimating the overall *"actual demand"*, i.e. the total *demand to be expected from the actual buyers in the planning period*. Given an estimate of the overall actual demand, the overall actual turnover and the actual contribution can be calculated by multiplying by price and contribution margin per product unit, respectively. A distinction has already been drawn between *actual* and *potential* buyers. As defined here, an *"actual buyer"* is *a buyer who will purchase the (generic) product in the planning period irrespective of marketing communication activities on the part of the companies marketing the product in the business area in question.*

In the second stage, the overall *"potential demand"* is estimated. As defined here a *"potential buyer"* is *a buyer whose possible demand for the product does depend on marketing communication activities on the part of the competing companies, i.e. on market development.* As indicated already, to a certain extent a company can stimulate latent needs and create new buyers in a planning period by converting potential buyers into actual buyers, i.e. by realizing a potential demand. The total potential turnover and potential contribution represented by the overall potential demand can be calculated by multiplying total demand with unit price and contribution margin, respectively.

The overall demand, turnover and contribution are calculated by adding up the estimated overall actual demand, turnover and contribution potentials, and the estimated overall potential demand, turnover and contribution, respectively.

This is illustrated by the following simplified example:

Let the total number of buyers in a business area be 100 000, of which 90 000 are actual and 10 000 are potential buyers. If estimated demand per buyer in the planning period is (on average) 10 product units, the estimated:

Overall actual demand	= 90 000 × 10 =	900 000
Overall potential demand	= 10 000 × 10 =	100 000
Overall demand	=	1 000 000

Given a price per product unit of $ 1 and a contribution margin of $ 0,5 per unit. In that case the estimated:

Overall actual turnover	= 900 000 × 1 =	900 000
Overall potential turnover	= 100 000 × 1 =	100 000
Overall turnover	=	1 000 000

And:

Overall actual contribution	= 900 000 × 0,5 =	450 000
Overall potential contribution	= 100 000 × 0,5 =	50 000
Overall contribution	=	500 000

The overall demand for a given product varies from one planning period to another. One very important determinant is the degree of product penetration. In the case of durable as well as non-durable products, low product penetration means that overall demand is relatively small. The number of actual buyers and potential buyers that can be converted into actual buyers is relatively low. As product penetration accelerates, so does the size of demand and the number of actual and "convertible" potential buyers.

In the case of non-durable products, demand will increase until saturation level is reached. All potential buyers have then become actual buyers and the demand potential is at its maximum. However, it was pointed out earlier, that the lifetime of durable products such as personal computers and video machines is always longer than a planning period. In such cases, enhanced penetration means that the number of households or businesses owning these products increases. As the stock of the product in a business area approaches saturation level, the demand stemming from first time buyers will decrease. When satu-

168 *Carrying out the task analysis*

Figure 10.1. Phases in the performance of a task analysis in a business area

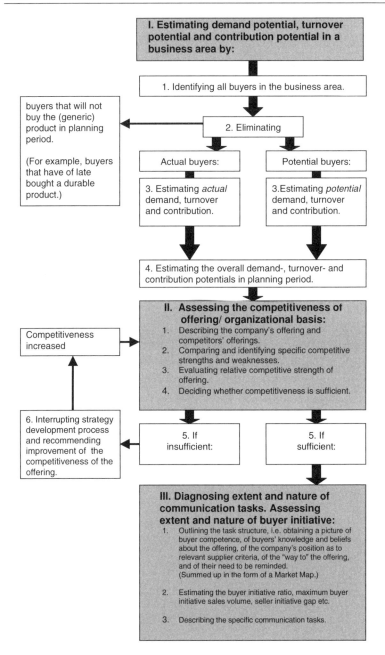

ration level has been reached, demand will depend on the need, willingness and financial ability of previous buyers to make replacement purchases, in short, on the lifetime of the product. For example, in periods of economic depression the number of car owners entering the market in order to replace their car in a given planning period tends to decrease dramatically.

Assessing the competitive strength of the offering and organizational basis

Assessing the competitive strength of the marketing offering or organizational basis comprises

a. identifying specific competitive strengths and weaknesses,

b. evaluating relative competitive strength as a whole (i.e. making comparisons with competitors' offerings and organizational bases), and

c. evaluating whether or not the company's offering or organizational basis is sufficiently competitive.

When making the assessment, planners make use of the insight provided by the analysis and the description of the planning premises as well as the results of new, supplementary analyses and investigations. At all events the evaluations have to be made on the basis of relevance/supplier criteria, possibly supplemented by relevant rewards and sacrifices.

The planner's work starts with listing and deciding on priorities concerning every material relevance and supplier criterion. He goes on to make a description of the company's offerings and organizational basis and those of its competitors on the basis of these criteria. By comparing the respective offerings and organizational bases he identifies specific competitive strengths and weaknesses. Based on the resulting insight he evaluates the relative degree of the company's competitive strength, and decides on whether or not it should be considered sufficient. This decision is, of course, largely a matter of personal judgment, based in part on intuition. In cases where the company's position is weak (or strong) in relation to all or most criteria, it should not be difficult to reach a conclusion. However, normally strengths as well as weaknesses are identified, making it necessary to make some kind of balanced evaluation. In such cases it may be useful to consider the extent to which strengths such as lower prices may compensate for weaknesses such as less favorable terms of delivery. It may also be of help to take into consideration the weight buyers put on the various criteria. In some cases certain competitive strengths related to especially important relevance and supplier criteria quite obviously outweigh certain weaknesses related to less important criteria.[31]

Diagnosing the extent and nature of the communication tasks

If – and only if – the competitiveness of the offering and the organizational basis is considered sufficient, the planner will continue with the task analysis in order to identify and clarify the extent and nature of the communication tasks.

A planner's work involves:

a. Surveying the *"task structure"* in the business area, i.e. providing *an initial, rough overview of the extent and nature of the communication tasks.*

b. Describing the *specific* communication tasks.

Outlining the task structure: The Market Map

The task structure can be outlined by estimating the distribution of buyers within three distinct categories with regard to

  - knowledge and beliefs about the offering, the "way to" the

offering and of the company's position as to relevant supplier criteria, and
- experience with the offering or the company.

The three categories are:

1. Buyers who are completely unaware of the existence of the offering or the company.

2. Buyers who have acquired partial, although insufficient knowledge, i.e. buyers who know that the offering or the company exists, and have some more or less realistic beliefs concerning the offering, the "way to" the offering and/or the company's position as to relevant supplier criteria.

3. Buyers with sufficient knowledge about the offering or the company.

The term *"sufficient knowledge"* is *not* used here to imply *complete knowledge*. Quite obviously, buyers make purchasing decisions without knowing everything about the offering or company in question. Most non-durable everyday commodities such as printing paper, lemonade, margarine, detergents and disposable diapers involve little or no financial and/or social risks. Consumers may, therefore, be expected to be willing to make a trial purchase based on a minimum of knowledge of the offering. Awareness of one or two favorable properties may be enough. Conversely, because of the financial and/or social risks involved, a most buyers want to know more before they decide to buy a house, a car, an item of furniture or a production machine. It is unrealistic to expect buyers in transformation markets to have complete knowledge of a potential supplier's position with regard to relevant supplier criteria before approaching the supplier and giving him an opportunity to make an offer. Moreover, buyers will tend to be satisfied with less product information about an offering whose supplier enjoys a good reputation. No general rules can be laid down to determine what is sufficient knowledge on the part of the buyers in any particular situation, although, it seems reasonable to assume that in general, sufficient knowledge includes knowledge of the offering and/or the organizational basis related to some important relevance and supplier criteria. Ultimately, each planner has to base his personal judgment about this question on the information available, prior experience and intuition.

The relative distribution of buyers between the above three categories forms a basis for outlining the task structure in the business area. This is because it is relatively easy to identify the extent and nature of the communication tasks in each of the categories:

1. Unaware buyers:
The number of standard communication tasks and tasks connected to "showing the way" to the offering correspond to the number of buyers in this category and the number of development tasks reflects the number of potential buyers. Where the business area in question belongs to a transformation market, there will also be transformation tasks to carry out. Unaware buyers cannot be expected to take buyer initiatives.

2. Buyers having a partial, insufficient knowledge:
Buyers in this category will not have bought the current offering or experienced the current organizational basis. Their beliefs, whether correct or incorrect, may be a function of such things as post-purchase experience with prior offerings, marketing communication activities in previous planning periods, multi-step communication effects in the form of word-of-mouth or sheer product visibility or a combination of any of these. The fact that these buyers' knowledge is insufficient may indicate the need to perform standard communication tasks as well as tasks connected to "showing the way" to the offering or company. Some development tasks may also need to be carried out. Mostly, however, this category calls for market utilization.

Although a potential buyer's knowledge is insufficient to make a purchase, it may form an adequate basis for making an inquiry. It may, therefore, be useful to estimate the degree to which buyers have overall *favorable, neutral* or *unfavorable attitudes* to-

Diagnosing the extent and nature of the communication tasks 173

ward the offering or company. The number of buyers with favorable or neutral attitudes may indicate the extent to which buyer initiative may be expected to occur.

3. Buyers having sufficient knowledge:
These buyers have bought and experienced the current standard or a customized offering or the organizational basis directly. The product in question will determine the kind of communication tasks that need to be performed.

Buyers of *non-durable, frequently purchased products,* such as toothpaste or corn flakes may be divided into three sub-categories, namely, buyers who have reacted in one of the following three ways:

- with preference,

- with indifference, i.e. they consider the offering neither better nor worse than one or more competing offerings, and

- with rejection.

There are, of course, no communication tasks in relation to buyers who prefer an offering or buyers who have rejected an offering because of dissatisfaction. However, communication tasks directed towards indifferent buyers will be aimed at reminding them of the offering. Both buyers holding a preference and indifferent buyers may place orders on their own initiative.

Analogously, in *transformation markets* characterized by a relatively high purchase frequency some buyers may be expected to develop a preference for a company while others might show indifference towards it or may reject it as a potential supplier. Relevant examples are services like hairdressing, market analyses and advertising campaigns. In the context of transformation markets preference means that the company is included in the buyers bidding list, *or* that the buyer-seller relationship has become so close, that no other potential supplier is invited to offer. The latter might be the case within the context of a strategic partnership. In any case, such preference means that standard communication tasks are non-existent. Rejection, of course, is tantamount to never being invited to offer. Buyers that have rejected the company as a potential supplier of customized offerings do not represent any communication tasks. Indifference means that the company may or may not be considered as a potential supplier, and that the latter has to undertake tasks which involve reminding the buyers in question. Obviously, both favorably disposed and indifferent buyers may make inquiries on their own initiative.

The relatively long lifetime and low purchase frequency of *durable products* makes it reasonable to assume that no buyers can have sufficient, experience-based knowledge of the offering or the company. Normally, both offerings and organizational bases are changed at a pace which makes repeat purchases of identical standard offerings or competence transformation on the basis of identical organization bases very unlikely. Consequently, the concepts of preference, indifference and rejection have little relevance. In general, therefore, in the context of durable products a buyer is either unaware or his knowledge is insufficient. There will be a considerable number of standard communication tasks and tasks connected to "showing the way", that number being a function of the total number of buyers among other things. The number of unaware buyers will determine the extent of development tasks. There will, of course, be transformation tasks to be undertaken in transformation markets. A favorable company reputation may lead buyers to make inquiries on their own initiative. Accordingly, it may pay to make an estimate of the existence of favorable, neutral or unfavorable attitudes among potential buyers.

Figure 10.2. illustrates how a task structure can be summed up in the form of a *Market Map*.[32] The map shown refers to a non-durable, standardized product. As will be seen, the map illustrates how the buyers in a business area are distributed with regard to the main and sub-categories discussed above. Based on the assumptions put forward about the existence of communication tasks in the various categories, conclusions can be drawn regarding the nature and extent of communication tasks in the business area in question.

This can be illustrated in the following way. If we assume a market in which the total number of buyers is 1 000 000, we can see from the box at the right-hand side of the map in Figure 10.2. that 40% of these are unaware buyers who present the company with virtually every kind of communication task. Many of these buyers have a lot to learn. According to the box in the lower left-hand side of the map, 30% or 300 000 buyers have partial or insufficient knowledge of the offering. 30% or 300 000 buyers have purchased the offering and have sufficient knowledge about it. In addition, the 15% of buyers who have reacted with indifference may be reminded that the offering exists. No communication tasks exist in relation to the 10% who prefer and the 5% who have rejected the offering.

The above example refers to a non-durable, standardized product. The Market Map may, however, be used in relation to any market. En example applying to a durable product will be shown below. As a diagnostic tool the Market Map indicates how the extent and nature of communication tasks facing the company develop through time. It reflects product penetration as well as the degree of penetration of the offering.

Describing the specific communication tasks

The insight provided by describing the offering or organizational basis and outlining the task structure constitutes the foundation for a more detailed description of the specific communication tasks that the company faces in relation to buyers with no or insufficient knowledge of a given offering or organizational basis. Unaware buyers represent standard communication tasks involving every important element in an offering, relevance criterion and supplier criterion. Nor do these buyers know "the way" to the offering. To the extent that they are potential buyers, specific development tasks will exist. As far as buyers with insufficient knowledge are concerned, every important element in the offering, relevance criterion and supplier criterion should be evaluated with regard to the degree to

176 *Carrying out the task analysis*

Figure 10.2. Summing up a task structure in the form of a Market Map

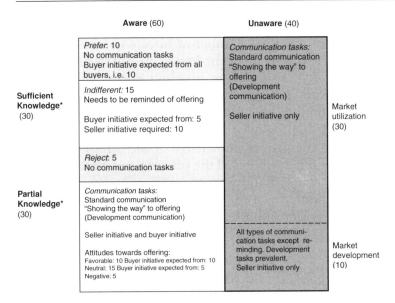

Figures, which are fictitious, indicate percentage of total number of buyers (= 1 000 000) in the market/business area. Brackets indicate that normally the communication tasks in question will not be present, but may nevertheless occur.

*: It is assumed that only buyers that have tried the offering may have sufficient knowledge. Buyers having partial knowledge have not tried the offering. Their partial knowledge may be based on such things as word-of-mouth or seller initiatives in previous planning periods.

According to the above figure buyer initiative may be expected from (10 + 5 + 10 + 5 =) 30% of the buyers. Consequently the buyer initiative ratio is 30/70.

See text for further comments and explanations.

which the relevant buyers may be expected to have any belief at all whether correct or incorrect. This means that for each main category of buyers a rather detailed description is given of every single communication task, its specific nature and the extent to which it exists.

For example: It may be that there are 50 000 buyers who are unaware that the price of the company's durable offering is $ 1 050. In that case, one specific standard communication task is:

"to convey the message that the price is $ 1 050".

Assessing the extent and nature of buyer initiative 177

The extent of this specific task is 50 000 buyers.
It may, furthermore, be that 10 000 of the unaware buyers do not know how to maintain the product properly. So, one specific development task concerns

"conveying information on product maintenance".

The extent of the task is 10 000 buyers.

We can envisage a situation in which 100 000 buyers have partial but insufficient knowledge of the relevance criterion, "design", relating to a company's offering, and that 20 000 of these 100 000 buyers entertain an incorrect belief about it. In that case, a specific communication task will be:

"to convey the correct product design".

The extent of this task is 100 000 buyers, 20 000 of whom have an incorrect belief about the offering.

Figure 10.5. in the last section of this chapter shows how the results of a description of specific communication tasks can be summarized in the form of a Market Map and a *"task profile"*.

Assessing the extent and nature of buyer initiative

The final step in a task analysis involves making a rough assessment as to the extent and nature of buyer initiative to be expected from the buyers. The purpose of such an assessment is to provide planners with a rough, initial idea regarding the degree to which the company's communication tasks can be performed through handling buyer-initiated orders and inquiries, the size of the buyer initiative sales, turnover and contribution potentials, and the seller initiative gap.
The relative importance of buyer initiative in a business area can be expressed by what is here termed the *"buyer initiative ratio"*, defined as:

178 *Carrying out the task analysis*

$$\text{Buyer initiative ratio} = \frac{\text{The maximum proportion of the buyers who can be expected to show buyer initiative in the form of orders or inquiries}}{\text{The proportion made up of the remaining buyers in the business area in question}^{33}} = \frac{\text{Maximum buyer initiative proportion}}{\text{Minimum seller initiative proportion}}$$

For example, if 50% of the buyers may be expected to show buyer initiative in the planning period, the buyer initiative ratio is 50/50. This also means that in relation to 50% of the buyers, seller initiative is a precondition for making sales. The buyer initiative ratio is, of course, an increasing function of the degree of market penetration of the offering/company.

The task structure provides a basis for assessing the maximum proportion of buyer initiative.

As far as *non-durable, standardized products* are concerned, the maximum proportion of buyers who may be expected to show initiative can be assessed as follows:

Maximum buyer initiative proportion =

　The buyers *preferring* the offering
+ some proportion of the total number of indifferent buyers
+ some proportion of the total number of buyers with insufficient knowledge but with *favorable* attitudes to the company or its offerings
+ some proportion of the total number of buyers with insufficient knowledge but who also have *neutral* attitudes to the company or its offerings.

Estimating the above proportions is not easy. Planners may, nevertheless, reason along the following lines:

Assessing the extent and nature of buyer initiative

Buyers who prefer an offering may be expected to show buyer initiative by placing orders. Indifferent buyers may also place orders. The extent to which they will do this is likely to be inversely related to the scale of competitors' marketing communication activities. Furthermore, it seems reasonable to expect that buyers with partial or insufficient knowledge, but who nevertheless have favorable or neutral attitudes will initiate sales by making inquiries. Buyers with favorable attitudes are more likely to show buyer initiative than buyers with neutral attitudes. Conversely, buyers with unfavorable attitudes to a company or its offerings will not normally initiate contact and the same will hold true of unaware buyers.

Figure 10.2. illustrates the proportion of buyers expected to show initiative. These are respectively:

10 (buyers who prefer the offering),
5 (indifferent buyers),
10 (with favorable attitudes), and
5 (with neutral attitudes),

Accordingly, the maximum buyer initiative proportion is 30 (= 10+5+10+5), and the buyer initiative ratio 30/70. This means that buyer initiative can be expected on the part of no more than 30% of all buyers, and that seller initiative is a precondition for making sales to the remaining 70%.

The seller initiative gap refers to the proportion of a budgeted total sales volume that has to be realized through seller initiatives, i.e. to the difference between a company's sales (volume) goal and a budgeted buyer-initiated sales volume. Thus, in a situation where a company's sales goal in a given planning period is 10 000 000 and 30% of the buyers are expected to show buyer initiative (estimated to buy no more than 3 000 000 product units), the minimum seller initiative gap will be 7 000 000.

Minimum seller initiative gap =

sales goal – maximum buyer initiative sales volume
= 10 000 000 – 3 000 000 = 7 000 000.

In this example, at least 70% of the sales goal has to be realized through seller initiative.

A maximum *order proportion* and a maximum *inquiry proportion* may also be estimated on the basis of a task structure. The term " *maximum order proportion*" refers to *the proportion of buyers showing initiative who may be expected to place orders.* It can be estimated as the proportion of buyers who prefer a company or its offerings + some proportion of indifferent buyers. Similarly, the term *"maximum inquiry proportion"* refers to *the proportion of buyers showing initiative who may be expected to make inquiries.* It can be estimated as a relatively large proportion of the buyers with favorable attitudes to the company or its offerings + some proportion of the buyers with neutral attitudes.

Using the figures in Figure 10.2. as an example:

Maximum order proportion (equal to 150 000 buyers)	= 10 + 5 = 15
Maximum inquiry proportion (equal to 150 000 buyers)	= 10 + 5 = 15

Consequently given that the average purchase per buyer in the period in question is 10 product units :

Maximum order sales volume	= 1 500 000
Maximum inquiry sales volume	= 1 500 000
Maximum buyer initiative sales volume	= 3 000 000

The same line of reasoning applies to *transformation markets* in the case of products with a relatively high purchase frequency, although, in such markets, buyer initiative occurs merely in the form of inquiries. Company reputation can be assumed to be the main source of buyer initiative in the case of both *standardized* and *customized durable, products.* Consequently, the maximum buyer initiative proportion can be estimated on the basis of assessments of the proportions of buyers with favorable and neutral attitudes towards the company. In some industrial markets, supply contracts may cover two or more planning periods. For practical purposes, such contracts applying to later periods are viewed as buyer-initiated, regardless of which party initiated the original contract.

An example

The course of a task analysis may be further illustrated with the following simple, fictitious example.

A company, located in N-land, imports plows. It introduced the K-model in the current year and plans to make it the core of its marketing offering in the forthcoming planning period. However, changes will be made to other elements in the offering in order to improve competitiveness. The company has one competitor, X.

Arrangements for distributing the K-plow have just been finalized by entering into agreements with 9 new dealers in the northern part of the country. According to the operating budget, the sales goal for the forthcoming planning period is 750 plows. The total number of buyers (farmers) is 100 000. Each of these owns one or more plows.

Based on these assumptions, a task analysis might take the following course:

1. It is estimated that in the planning period in question, 3 000 of the 100 000 farmers will buy a new plow. In other words, the estimated demand is 3 000. Since product penetration is 100%, the company's task is one of market utilization only (actual demand and actual buyers), although it must be borne in mind that certain development tasks concerning use and maintenance may exist.

182   *Carrying out the task analysis*

The trade price is $ 3 200 and the contribution margin per unit $ 1 200. That is, estimated:

Overall actual turnover   (= 3 000 * 3 200) = $ 9,6 mill.
Overall actual contribution (= 3 000 * 1 200) = $ 3,6 mill.

2. In order to be able to evaluate the competitiveness of the offering,

   - the most important relevance criteria and their relation to various elements in the offering have to be identified,

   - both the company's offering as well as that of competitor X have to be described in relation to the identified relevance criteria and their respective elements.

3. The offerings have to be compared with a view to

   - identifying specific strengths and weaknesses,
   - evaluating the overall relative competitive strength of the company's offering, and
   - deciding whether or not competitive strength is sufficient.

Box 10.3. illustrates this identification and evaluation process. Column 2 suggests that the farmers have nine important relevance criteria:

1. Molding ability, i.e. ability to turn the sod correctly,
2. sideways stability, i.e. ability to make straight plow furrows,
3. tractive power required,
4. plowing speed,
5. time and skill required with regard to setting the plow correctly (incorrect setting reduces performance drastically),
6. setting service, i.e. service provided with regard to setting the plow correctly,
7. price,
8. speed of spare part delivery – and
9. ability to deliver spare parts on time (as promised).

An example 183

Column 1 shows seven relevant elements in the offering:

1. Design of plowshare (moldboard) (product property),
2. setting mechanism,
3. setting service,
4. price,
5. time of delivery of spare parts – and
6. ability to deliver spare parts on time.

A comparison of the two columns shows that some elements in the offering and relevance criteria correspond, while others do not. The farmers cannot evaluate the design of the plowshare directly. In their experience, what counts is molding ability, sideways stability, required tractive power, and plowing speed. Therefore, these four relevance criteria have to be "translated" into one element in the offering, namely, "the design of the plowshare". The same is true of the relevance criterion "time and skill required with regard to setting the plow correctly" and the element "setting mechanism". On the other hand, there is a complete concurrence as regards ability to deliver spare parts on time, price, setting service, and time of delivery as regards spare parts.

The offerings of the company (OK) and that of competitor X (OX) are described in column 3 and 4, respectively, in Box 10.3. The offerings are compared in column 5. A plus symbol (+) is used to indicate "good/better" and a minus symbol (-) indicates "poor/poorer". It appears that the offerings are identical as regards molding ability and ability to deliver spare parts on time. OK has a strong competitive position compared to OX as regards sideways stability, plowing speed, setting service, and time of delivery as regards spare parts. However, X has a lower price and less time and skill are required to set the plow correctly.

Some of the differences are commented on in further detail. For example, the K-plow requires 20% lower tractive power and its possible plowing speed is 10% higher, while spare parts can be delivered four days sooner. Furthermore, K alone offers

184 *Carrying out the task analysis*

Box 10.3. Evaluating the competitiveness of the K-plow offering

Elements in the offering: (1)	Relevance criteria: (2)	OK (3)	OX (4)	Competitive strength of K-plow: (5)
Design of plowshare	Molding ability	+	+	0
	Sideways stability	+	-	+
	Tractive power required	+	-	+ (20% less)
	Plowing speed	+	-	+ (10% faster)
Setting mechanism	To set the plow correctly:			
	Skill required	-	+	-
	Time required	-	+	- (twice as long)
Setting service	Setting service	+ (free of charge at one weeks notice)	- (no service)	+ (considerable strength)
Price	Price	- ($ 3 200)	+ ($ 3 000)	- ($ 200 higher)
Time of spare part delivery	Time of spare part delivery	+ 2 days	- 5 days	+ (3 days shorter)
Ability to deliver spare parts on time (as promised)	Ability to deliver spare parts on time (as promised)	90%	90%	0

a setting service free of charge at one week's notice. On the other hand, X's plow costs $ 200 less than the K-plow.

On the whole, OK appears to be sufficiently competitive.

A survey has shown that

- 40% of the 3 000 farmers who actually intend to purchase a plow are completely unaware of the K-plow/OK, while
- 60% have partial, insufficient knowledge about it, including some incorrect beliefs.

45 % of these farmers have a neutral attitude towards company K. As intensive competitive communication activities are expected to be carried through in the planning period, these buyers

An example 185

cannot be expected to initiate inquiries. However, the positive attitudes among the remaining 10% may be a source of buyer initiative. In all probability, the 5% who have negative attitudes will not show buyer initiative.

The task structure indicated by the survey shows that the company is faced with a considerable number of communication tasks. None of the buyers have sufficient knowledge of the offering. The largest possible buyer initiative ratio is 10/90, in other words, only relatively modest buyer initiative can be expected. The maximum buyer initiative sales volume is 300 K-plows. Accordingly, the seller initiative gap is 750 – 300 = 450 plows.

Box 10.4. contains information demonstrating the extent and nature of the specific communication tasks. Columns 3, 4 and 5 show the relative proportion of farmers who have correct, incorrect or no beliefs about the offering as far as the various relevance criteria are concerned. The box speaks for itself. It is clear that the buyers are unaware of or have incorrect beliefs about some important properties of the offering. The percentages of those who are aware of the lower tractive power required, the 10% higher plowing speed and the free setting service (20%, 20% and 5% of the buyers respectively) are especially low. Furthermore, only 50% have a correct belief about the price, and as many as 50% believe that it is higher than it really is. Also, a large proportion of the buyers have incorrect beliefs about time of delivery of spare parts (30%) and ability to deliver spare parts on time (40%).

In addition to this, interviews with dealers have indicated that buyers lack the necessary knowledge and skill to set and maintain the plow (development task). It is also probable that as many as 60% of buyers need to be "shown the way" to the offering and especially to the new dealers in the northern part of the country.

Figure 10.5. illustrates how the extent and nature of the specific communication tasks may be visualized in the form of a task profile.

186 *Carrying out the task analysis*

Box 10.4. Buyers' beliefs about the K-plow offering

Elements in the offering:	Relevance criteria:	Have correct beliefs:	Have incorrect beliefs:	Have no beliefs:
		Relative distribution of 3 000 buyers (%):		
Design of plowshare	Molding ability	50		50
	Sideways stability	50		50
	Tractive power required	20		80
	Plowing speed	20		80
Setting mechanism	To set the plow correctly:			
	Skill required	40		60
	Time required	40		60
Setting service	Setting service	5		95
Price	Price	10	50	40
			Believe the price is $ 2-300 higher than it is.	
Time of spare part delivery	Time of spare part delivery	20	30	50
			Believe time of delivery is 2-7 days longer than it is.	
Ability to deliver spare parts on time (as promised)	Ability to deliver spare parts on time (as promised)	10	40	50
			Believes probability of delivery on time is lower than it is.	

Working with the task analysis normally gives planners new insights into such things as the number of buyers in a business area, the size of demand to expect in the forth-coming planning period, the likely extent of buyer initiative, the buyer initiative sales volume etc. Such new insights may lead planners to revise some of the estimates made in the initial analysis and description of the planning premises.

An example 187

Figure 10.5. A task profile: Visualization of the nature and extent of specific communication tasks in the K-plow example

Proportion of buyers with no knowledge of or incorrect beliefs about the offering (%)

	0	10	20	30	40	50	60	70	80	90	100

1. Conveying the offering

Development task:
Use and maintenance ⎯⎯⎯⎯⎯⎯⎯⎯⎯⎯⎯⎯⎯⎯⎯⎯⎯⎯ (to ~90)

Standard communication tasks:
Molding ability ⎯⎯⎯⎯⎯⎯ (to ~40)
Sideways stability ⎯⎯⎯⎯⎯⎯ (to ~40)
Tractive power required ⎯⎯ (to ~20)
Plowing speed ⎯⎯ (to ~20)
Setting mechanism:
  Skill required ⎯⎯⎯⎯⎯⎯ (to ~40)
  Time required ⎯⎯⎯⎯⎯⎯ (to ~40)
Setting service —
Price ⎯⎯ _ _ _ _ _ _ _ _ _
Time of spare part delivery ⎯⎯⎯⎯ _ _ _ _ _ _
Ability to deliver spare parts on time _ _ _ _ _ _ _ _ _ _ _

Transformation tasks: None

2. "Showing the way" to the offering

9 new dealers ⎯⎯⎯⎯⎯⎯⎯⎯⎯

3. Reminding of the offering None

⎯⎯⎯⎯⎯⎯ : No knowledge

_ _ _ _ _ _ : Incorrect beliefs

This figure is based on Box 10.4.

11. Developing a target group strategy: Prioritizing buyer segments and selecting target groups

Provided that the offering is sufficiently competitive, the planning process proceeds with

selecting which tasks to consider in relation to which buyers in the planning period, i.e. with developing a target group strategy.

Viability and profitability criteria. Target groups

The selection of communication tasks is made with due regard to the following:

1. which and how many tasks it is possible and/or desirable to perform, given the company goal and the present state of the organizational basis.

2. how resources can be used as profitably as possible.

In other words, communication tasks are selected to take account of viability criteria as well as profitability criteria.

Viability criteria may have to do with such matters as the financial resources available, with the competence of management and staff, and with organizational culture. For instance, a company may be unable to tackle certain development tasks due to lack of necessary liquid assets and certain competencies. Such a company may not have sufficient capacity to give incompetent buyers' insight into relevance criteria, to train them to use complex products such as consulting services in strategic management. A company's sales goal or available production capacity may limit the number or range of communication tasks it should attempt to tackle. Normally sales volume is proportional to the number of buyers communicated with, i.e. to the number of communication tasks completed successfully. Consequently, the sales goal sets limits to the number of segments it is appropriate to communicate with since it would be pointless for a company to attempt to create demand beyond its own productive capacity to meet it.

Profitability criteria are used with the purpose of allocating resources in such a way that the most profitable tasks are given the highest priority, while unprofitable tasks are avoided. It has already been pointed out that the contribution and costs connected to performing various communication tasks may vary considerably. Profitability criteria relate to differences in profitability. They indicate contribution that might be obtained or costs that might be incurred in communicating with various categories of buyers. For example, it seems reasonable to assume that the contribution gained is positively related to such things as the level of buyers' demand in the planning period, and to their ability to influence other buyers to make purchases. Especially in industrial markets, costs incurred by using personal face-to-face communication may vary considerably depending on where buyers are located. Communicating with buyers who are heavily exposed to competitors' marketing communication may even be unprofitable. In short, profitability depends quite heavily on task selection. Since communication tasks are related to buyers, *the selection of tasks is tantamount to selecting which buyers to communicate with*.

In order to canalize resource use in the desired direction, all buyers in the appropriate business areas are segmented and prioritized with regard to potential profitability. Segments are selected in order of profitability, and those given the highest priority constitute the *target groups* in the planning period. Since it cannot exceed production capacity, the sales goal is used as a basis on which to determine an adequate number of target groups. For example, if a sales goal is 30 000 product units, and the two most profitable segments represent an actual demand of 600 000 units, two target groups with a combined demand amounting to 20 times the sales goal may be considered adequate.

Even though a target group is the result of a segmentation process based on a set of profitability criteria, in most cases its members will be more or less heterogeneous as far as other important characteristics are concerned. Where this is so, a planner may have to divide a target group into more homogeneous *sub-(target) groups*, before it is possible to develop effective content, symbolization and media solutions that are appropriate to each of them.

Segmenting and prioritizing: The procedure

Figure 11.1. outlines the segmenting and prioritization procedure to be carried through in relation to each business area. The procedure applies to dealer as well as end-buyer segments, although the discussion and examples in this and the following two sections relate to end-buyers.

The procedure entails the following steps:

1. Some communication tasks – and thereby buyer segments – are ruled out on the basis of viability criteria.

2. The remaining buyers in the business area in question are segmented on the basis of (relatively few) profitability criteria.

In principle, precise evaluation of potential profitability to be derived from communicating with different buyers depends on the number of profitability criteria applied. In other words, the greater the number of profitability criteria applied the greater the number of segments. However, working with many criteria may be quite impractical. For one thing, multi-dimensional cross-tabulations require a lot of information and information processing capacity. In addition, information over-load can easily cloud perspective. For these reasons, it is generally preferable to operate with a relatively limited number of criteria and segments.

As profitability criteria may and often do point in opposite directions, the final priority of a segment rests on a total evaluation. For example, the buyers in an industrial business area may be sub-divided into three segments according to total annual demand for the product in question. This segmentation will make it possible to distinguish between "heavy", "medium" and "light" buyers and provide a basis for giving appropriate priority to each group. If, however, competition for heavy buyers is particularly strong, a reasonable conclusion might be that medium buyers should be given highest priority.

The segments are sorted with regard to profitability and a number of target groups are selected in order of profitability and with regard to the company's sales goal. The buyers in the selected target groups are those with whom the company has chosen to communicate in the forthcoming planning period. It should be emphasized that a segment need not necessarily consist of more than one buyer. It is quite possible that a segmentation process leads to the conclusion that it would be most practical *to consider each buyer as a separate segment*. This may occur especially in industrial markets consisting of relatively few large and heterogeneous buyers. While the term *"target buyer"* is more precise than target group in such instances, for the sake of simplicity, the term *"target group"* will be used in the following discussion to refer *to prioritized segments consisting of one or more buyers.*

The strategic planning task of selecting a target group strategy involves subjecting each business area to the above procedure. The final decision on a strategy is based upon a total evaluation and prioritization of potential target groups across all business areas.

Segmenting buyers and prioritizing target groups is a complex "search-and-learn" process. There are no formulae to help the user. Evaluations can be made in more "mechanical" ways, for

Segmenting and prioritizing: The procedure 193

Figure 11.1. Developing a target group strategy

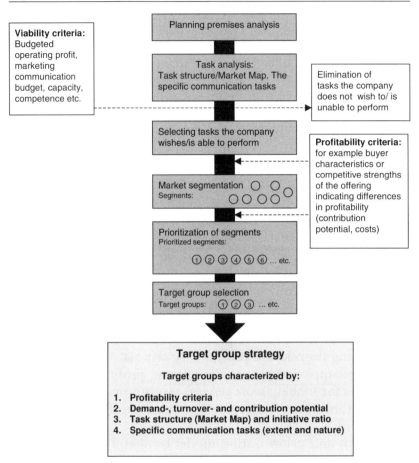

example, by expressing the relevant profitability criteria on some kind of quantitative scale, giving priority points to the various segments based on the scale, adding up the points and prioritizing in accordance with the sums arrived at. However, the real situation is usually too complex to be represented in this way and such an analysis would fail to capture important qualitative elements. Accordingly, other modes of problem solving have to be followed. Even rules-of-thumb may prove helpful. For instance, if some criteria are obviously more important

194 *Developing a target group strategy*

than others, a practical first step may be to use these as a basis for segmenting. Once that has been done, a planner may consider whether or not any of the less important criteria are nevertheless relevant. No more detail should be incorporated into the analysis than is consistent with maintaining perspective. Many – if not most – evaluations will be based on experience, common sense and intuition. The planning task is finished when the planner becomes convinced that a certain target group strategy is sensible and that he is capable of arguing in favor of it on the basis of viability and profitability criteria.

Identifying, selecting and using viability and profitability criteria is a crucial planning task. The literature on marketing and buyer behavior offers numerous ideas as to potentially relevant criteria, but no general and complete survey exists. This means that it is up to planners to draw on their theoretical and practical marketing knowledge in order to find appropriate solutions in each planning situation.

The remaining part of this chapter contains:

- outlines of two possible procedures that can be used when searching for relevant profitability criteria.
- some examples of potentially relevant profitability criteria.
- reasons for making *some* general assumptions about searching for and identifying target groups from the "most profitable end".
- a search and prioritization model termed *The Prioritization Path*.
- a discussion about how to coordinate the selection of end-buyer and dealer target groups.

On profitability criteria

Two possible search procedures

In his search for relevant profitability criteria a planner may follow two different paths:

1. He may start from a notion of a possibly relevant criterion and ask whether that criterion can be assumed to give any indications about contribution potential and/or costs, i.e. profitability. For example, in an industrial market, the planner might ask whether a buyer's annual turnover indicates the size of the contribution potential, or whether the fact that his company has a strong relationship to a buyer means that communication costs are relatively lower.

2. He may take contribution potential and costs as his point of departure and try to get ideas of relevant criteria.

Criteria based search

In a criteria based search it may be useful assume that in principle, profitability criteria may relate to:

a. characteristics of buyers as individuals,

b. characteristics of buyers' social and physical environment,

c. the competitive strength of the offering, and the company's position with regard to relevant supplier criteria, and

d. the degree to which buyers are exposed to competitors' marketing communication.

Where individual characteristics are concerned, a distinction may be drawn between psychological and social characteristics. Psychological characteristics may be either cognitive (intellectual) or motivational (affective or emotional). Cognitive characteristics relate to such things as knowledge and perceptions of reality, e.g. relevance criteria and beliefs about companies and their offerings. Motivational characteristics relate to needs, emotions, and attitudes, e.g. towards a company or an offering.

Potentially relevant sociological characteristics include group membership, the relevance of which rests largely on an assumed influence of group norms and group status on an individual's purchasing behavior. It is generally thought that group norms are an important source of relevance criteria. Social status may be assumed to provide some indication of a person's influence on the perceptions, attitudes and behavior of other group members.

Advertising literature tends to focus on easily measurable (quantifiable) buyer characteristics such as gender, age and education. These are widely assumed to be *indicators* of more relevant but less measurable (or immeasurable) psychological or sociological characteristics. For instance, age is sometimes assumed to correlate with certain attitudes, which in turn may be supposed to influence buyers' purchasing decisions. Indicators typically considered relevant in relation to markets for consumer products are economic-demographic characteristics such as gender, age, degree of urbanization with regard to location of residence, type of residence (owner-tenant flat, private house etc.), family size, family role (father, mother etc.), income, property, and family life cycle.

Further examples of frequently used characteristics are buyers'/families' total consumption of non-durable products and ownership of durable products.

Examples of segments based on such easily measured characteristics are:

"women between 15 and 25 years of age, living in urban areas",

"women between 26 and 45 years of age, living in urban areas",

"women between 26 and 45 years of age, living in rural areas",

etc.

Standardized surveys of the coverage of different impersonal mass media such as newspapers, magazines, TV- and radio programs, and commercial films are based exclusively on such easily measured characteristics.

Contribution and cost based search

Following this procedure, it may be useful to view a contribution as dependent on:

- The probability that buyers will respond to the company's marketing communication, i.e. that they will become aware of it, interpret it, remember the contents, buy as a result of it, and experience the full potential of the offering. In the case of non-durable products, for example, this means reaction with preference rather than indifference, and indifference rather than rejection.

- The contribution potential when buyers respond to the company's marketing communication by purchasing an offering and subsequently experience its full potential.

The following may serve as examples of criteria indicating probability of response and contribution potential, respectively:

1. Criteria indicating the probability of response:

Motivation is one example of a potentially relevant profitability criterion, which may be supposed to indicate the probability of response. In the literature dealing with buyer behavior and mass communication, motivation is seen as an important determinant of an individual's receptiveness to communication messages. Motivation – often defined as a feeling of an unsatisfied need or an unsolved problem – is supposed to be a function of a buyer's individual characteristics as well as his social and physical environment. For example, the fact that a company is losing money may make its top manager more interested in information on certain consulting services. A company in need of a partner with which to collaborate may be assumed to be more receptive to information that may lead to a dialogue, which may in turn lead to a close buyer-seller relationship. Faulty gutters on the roof of a family house may motivate its occupants to look for information on relevant offerings. Changing their place of work may make people more susceptible to marketing communication messages about such things as neighboring gas stations and fast food restaurants. Motivation is a state that changes over time.

Motivation is certainly a relevant profitability criterion. Whether or not a buyer seeks information actively depends, among other things, on his motivational state. Furthermore, motivation is assumed to influence whether or not a buyer becomes aware of a communication message such as an advertisement, how the message is interpreted, and whether or not and how it is remembered. Marketing communication might sometimes motivate a buyer who has not previously been motivated. The question of whether or not buyers can be motivated by marketing communication is an extremely important one in connection with decisions regarding market development.

Normally motivation varies considerably among buyers in a business area. In most cases, however, the motivational state of buyers is difficult to establish directly. One possible method involves the use of indicators. For example, a bank may assume that people who are moving house will be motivated to find a bank that is conveniently situated in their new neighborhood and will therefore be more interested in information about bank offerings than they would otherwise be. Furthermore, the fact that a buyer makes an initial contact on his own initiative indicates susceptibility and a relatively high probability of responding by purchasing. It has already been pointed out that buyer initiative indicates that a buyer has at least some knowledge about the company and a positive attitude towards it.

According to a related, well-known hypothesis, an individual's susceptibility to marketing communication depends on whether the *problem solving* process leading to a purchase is *extensive, limited or habitual*. Extensive problem solving is characterized by active information seeking and a relatively thorough evaluation of several offerings. When problem solving is limited, no information seeking takes place, but the buyer may nevertheless be receptive to marketing communication messages. Habitual problem solving means that virtually no resources are spent on making purchasing decisions. Buyers' receptiveness is low, even when marketing communication messages are about offerings that are clearly better than those bought habitually.[34]

The competitiveness of an offering is a crucial source of communication contents. Accordingly, the more competitive the offering is in relation to a buyer's relevance/supplier criteria, the higher the probability of response. For example, a supplier of hair-shampoo may find the best match between relevance criteria and product properties among young women between 15 and 25 years of age. This means that buyers belonging to this age segment are those most likely to respond by purchasing, preferring and experiencing the full potential of the offering.

It seems reasonable to suppose that potential buyers are more likely to respond to one company's marketing communication by purchasing the less they are *exposed to competitors' marketing communication* – and vice versa. In an industrial market a buyer's location may serve as a useful indicator of competing communication activities. For example, many building contractors tend to focus their attention on buyers who are located near or in the region of the building company's own headquarters.

Taking *the nature of the communication tasks* as a starting point may also produce useful ideas. For instance, the greater the amount of information to be conveyed and the more the buyer has to learn, the less likely potential buyers are to become aware of and to interpret information adequately and therefore to purchase the offering. For example, learning to fill requisite user or consumer roles may be quite a demanding task for incompetent buyers. This hypothesis supports a strategy which puts market utilization before market development, and buyers with some knowledge of the offering or company before buyers who are unaware of these. Finally, potential buyers with favorable beliefs about a company are likely to be more receptive to communication messages about new offerings than those with negative attitudes to the company making them.

2. Criteria indicating the contribution potential:
A buyer's *total actual or potential demand in a given planning period* may be used as an example of a criterion which can indicate

the seller's contribution potential. When there is insufficient information about total demand, various indicators might be used. For example, in a market for non-durable everyday commodities, relevant indicators might be family size or age. A large family consumes more than a small one, and young families are larger than older ones. In an industrial market overall turnover or number of employees might serve as indicators of the contribution potential.

Another example is *a buyer's influence on the purchasing decisions of other buyers*. Theoretical work as well as practical experience bear out the assertion that buyers vary considerably when it comes to influencing others, whether by enhancing product visibility or by contributing to two- or multi-step word-of-mouth processes. Car owners who drive long distances each year expose their car to a considerably larger number of potential buyers than do weekend drivers. A well-known hypothesis drawn from mass communication and buyer behavior theory states that buyers may be divided into "opinion leaders" and "followers". Followers view opinion leaders as "experts" within one or more subject areas and tend to seek their advice. The source of an opinion leader's know-how may be no more than general interest or the fact that he has just bought a relevant offering and is believed to possess a sufficient knowledge about it. Opinion leaders may be found in all kinds of areas from health food to ladies' fashions. In markets for agricultural machines such as plows and harvesters, younger farmers may function as opinion leaders by virtue of more recent and superior education. In an industrial market, some especially innovative companies may be regarded as "experts" in areas such as new raw materials or new production technologies. Because information on a buyer's actual influence on other buyers may be hard to obtain, indicators such as company size, education or age may have to be used.

Certainly, the potential influence of some buyer's on the purchasing behavior of others is an important relevance criterion for at least two reasons. The first is that other buyers' purchases may be attributed to influential buyers. The second is that by showing and communicating about an offering, influential buyers may reduce or even eliminate the need for marketing communication activities, thereby saving the company communication costs.

One example of a potentially relevant criterion indicating costs relates to whether or not buyers require market development. It was argued above that market development normally incurs higher costs than does market utilization. Another example of such a criterion concerns communication based on buyer initiative, which incurs lower communication costs than that based on seller initiative. According to a well-known hypothesis, communicating with existing customers is more cost-effective than communicating with new customers. One reason for this is that the cost incurred in contacting a familiar buyer is relatively lower. Another reason is that the communication cost per unit is reduced through time due to the effects of learning. In industrial markets especially, marketing communication costs and transportation costs are likely to be directly proportional to the distance between buyer and company.

The Prioritization Path: A search and prioritization model

It was pointed out earlier that there are no formulae that can tell us how buyers should be segmented and prioritized. This is not to say that no general assumptions can be made about how an effective search for target groups might be carried out. A number of such assumptions are embedded in the model presented in Figure 11.2. under the heading: *The Prioritization Path*.

The course of the Prioritization Path

As appears from Figure 11.2. the Prioritization Path runs from left to right, starting with buyers who may be expected to place orders on their own initiative, and ending with potential buyers. The path should be interpreted as follows.

When searching for target groups planners should:

1. Search first *among buyers expected to show buyer initiative* in the form of orders, and inquiries.

Several arguments in favor of giving top priority to these buyers have been stated already. These indicate a high probability of making a sale as well as low communication costs.

2. Search secondly among segments consisting of *actual buyers requiring seller initiative*.

In relation to actual buyers development tasks are simpler or non-existent and therefore incur low costs or no costs at all. These buyers are already "in the market" for the product in question and thus more susceptible to marketing communication. Moreover, their overall demand and contribution potential is almost certainly above average.

Among actual buyers, priority should be given to

- buyers with sufficient knowledge (e.g. indifferent buyers) or with some, but insufficient knowledge of the offering/ company in preference to

- buyers who are unaware of the company or its offering.

This prioritization rests on the assumption that the greater the buyer's prior knowledge of the offering or company, the fewer are the communication tasks and, consequently, the lower are the company's communication costs. Some buyers may simply need to be reminded of the offering. Some will know "the way to" the offering or company. Hopefully, some buyers already have a favorable attitude towards the company or its offerings, stemming from positive experiences with previous offerings or favorable word-of-mouth. All existing "good customers" belong to this buyer segment. Buyers who are unaware of the company or its offering, on the other hand, represent a greater number of communication tasks, many of which will be more demanding. These buyers have to learn about all the properties of the offering or company from scratch.

3. Lastly, search among *potential buyers*.

The probability that any one potential buyer will react to marketing communication is relatively low. Costs connected to market development are relatively high. The communication tasks range from more or less demanding development tasks to extensive standard communication tasks, and tasks connected to "showing the way" to the offering or company.

Using the Prioritization Path as a planning tool
Basically the Prioritization Path involves giving priority to

- buyer initiative before seller initiative,
- market utilization before market development, and
- buyers with some knowledge of the offering or company before buyers who are unaware of these.

By using the Prioritization Path as a tool planners may enhance the likelihood of identifying relevant buyer segments in an appropriate order of priority. *No greater claims are made for the validity of the model.*

When necessary, additional criteria may be applied at each stage of the search process, for the purpose of further segmenting and prioritizing. These criteria may concern contribution potential, competitive strength, exposure to competitors' marketing communication etc. At every stage, some segments may be dropped. Even buyers showing initiative have to be filtered, *sorted* in segments, and prioritized. For example, buyers contacting the company on their own initiative may be excluded from the target groups on grounds such as small contribution potentials or inability to pay. The search along the path ends when a sufficient number of target groups have been identified to satisfy the requirements of the company's sales goal.

A number of circumstances will determine how "far" one has to move along the path in order to identify a sufficient number

Figure 11.2. The Prioritization Path

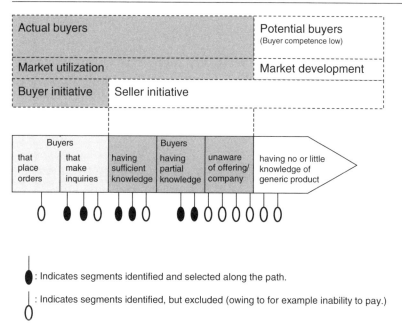

of target groups. Examples of such determinants are the competitive strength of the offering, the extent of competing communication activities, and the size of the various buyer segments. Furthermore, where the degree of penetration of the offering is low, the target groups may have to include a considerable number of buyers who are unaware of the company or its offerings. On the other hand, if the degree of penetration of the offering is near maximum, the target groups may consist merely of buyers expected to show initiative. In cases where product penetration is low, the target groups may have to include potential buyers if a budgeted sales goal is to be realized.

The Prioritization Path emphasizes the importance of buyer initiative, which ties in with the view that *a company's most important target groups are found among buyers who show initiative.* The approach to segmentation of buyers and prioritization of target groups embedded in the model is in sharp contrast with that which is dominant in other marketing communication literature, which focuses exclusively on buyers requiring seller initiative.

It should be noted that information on the following questions related to each of the target groups can be drawn from the task analysis:

- estimated demand, turnover and contribution potential, and

- relevant communication tasks, i.e. task structure/Market Map, buyer initiative ratio, and specific communication tasks (task profile).

Coordinating the selection of end-buyer and dealer target groups

Where a company's product is marketed through dealers, its planners face the task of developing a target group strategy which takes account of all links in the distribution chain. In principle, the concepts and procedures discussed above apply to segmentation and prioritization of dealers as well as of end-buyers. However, when using the Prioritization Path in relation to those markets that are characterized by intermediate trade, it must be remembered that buyer initiative may stem from dealers (as opposed to end-buyers) only.

While segmentation and prioritization leading to dealer and end-buyer target groups are separate processes, these still need to be *coordinated*. This is done by selecting the end-buyer target groups first and by letting these groups constitute a premise for the selection of dealer target groups. In addition to other profitability criteria, dealers should be evaluated on the basis of criteria such as those given below:

a. Coverage of the end-buyer target groups, i.e. the extent to which they attract end-buyers in the selected target groups. In markets for non-durable consumer products, for example, coverage may have to do with such things as geographical location of stores.

b. Intention and capability with regard to developing and implementing a competitive offering including the company's product. As previously emphasized, a dealer's offering is influenced by the company's offering to him, but will ultimately be determined by the elements that the dealer himself contributes to the total offering. For instance, a cycle dealer's offering might consist of a bicycle manufacturer's competitive model, combined with the dealer's own competitive (or non-competitive) repair service and complaint handling.

c. Intention and capacity with regard to taking the necessary seller initiative in order to convey the offering to end-buyers in the selected target groups.

d. Extent of exposure to buyer-initiated orders and inquiries on the part of end-buyers in the selected target groups.

e. Intention and capability with regard to competent handling of buyer initiative.

The higher a dealer scores on these criteria, i.e. the *stronger* he is, the higher his priority, and vice versa.

When dealers are (very) strong, the vendor company will not need to direct seller-initiated communication activities at end-buyers. A "push-strategy" will be adequate. Communication efforts will be directed at selling to the dealers, who may be expected to do the rest of the job. Weak dealers, on the other hand, call for a "pull-strategy" whereby the company spends (considerable) resources on seller initiative directed at the end-buyer target groups in order to create inquiries that "pull" the product "through" the dealers. In most markets, dealer strength lies somewhere between these extremes, and effective strategies combine "pull" with "push". However, in the absence of other considerations, dealers in a coordinated selection of dealer and end-buyer target groups should be accorded priority corresponding inversely to the need for "pull". In a nutshell, strong dealers mean higher sales volumes and lower communication costs.

It should be noted that several of the above criteria relate to buyer competence. Dealers with low scores may be considered unable to fulfill the required user role, since they cannot exploit available marketing tools in a purposeful manner. In such cases, the vendor company will have to undertake development tasks itself. It should also be mentioned that otherwise competitive offerings to weak dealers may easily become more costly. This is due to a greater need of support in the form of such measures as:

- training programs related to acquiring adequate product knowledge.
- training programs related to service provision.
- financial advertising support.
- free communication material such as brochures and placards.

All the target groups given top priority on the Prioritization Path will consist of dealers, since only these can show buyer initiative directed at the company. The subsequent results of following the path will depend to a large extent on dealers' strength. Where there are many strong dealers in a business area, it may not be necessary to employ any resources at all on communicating with end-buyers. However, when communication activity directed at end-buyers is an important relevance criterion with strong dealers, the vendor company may nevertheless have to employ resources for this purpose. A familiar example of this occurs when supermarket chains treat consumer advertising as a precondition for dealing in a brand. A normal "push" and "pull" situation will thus include a mixture of dealer and end-buyer target groups.

The discussion in Chapter 10 implied that a task analysis will cover all the buyers in a business area. However, while there are good reasons for considering all buyers the first time a task analysis is made, it may nevertheless be practical to narrow down coverage at a later stage. Some buyers might be left out of consideration for reasons that become apparent as a result of subsequent experience. For example, a planner may have learnt that due to heavy costs connected to market development, potential buyers can be ignored for several planning periods to come. There may be geographical areas where an offering is not likely to be available in the near future. Situations may even arise in which it makes sense to limit a task analysis to certain obvious target groups.

12. Developing a content strategy

The target group strategy lays down guidelines for prioritizing segments of buyer. This is tantamount to selecting communication tasks for the company to consider. The next step in the planning process involves

developing a content strategy,

i.e. identifying, prioritizing, selecting and clarifying communication content. This is tantamount to *selecting which communication tasks should be carried out.*

Impact of content strategy on symbolization and media strategy

In the strategy development process, the content strategy has the following two functions:

a. It forms the basis of content symbolization. Obviously a specified content is the root of any decision regarding the use of specific symbols in advertisements, letters, films, spoken sentences etc.

b. It constitutes an important premise for the development of the media strategy. One of the reasons for this is that media differ with regard to symbolization capacity, i.e. capacity to carry various kinds of symbol structures. For instance, if it is considered necessary to convey color as a product property, the telephone will be considered an inappropriate medium. Similarly, complex messages may require the use of personal communication media, as where someone uses spoken words (auditory symbols) in combination with visual symbols on a flip-over, overhead projector or video. Where potential buyers are only marginally motivated, it may be necessary to use quite "intrusive" media such as personal telephone calls in order to secure their attention to messages aimed at enhancing buyer competence. Decisions regarding media use must therefore be made with due regard to content strategy so that content, symbolization and media correspond with each other.

It should be noted here that the words "intrude", "intrusive" and "intrusiveness" normally carry negative connotations, implying an unwanted entry or interruption. However these terms are used here in a technical sense, to describe media that are difficult to ignore or overlook in the first instance.

A communication model and the concept of "content"

The model in Figure 12.1. will serve as a basis for outlining the content strategy development process and for a further clarification of the concept of "content".

The model applies to one buyer and illustrates the course of a *seller-initiated* communication process. The purpose of the seller's initiative is to persuade the buyer to purchase a durable product or to make a trial purchase of a non-durable one. However, as will be argued below, in principle the model applies to buyer-initiated communication processes as well.

1. Running from left to right in the figure, the process starts with the buyer being exposed to a combination of communication symbols, through a medium such as a newspaper or magazine advertisement, TV-commercial or telephone message. As already indicated, exposure means that the buyer has the opportunity to hear or see the communication symbols. A necessary condition for communication is, however, *"initial awareness"* on the part of the buyer, which means

A communication model and the concept of "content" 211

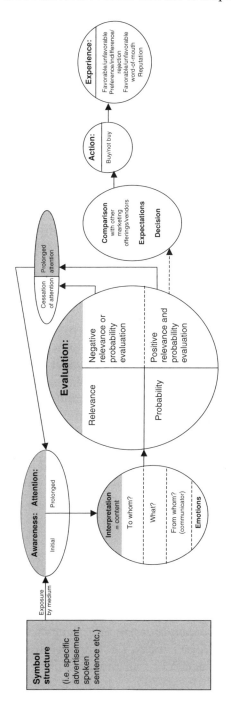

Figure 12.1. A communication model

that the *buyer pays attention to at least one of the symbols*, such as a word, a headline or a picture. The buyer interprets those symbols which do in fact capture his attention and ascribes "meaning" or "content" to them. In this context, "meaning" and "content" are synonymous.

2. A buyer's *"interpretation"*, i.e. contents, may concern:

   a. *Who* the communication is *addressed to*: Whether it is intended for the buyer in question?

   b. *What* the communication is about, e.g. about properties of an offering, a company's position with regard to relevant supplier criteria, "the way" to an offering etc.

   c. *Who the communicator is*, i.e. who is the source of the communication.

3. The interpretation process may give rise to feelings on the part of the buyer. Communication symbols may, for instance, give rise to a "foretaste" of certain types of satisfaction connected with the offering. For example, a color picture of a juicy steak might arouse hunger and feelings associated with eating it. Such emotions or feelings may be thought of as *"emotional content"* as opposed to *"cognitive content"* defined above as *"interpreted meaning"*.

4. A potential buyer will subject message content to a process of judgment or *evaluation* with regard to its

   a. relevance, and
   b. probability.

"Relevance evaluation" has to do with the following two questions:

- *whether or not the content concerns something that can wholly or partly satisfy the buyer's needs*, i.e. improve his "total situation" in terms of sacrifices and rewards.

- whether or not the content *deals with something the buyer does not know already*, for example, that a better product and a shorter delivery time can be obtained at the same or a lower price.

"Probability evaluation" has to do with *a buyer's judgment about how probable it may be that a "message" corresponds with reality.* For example, whether a claim that "X Color TV has the best color picture on the market and costs only $ 70" is true.

It is assumed that the buyer's interpretation relating to who is the addressee and who is the communicator will partly determine:

   - whether he will pay more attention.
   - whether he will continue to be aware of the message.
   - the extent to which he will judge the message relevant to his needs.

These hypotheses will be further elaborated below.

5. A potential buyer's *"prolonged attention"* to a message, for example, *whether he goes on reading an advertisement*, depends on whether he continues to judge its content both relevant and credible. When he decides that it is not relevant or not credible, he will cease to pay attention to it. In that case, he will only process or interpret some of the symbols in the message – and, by directing his attention elsewhere, remain unaware of the rest. The longer he pays attention, the more symbols he will interpret.

6. The interpretation process – and the possible feelings arising from it – give rise to *expectations. Comparisons* are made continuously with other known offerings and suppliers. This comparison process interacts with and influences the outcome of the process of evaluating for relevance and probability in a positive or negative direction. The more favorable the offering seems, the more positive the evaluation. How-

ever, if the offering seems "too good to be true", the evaluation for probability may be influenced in a negative direction.

7. The total process of awareness, attention, interpretation, evaluation and comparison may lead to a (trial) purchase. A purchase brings favorable or unfavorable post-purchase experiences which, in turn, determine whether the buyer responds with preference, indifference or rejection (in the case of non-durable products), with favorable or unfavorable word-of-mouth etc.

In order for the model to be understood correctly, it should be emphasized that, as it appears in Figure 12.1, it seems to apply only to episodes where a buyer is exposed once to one specific combination of symbols. However, expectations and purchasing may, of course, also be a result of repetitive exposures to the same combination of symbols, for instance, to the same TV-commercial, or of two or more subsequent exposures to different symbol structures, e.g. several telephone conversations.

Furthermore, the model should not be understood as implying that trial purchases of non-durable products or purchases of durable products cannot take place without at least *some amount* of information processing and comparison of the offerings in question with competing offerings. The model should rather be interpreted in light of the point made earlier, namely that sufficient knowledge of an offering does not imply complete knowledge. Obviously, buyers frequently make purchasing decisions without knowing everything about the offering or company in question. Some advertising theories imply that purchases – including trial purchases – of non-durable products can be triggered with a minimum amount of information processing. These theories will be dealt with later in this chapter.

Finally, as indicated above, the model applies, in principle, both to buyer-initiated and to seller-initiated communication processes. The only difference is that since the buyer himself makes the initial contact he is certain to be aware of the seller's message at the outset. Prolonged attention then depends on the interpretation process. The buyer may take the initiative to discontinue a telephone conversation or may lose interest and stop listening.

Outline of the strategy development process

The following sections outline and elaborate on the content strategy development process. The discussion will focus mostly on cognitive content. Therefore, unless a different meaning appears from the context, in the text below "content" denotes "cognitive content". For the sake of simplicity, the discussion focuses on standard communication and communication with the purpose of "showing the way" to and reminding of a standardized offering. Content strategy development in transformation markets is discussed later in this chapter.

Identifying, prioritizing and clarifying content elements

Developing a content strategy involves identifying, prioritizing and clarifying the following kinds of content:

a. core content, and
b. facilitative content.

Core content refers to the offering and to "showing the way" to the offering or company. Its function is to give the buyer sufficient knowledge about the offering and the "way to" the offering by doing one or more of the following:

- supplying new information.
- correcting misconceptions.
- reminding the buyer of the offering.

Appropriate content elements are provided by the task analyses made in relation to the various target groups. Conveying core content is tantamount to carrying out corresponding communication tasks. In other words, communication tasks and core content are two sides of the same question. The term *"emo-*

tional core content" refers to *"foretastes" of feelings of satisfaction connected to consuming or using the offering* (emotional rewards and sacrifices).

"Facilitative content" does not refer to the offering itself, but *serves to facilitate the communication process* in order to enhance the likelihood that the buyer will respond by purchasing the offering. The process of selecting facilitative content elements is based on hypotheses about what will make the buyer aware of the message – or more likely to believe it – and so on. Credibility may, for instance, be increased by conveying references to specific buyers who have already purchased and experienced the offering, or by referring to a large and growing market share. *"Emotional facilitative content"* may refer to such things as feelings of having fun (humor). Such feelings may be assumed to make it more likely, for instance, that potential buyers will be aware of the message.

Potentially relevant content elements are *prioritized*. The media as well as the susceptibility of buyers set limits as to how much can and should be conveyed. A buyer may have limited time to spend with a salesman. Advertisements have obvious limits. Regardless of their size, they cannot convey all relevant messages. However, since complete knowledge is seldom necessary, buyers are often prepared to make a trial purchase if they are aware of one or two competitive product properties. There will also be limits to how much information some buyers are willing to process. Strongly motivated buyers who are actively seeking information on cars or houses obviously require more extensive core content than marginally motivated buyers of shoe polish.

Prioritizing offers a basis for deciding which content elements to *select* and emphasize in various situations. What should be accentuated in an advertisement or a brochure? What core content elements should be conveyed in a short telephone conversation with a potential customer making an inquiry? What facilitative content elements should be used in order to enhance the probability of initial awareness? On the one hand, the selected content should be sufficient to bring about the intended

Outline of the strategy development process 217

reaction on the part of the buyer. On the other hand, "drowning" the buyer in messages or using resources on unnecessary content elements should be avoided.

Depending on the richness of detail in the task analysis, selected and prioritized content elements may need further *clarification* in order to create a useful basis for selecting efficient communication symbols. Where core content regarding "the way" to the offering is concerned, clarification efforts might be directed towards such tasks as:

- providing information about the type of dealers who carry the offering.
- publishing dealers' names and addresses.
- giving the company's address and telephone number.
- informing inquirers when to call and who to ask for.

The seller may have to clarify such properties of the offering as the degree to which it satisfies a specific relevance criterion or whether it will entail particular sacrifices or rewards. For example: the plowing speed of a plow, Z, is x km/h, which is 20% higher than that of competing plows. The higher speed saves Y working hours per year. A task relating to facilitative content might involve specifying exactly which references to use in order to make it more likely that a buyer will believe the seller's claims.

The content platform: Concept and functions

The content strategy arrived at is stated in a *"content platform"*. This *describes the relevant core and facilitative content elements and priorities in relation to each target group – and may also include descriptions of emotional content elements.* The content descriptions may serve as *"content goals"*, i.e. *goals concerning what to convey to the buyers in the various target groups.* The aim of the symbolization strategy and the media strategy is to realize these goals.

The use of the content platform in the subsequent strategy development process depends on the type of medium chosen, as well as on which party initiates the communication process. In seller-initiated communication through *impersonal mass media* such as newspapers, magazines, TV, radio, and posters, the content platform governs symbolization directly. For example, instructions for assignments ("briefings") to advertising agencies are based directly on the content platform: The company wants symbolization – or "creative" – solutions that will convey a specified core and facilitative content effectively and precisely to the target groups in question.

The content platform represents neither more nor less than can reasonably be prepared in advance with regard to identifying, prioritizing and clarifying communication content. In seller- or buyer-initiated communication through *personal media* or *individual, impersonal media* such as mail and facsimile, it would serve no purpose to bind salesmen or other staff to specific instructions regarding content goals. This principle applies to initial contacts as well as communication episodes connected to handling and following up both buyer- and seller-initiated orders and inquiries. The relevant conditions surrounding the many contact episodes that can take place during a planning period are largely unpredictable. Accordingly, each episode represents a potential for *learning more* about the buyer on the spot. Personal communication episodes involving dialogues are particularly important sources of information for the seller. Staff members can ask buyers questions and listen to their answers. In this way more can be learnt about such things as the buyer's needs, relevance and supplier criteria, knowledge about the relevant offering, and, consequently, about the communication tasks to be carried out in relation to those particular buyers.

The content platform does not function as a straitjacket imposed on seller- or buyer-initiated communication through personal media or individual, impersonal media. On the contrary, it serves as a basis for developing the staff's *"content competence"*. The platform provides broad guidelines about the priority of selected content elements that are appropriate to members of various target groups in various situations. It indicates what kind of questions to expect from buyers making inquiries and suggests answers to these questions. The *"content preparedness"* of the company is *a measure of the degree to which employees and managers concerned know and understand the platform.* However, in each single contact episode the interacting employee or manager must himself make final decisions about what content elements to prioritize. He will base these on the content platform *and* on additional knowledge about the buyer, acquired through communication episodes. Such additional knowledge may even justify focusing content elements that have been given low priority in the platform. A high level of content competence involves the ability to learn on the spot and to *customize* content to the conditions surrounding a particular communication situation. Such competence requires thorough knowledge not only of the content platform but also of the characteristics of the target groups and of the competitive strength of the offering or organizational basis. A highly competent staff member will be familiar with the results of the task analysis and will know how to identify communication tasks and how to identify, prioritize and clarify content elements.

Two hypotheses serve as guiding principles for the following discussion about identification, prioritization and clarification of core and facilitative content elements. The model in Figure 12.1 provides a starting point for this discussion:

1. Conveying content to a buyer can only take place as long as he accepts that the seller's message is relevant and credible. Initial awareness is not enough. This principle needs emphasizing in order to counter the advertising industry's one-sided focus on initial awareness.

2. Content elements should not raise unrealistic expectations with the buyer. Promises that cannot be kept should not be made.

It has already been pointed out that unfulfilled expectations aroused by exaggerated, ambiguous or simply incorrect claims produce and may even reinforce negative reactions. Disappointment following from unrealistic expectations may even cause the experience of a given set of properties to be less favorable than it would otherwise have been. For example, the reaction to a non-durable offering may be rejection instead of indifference, or indifference instead of preference. Not only do unrealistic expectations spoil the relationship between buyers and companies in the short run. In the longer run disappointments will undermine the company's wider reputation as well as that of marketing communication in general. The advertising industry's characteristic practice of exaggerating and boasting is ultimately self-defeating.

Clarifying, prioritizing and selecting core content

Task analysis is the starting-point for developing a content platform in relation to a given target group. Each communication task that is identified represents a potential content element. In order to create a basis for selecting core content the potential content elements need to be prioritized. In many cases, clarification will also be needed.

Clarifying core content

Clarifying content related to "showing the way" to and reminding of the offering is normally a relatively easy task.

The object of the communication task of *"showing the way"* is to give buyers precise instructions about how, where and when purchases can be made or further information about offerings can be obtained. This may include giving postal, e-mail and Internet addresses, phone and facsimile numbers, indicating when phone lines and stores are open, listing staff who can be consulted and saying when they are accessible.

When addressing the task of *reminding* buyers of the offering, content should be shaped with the aim of making the offering or company easily recognizable to the buyer. A clarification process might result in a company or brand name or logo. In a market for non-durable products the process might lead to a combination of product (package) and brand logo. Other examples are content elements such as: "X for dish washing!" or "Call us today on ZZZZZ! Y – the leading supplier of steel constructions".

Clarifying, prioritizing and selecting core content 221

Clarifying core content related to *standard communication tasks* often represents greater challenges.

The first task of clarification in *standard markets* might be to spell out exactly what is to be conveyed about how specific properties of the offering satisfy specific relevance criteria and to what degree they do so. For example: Should plowing speed be given in kilometers per hour? How should a plow's sideways stability be described? A second clarification task might be to help the buyer to "translate" offering properties into related sacrifices and rewards in cases where it cannot be assumed that he will be able to do this for himself. If a feature of the K-plow is that it requires low tractive power, precisely what does that mean in terms of operating costs connected to such things as fuel, service, repairs and working hours saved? What are the consequences of a clearly competitive "3 day delivery" as regards time and money saved and irritation avoided? One way of clarifying relevant sacrifices and rewards may be to describe the emotions and feelings one aims to arouse (emotional content).

In *transformation markets* clarifying core content related to standard communication tasks might be a matter of describing the company's exact positions with regard to relevant supplier criteria. For example, "project management" is likely to be an important criterion in the market for customized steel constructions (e.g. buildings, bridges, and TV antennae). In that case, clarification might involve giving a detailed description of the company's organization in the area of project management. For instance, the substance of the company's message might be that it has implemented guidelines to ensure that only one person with wide authority is responsible for a project from its inception to its completion. The buyer thus knows that he can always expect to deal with one specific person who is able to make any decision and take whatever steps may be necessary to ensure delivery. Clarification might also aim to help the buyer «translate» supplier criteria into relevance criteria or relevant sacrifices and rewards. What, for instance, will be the consequences of the project management organization and guidelines in terms of more flexible, appropriate and prompt treatment of possible complaints (relevance criteria) and less irritation and saving of time (sacrifices)?

In cases where the product is marketed *through a distribution chain* with one or more intermediate links, clarification might be tantamount to describing derived sacrifices and rewards. For example: What does the company's end-buyer service, relating to setting the K-plow correctly, represent in the form of time saved, lower costs and a more competitive offering on the part of the dealer?

In principle, content clarification should aim at stating the relevant sacrifices and rewards that will follow from an offering in the clearest possible terms to buyers who may not be capable of doing this for themselves. In this way a basis is created for conveying the buyer's total experience or (net-) buyer value to be expected from the offering. However, in many cases this aim may be difficult to achieve, and partial descriptions are all that can be expected. The relationship between the properties of an offering, its relevance criteria and consequent sacrifices and rewards may be too complex. For example, in the market for concrete constructions a buyer's perception of what is fair treatment in connection with notification of defects may be assumed to be a function of guidelines regarding complaint handling and project management *as well as* the competence of project managers.

A further difficulty will be encountered when attempting to give an exact description of product performance in cases where buyers use the product in widely varying conditions. For instance, the molding ability of a plow depends on the nature of the soil as well as on the contours of the ground. In such cases a satisfactory solution might be to describe the molding ability under certain clearly defined conditions. The buyer may then make appropriate adjustments to the manufacturer's assessment of plow's performance in the light of his knowledge of the soil and contours of his fields. Finally, it may be difficult to describe qualitative sacrifices and rewards such as effort, irritation, enjoyment, sense of security and so on. In contrast to this, quantitative sacrifices and rewards in the form of such things as price, rate of interest and plowing speed are relatively easy to describe.

Clarification in connection with *development tasks* may concern anything from making buyers aware of the existence and relevance of a product to informing about use and necessary user competence. For example, a couple of decades ago, potential buyers of safety glass knew relatively little about the product. At that time, relevant clarification tasks might have consisted of explaining reasons for using it and areas of use, for instance, in doors and windows and as building material in fronts, walls and roofs.

Clarification might also have dealt with "strength" as a relevance criterion and spelt out the implications of this criterion in relation to sacrifices such as "personal injuries" as a consequence of walking into a glass door or wall. A possible task might also have been to explain the relationship between "production facilities" (supplier criterion) and certain product properties such as uniform quality and smooth edges (relevance criteria).

Prioritizing core content

Normally the task of prioritizing core content elements in the context of *reminding of the offering* is relatively easy. The relevant content is necessarily rather limited (a slogan, a logo etc.). Content relating to «*showing the way*» to the offering should always be given high priority. Knowledge of "the way" is a precondition for making both inquiries and purchases.

In relation to *standard communication tasks* it seems reasonable to give content elements priority proportional to the following:

a. The *degree of importance* that buyers in the target group in question attach to the properties of the offering, relevance criteria or to sacrifices or rewards or supplier criteria that the content element relates to.

b. The *competitive strength* of the offering or company in terms of properties, relevance criteria, sacrifices and rewards or supplier criteria to which the content element relates.

c. The proportion of buyers who *lack knowledge of* or have *incorrect beliefs* about the properties of the offering, relevance criteria, supplier criteria, sacrifices and rewards to which the content element relates.

Decisions must, of course, rest on a total appraisal of relevant content elements based on these criteria. Top priority should be given to elements relating to those properties of the offering or company:

- which matter most to buyers.
- in relation to which competitive strength is good.
- about which buyers have little knowledge.
- about which buyers have incorrect beliefs.

High priority should also be given to conveying *emotional* content elements which can substitute or support *cognitive* content elements relating to significant sacrifices and rewards.

The purpose of prioritizing content elements on the basis of the above criteria is to persuade buyers that a company's offering is relevant to them. However, it does not necessarily follow that all buyers will recognize that it is so. In the context of market utilization and standard communication, motivation among buyers can be relatively high. Product knowledge is good, buyer competence is relatively high, and actual demand is relatively high. However, in the context of market development, the relevance of the content may be merely potential. This is because buyers may lack the product knowledge and competence necessary to be motivated and, consequently, susceptible to marketing communication. The implications for media strategy are that it may be necessary to use relatively "intrusive" media such as personal visits and telephone calls in order to secure initial awareness and prolonged attention. Finally, indifferent buyers are unlikely to wish to be reminded of an offering or company that they judge to be no better or worse than others they know of. However, as prioritized content is always limited to a slogan or a logo, initial awareness will often be sufficient to trigger a purchase.

Facilitative communication content

Various kinds of facilitative content

It was pointed out earlier that the purpose of using facilitative content is to ease the communication process and thereby make it more likely that buyers will respond by purchasing the offering in question. This is the thinking behind the well-known hypothesis which predicts that emphasizing *novelty in* an offering will increase the probability of initial awareness as well as prolonged attention. Buyers may think that new offerings are more likely to satisfy their needs.

We may distinguish between four different kinds of facilitative content and refer to them as:

1. addressee-indicating,
2. emotional,
3. credibility-enhancing, and
4. action-encouraging content.

The purpose of using "*addressee-indicating content*" is to make it easier for the buyer to realize that one wishes to communicate with him. Examples of such content are advertisement headlines saying "Planning to build a new house?", "Women between 25 and 40!" and "To all managers striving to increase profitability". The addressee may be an individual or a category of person that is defined on the basis of shared problems, needs or plans – or according to demographic criteria such as age, gender or type of job. Addressee-indicating content makes initial awareness more likely.

The aim of using *emotional facilitative content* is to secure buyers' initial awareness and prolonged attention, while making them well disposed towards an offering or company. A positive response to an advertisement (sometimes referred to as "ad-liking") is widely assumed to be an important content dimension in this connection. Entertaining content in the form of humor is widely used in advertising. Although emotional facilitative content may achieve these objectives, it will always risk diverting buyers' attention away from core content. Entertaining content, in particular, should therefore be used with some caution.

There are a number of ways of marking the core content as credible (in the sense of "deserving credence") and thereby increasing the chances that buyers will evaluate it favorably. Examples of *"credibility-enhancing content elements"* are references to "a large (50%) market share" or "rapidly increasing sales volume and market share". The rationale behind such content elements rests on the assumption that the core content will be identified as credible in the above sense – and therefore worthy of further consideration – because many other buyers have found the offering or company competitive and have responded accordingly.

One important kind of credibility-enhancing content relates to the *"perceived communicator"*, i.e. *the person, organization or institution that the buyer perceives as the source of the interpreted core content*. The well-known "communicator effect hypothesis" states that the credibility of the source rubs off on the message. According to this hypothesis a credible communicator is honest as well as competent.

Perceived honesty is closely related to whether or not the communicator may be expected to act out of self-interest. For this reason a vendor company will always be at a potential disadvantage, since it is obvious that it stands to gain from selling its offering to the buyer. However, it is obvious that a company's credibility, in the sense of its reputation for integrity and reliability, will depend largely on buyers' direct experience when dealing with it.

One way of strengthening the credibility of message content is to make use of *"co-communicators* Potential co-communicators are *persons, organization or institutions whose integrity the buyer perceives as beyond dispute, and who are willing to make (positive) statements about the offering or company.* Impartial institutions such as laboratories which test food product ingredients or textile wear resistance and recognized experts within fields such as health care are typical examples of such co-communicators. Buyers with whom a company has good relations and who have recently purchased an offering are also often regarded as effective co-communicators. Such buyers are unlikely to be suspected of communicating out of self-interest and are highly competent in the sense that they have direct experience of with the company. Co-communicators' statements may be content elements in advertisements, brochures and billboards. In industrial markets credibility-enhancing content elements often take the form of *references* combined with descriptions of the delivered offering. Such references may, in turn, give rise to statements made on buyers' request.

Finally, admitting past and present mistakes and weaknesses may also strengthen credibility. By conveying both advantages connected to the offering/company and weaknesses, the message *demonstrates honesty*. Examples of relevant content elements are statements such as "We know that our treatment of complaints have been poor in the past. However, ...", or "Our offering has two main disadvantages. The price is approximately $ 200 higher than ...".

"*Action-encouraging facilitative content*" is aimed at making sales more likely by specifying what the buyer – and perhaps, the vendor company – should do as a result of the communication process. Content elements may take the form of an invitation to call on a dealer or to make a phone call, send a facsimile or an e-mail to a particular staff member in order to get more information or to make a purchase. In the context of two-way-communication, such content may amount to inviting a buyer to make a purchase or suggesting an arrangement for following up a meeting.

Prioritizing facilitative content

In the context of seller initiatives, addressee-indicating and action-encouraging content elements should in general be given a high priority. The same is true of action-encouraging content elements in the context of following up orders and inquiries. The significance of such elements is obvious, and there is usually sufficient space or time available to convey them in the media.

The need to strengthen credibility and the availability of suitable co-communicators will determine the extent to which a company should give priority to credibility-enhancing content. For example, a recently established unknown company is likely to need co-communicators more than a well-established, reputable company. Emotional facilitative content may be relevant especially in situations where the buyers show little or no interest in a company's products. For example, humor might be needed in order to catch the attention of potential buyers of a new product.[35]

Selecting communication content in the context of low involvement. Three hypotheses

In Chapter 11, it was suggested that, in the absence of other considerations, segments consisting of non- or only marginally motivated buyers should be given a correspondingly low priority as target groups. However, such target groups are very much in focus in the advertising literature. A number of hypotheses have been formulated explaining how advertising can trigger *trial purchases* of non-durable branded products by otherwise non- or merely marginally motivated consumers.

Low-involvement behavior is characterized by minimal information processing on the part of the buyer. For example, he buyer buys without making any comparisons with competing brands. Such low-involvement behavior – as opposed to high-involvement behavior – is supposed to be what most people show when they purchase products, which they consider to be unimportant, especially in terms of the financial and social risk. In short, these products are cheap and have no "badge value" affecting buyers' self perception or group membership. It is widely assumed that products may be classified as either low- or high-involvement products.

Three low-involvement hypotheses and their implications as to content selection will be touched upon here:

According to the *brand salience hypothesis* repetitive exposure to TV-commercials focusing on one single brand feature may increase brand salience among buyers and thus enhance their overall evaluation of the brand. A high level of brand salience can cause consumers to try the brand in question. The hypothesis implies that an advertising content consisting of short, simple messages focusing on one brand attribute (slogan) and on brand name/logo, packaging or a slogan is enough to bring about trial purchases.[36]

The *elaboration-likelihood hypothesis* (ELM-hypothesis) states that high and low-involvement are associated with different information processing *routes*.[37] Where there is low-involvement, buyers will tend to use *peripheral routes* or *cognitive shortcuts* in their information processing. Such information processing is superficial and purchasing decisions depend on the use of various *indicators*, such as whether or not:

- a buyer likes an advertisement or TV-commercial
- whether or not a buyer thinks an advertisement or radio-commercial is entertaining in the sense that it is funny or has good music
- a credible co-communicator is advocating the brand (even though the buyer does not trouble himself to consider carefully exactly what the co-communicator is claiming)
- a seemingly large number of product advantages or arguments in favor of the brand are listed (even though the buyer does not make any effort to assess these advantages critically).

The more positive the buyer perception of such an indicator, the more likely he is to make a trial purchase when he comes across the brand in a shop. The ELM-hypothesis implies that content should be relatively limited, focusing on one or, at most, a few indicators. Credibility-enhancing and emotional facilitative content elements are likely to be given high priority at the expense of core content.

According to the *mere exposure hypothesis* (repetitive) exposure to advertising for a brand enhances the buyer's overall evaluation of that brand, which, in turn, leads to trial purchases. One explanation for this is that as an effect of repetition, the brand becomes increasingly *familiar*. As a result, the buyer is more likely to perceive it as *reliable* and go on to make a (trial) purchase. The familiarity-reliability hypothesis implies that repeated short, simple messages which have very limited content and focus on brand names, logos, packagings or slogans are enough to bring about sales.[38]

The three low-involvement hypotheses may be taken as a supplement to the model in Figure 12.1. and the discussion in the preceding paragraphs in this chapter.[39]

Clarifying, prioritizing and selecting content in transformation communication

By definition, the offering and the communication tasks that face a company cannot be known before a transformation communication process starts. In the course of dialogues between buyer and seller, both parties have to discover each other's needs and problems, relevance criteria, communication tasks and so on, in a process of piecemeal learning. Consequently, where transformation communication is concerned, developing a content strategy consists of enhancing a company's content preparedness by developing the content competence of its staff. This means the ability of appropriate managers and employees to identify, clarify, prioritize, select and convey relevant core and facilitative content elements in the course of any dialogue. In the context of transformation communication the content platform takes the form of a description of those specific understandings, knowledge and skills that constitute optimal staff content competence and organizational content preparedness.

A staff member's content competence includes a basic understanding of his dual role as an offering developer and communicator as well as of the various factors that should be taken into consideration connected to communication and offering development. Furthermore, it includes such things as thorough knowledge of the relevant capabilities, competencies and capacity of the organizational basis as well as the ability to see how these can be transformed into a competitive customized offering. As indicated in Chapter 5, transformation communication may affect the strength of a buyer-seller relationship to the degree that a customized offering implies buyer-specific changes in the organizational bases of the two parties (e.g. joint investments in new production technology). Therefore, content competence may also include the ability to make decisions about whether or not solutions implying enhanced bonds and switching costs should be considered, and if so, what kind of buyer-specific changes would be acceptable. Transformation communication also takes the shape of negotiations for long-term supply contracts and strategic alliances.

Summing up

Figure 12.2. sums up the process leading to a content platform covering all relevant target groups.

It should be emphasized that in some instances, buyers in a target group may differ widely with regard to such things as relevance or supplier criteria, the importance they attach to the various criteria, their knowledge of the offering or company, and their post-purchase experiences. In such cases the target group should be sub-divided into two or more content groups, and a content platform should be developed relating to each of these sub-target groups. In markets with few large and heterogeneous buyers it may even be practical to develop individual content platforms relating to each of the buyers in a target group. In transformation markets such as the market for ships, offshore production platforms or large constructions in steel or concrete, standard communication would have to be customized to the individual buyer, for example, in the form of oral presentations of the company. For the sake of simplicity the term *"content groups"* is used here to denote *groups as well single buyers in relation to whom specific content platforms are developed.*

Obviously, the more target groups are sub-divided, the more a company will adopt a strategy of using individual and personal media and selective mass media aimed at few buyers. The cost of exposing a large number of buyers to irrelevant contents may easily become too high.

Figure 12.2. A content platform: Development and functions

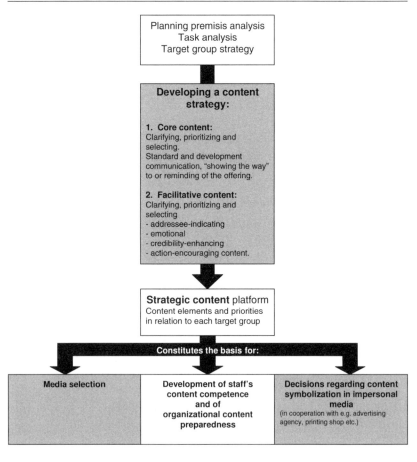

13. Developing a media strategy: Task, media and media characteristics

Given the selected and prioritized target groups and the content platform, the next step in the planning process involves

developing a media strategy.

A media strategy is viewed here as consisting of two sub-strategies, i.e.

- a buyer initiative media strategy, and a
- a seller initiative media strategy.

The aim of the buyer initiative media strategy is profitable utilization of the buyer initiative sales potential, while the aim of the seller initiative media strategy is a profitable closure of the seller initiative gap. The development of a media strategy calls for consideration of both sales (volume) effects and media costs.

As indicated already, developing a media strategy involves dealing with the following three questions:

- which *media* to use for receiving, handling and following up *buyer initiatives* and taking *seller initiatives*.

- to what *extent* the selected media should be used.

- *when* the selected media should be used (timing).

In many cases a combination of two or more media is required to convey the appropriate content. For instance, in an industrial market, initial contact with potential customers might be established by a letter drawing attention to a few highly prioritized messages and suggesting a personal meeting. Telephone calls might be used to make appointments with interested buyers, personal calls to convey further content elements and take possible orders. Incoming telephone calls may have to be followed-up. In such cases a company will have to consider

- the *order* in which appropriate media should be used.

An additional task may be that of

- *referring* the buyer *from one medium to another.*

The following sections of this chapter deal with the task of media strategy development, with the choice of suitable media, and with media characteristics that may be considered when making choices. For the sake of simplicity, this discussion (and that in Chapter 14) is confined to standard communication in markets in which the offering is sold directly to the end-buyer. The *process* of strategy development is discussed, on the same assumption. The last two sections of Chapter 14 deal with media strategy development connected to transformation communication and markets in which the offering is marketed through one or more intermediaries.

The media

An overview of marketing communication media was given in Box 2.4.

Buyer and seller initiative media

A relevant distinction can be drawn between

- buyer initiative media, and
- seller initiative media.

Buyer initiative media can be used by the buyer in order to contact and communicate with the vendor company, while seller initiative media can be used by the vendor company in order to contact and communicate with the buyer. Box 13.1. shows that, with few exceptions, individual media are associated with buyer initiative. This is because buyer initiatives are generally directed towards individuals. Exceptions are advertising media such as newspapers, which can be used to invite tenders. Dispositions made by both parties will partly determine which buyer initiative media are at a buyer's disposal in relation to a specific vendor company. Postal communication or calling on a member of the company's staff are options open to virtually any buyer, while use of such media as stationary or mobile telephones, facsimiles or e-mail is only possible if both parties have invested in appropriate equipment.

Controllable and uncontrollable media

A distinction may be made between the following two categories of seller initiative media:

- controllable media, and
- uncontrollable media.

Some media are *"controllable" media* in the sense that the company can decide exactly which buyers to contact. This is the case with all personal media as well as with all individual impersonal media. For example, the company has complete control as to which buyers to call on, phone, write to or invite to a seminar. Such media may be said to be 100% selective as regards exposure of the relevant target group. An added feature of such media is that they only convey the seller's marketing communication and not those of his competitors.

Other media, i.e. impersonal mass media, are *"uncontrollable" media* in the sense that the company has no influence whatsoever on their exposure of relevant target groups. The existence of newspapers, magazines, cinemas, TV programs, radio programs, shops etc. rests on their catering for functions other than that of conveying marketing communication content. However, a company can choose to use a mass medium as it is, accepting a lower degree of selectivity, and thereby paying for exposure to buyers who are of little or no interest to it. Most

236 *Developing a media strategy*

such uncontrollable media will usually contain competing contents. For example, newspapers and magazines will often carry advertisements for competitors' offerings. Obvious exceptions are e.g. billboards, posters, and direct mail.

The elements of a media strategy. Action planning and preparatory planning

Since the seller initiative gap is the point of departure for the development of any seller initiative media strategy, it follows that a buyer initiative media strategy has to be developed before embarking on a seller initiative strategy.

The elements of a buyer initiative media strategy

Developing a buyer initiative (media) strategy involves selecting buyer initiative media and adapting the capacity of staff, and communications equipment to meet the extent of buyer initiatives as and when necessity arises during a planning period. The aim of the strategy is to secure satisfactory accessibility, handling and follow-up of buyer-initiated orders and inquiries.

As the occurrence of buyer initiative cannot be determined by the company, but merely be approximately estimated, it serves no purpose to bind staff members to specific instructions regarding media use. This means that, as the buyer initiatives actually occur, managers and employees must be relied on to make final decisions regarding which of the available media to use, in which order, to what extent and when. Each single contact episode represents a potential for on the spot learning. It is imperative for companies to utilize this learning potential, since it represents the only realistic basis for making such decisions.

In the light of the above, we can see that strategic media planning related to buyer initiative is *"preparatory planning"* concerned with arranging and maintaining a state of *"media pre-*

paredness". Buyer initiative media are selected, and decisions are made regarding media capacity. As far as concrete media use is concerned, a preparatory plan contains what can reasonably be prepared á priori. Broad guidelines are drawn up in the form of suggestions for how to use the media in various situations. For example, in an industrial market a suggestion might be to use personal meetings when handling and following up large buyers, and telephone, facsimile, or e-mail when handling and following up small buyers. Such broad guidelines may be supplemented with more concrete working models and examples. The purpose of preparing guidelines, working models and examples is to provide a basis for enhancing the *"media competence"* of staff. Such competence comprises knowledge about and skills related to using the available media as well as the ability to make sensible decisions with regard to selection of media and timing of their use. Since decisions have to be made at the same time about choice of content elements, selection of appropriate media and timing of their use, it is also imperative that staff have sufficient knowledge of the content platform. Thus, media competence and content competence are mutually dependent. On its own, each kind of competence is partial and insufficient.

In order to be able to decide which media are appropriate to convey specific contents and to estimate the required media capacity, it is necessary to make some rough *preliminary assumptions regarding content symbolization*. These will also form a necessary basis for realistic estimates of the total use of the various media, which, in turn, will provide a basis for estimating media costs. Among the estimates required in order to be able to budget media costs are those relating to such things as the total number of

- facsimiles sent and received in the planning period.
- telephone calls made and received.
- meetings held.

Estimates may also include the length or duration of these and similar items.

238 Developing a media strategy

Box 13.1. Media categories

Type of medium:	Buyer initiative media:	Seller initiative media: Controllable:	Uncontrollable:
Personal media:			
Mass media:			
Meeting (face-to-face)	X	X	
Telephone conference		X	
Video conference		X	
Individual media:			
Meeting (face-to-face)	X	X	
Telephone conversation	X	X	
Interactive use of the Internet	X	X	
Impersonal media:			
Mass media:			
Newspapers	X*		X
Magazines			X
Trade press			X
Periodicals			X
Sponsoring media in connection with e.g. sport and cultural arrangements			X
Telephone books/ Yellow pages			X
Cinema commercials			X
Cinema slides			X
Television commercials			X
Radio commercials			X
The Internet (home page etc.)			X
In-store-media			X
Billboards			X
Addressed and unaddressed direct mail			X
Individual media:			
Mailing service (letters etc.)	X	X	
Facsimile	X	X	
The Internet/ E-mail	X	X	

X: Indicates type of medium.
*: Invitations to tender only.

The elements of a seller initiative media strategy

Taking seller initiative means initiating contacts with buyers, which may result in orders or inquiries. Accordingly, media planning related to seller initiative involves developing:

1. an action plan for producing initial contacts. This will embrace choice of media, extent, order and timing of media use.

2. a preparatory plan for receipt, handling and follow-up of resulting orders and inquiries.

The nature of the preparatory planning process is, in fact, identical the one discussed above in relation to buyer initiative, the only difference being that orders and inquiries are products of seller initiatives in the planning period in question. The point of departure for developing an action plan for producing initial contacts is an "*overall exposure goal*".

In order to produce a number of orders and inquiries sufficient to close the seller initiative gap, an overall exposure goal must specify the following:

- *the number of buyers in the various target groups* that should be exposed to various content symbolizations (advertisements, presentations etc.),
- *how often* these buyers should be exposed – and
- *when* these buyers should be exposed.

The above points show that the overall exposure goal builds on "*sub-exposure-goals*" connected to each target group.

Four kinds of decision have to be taken when developing an action plan for realizing the overall exposure goal:

- deciding which media to use.
- deciding to what extent the various media should be used.
- deciding in which order to use the media.
- deciding on the timing of media use.

These will now be considered in turn.

a. Deciding which media to use:
Depending on the situation, media use may be specified by referring to broad categories such as magazines, newspapers, telephone, and face-to-face meetings, or to narrower categories such as women's magazines, mobile telephones and bleepers.

b. Deciding to what extent the various media should be used:
The scale of use of controllable media may be specified directly by listing buyers to contact and the media to be used in each case – e.g. phone calls, personal calls, e-mails, and letters – with what frequency. The scale of use of uncontrollable media has to be specified for each type of medium, as indicated below:

- Newspapers, magazines etc.: Number of newspapers etc. and number of insertions.

- Cinema commercials: Number of cinemas, number of showings per day and the duration of the commercials themselves.

- Posters: Number of posters, how long they are to be displayed.

- Shop media: Number of shops, length of showing period(s).

- Exhibitions: Number of exhibitions, how long they are to be displayed.

- Direct mail (addressed/ unaddressed): Number of recipients and mailings.

- TV and radio: Choice of channels and programs. Frequency, duration and number of showings.

c. Deciding in which order to use the media:
Where appropriate contents cannot be conveyed through one

single medium, the overall exposure goal must specify the order in which content elements should be conveyed in each of the media chosen. In this connection, there will be a communication task of referring the buyer from one medium to another.

d. Deciding on the timing of media use:
The range of options for timing the use of broadcast or printed media, such as television, newspapers, magazines and trade journals, will depend on such factors as when and how often these are scheduled or published. Timing will also depend on the order in which it has been decided to use various media.

In order to be able to decide which media are needed to convey relevant contents and to estimate media costs, some rough *preliminary assumptions regarding content symbolization* are needed. Assumptions might relate to for example the size of magazine advertisements, the use of color in advertisements, the length of facsimiles or the duration of TV commercials, telephone conversations and meetings. It goes without saying that such assumptions may prove wrong at the later stage in the planning process dealing with symbolization strategy. In that case planners will have to revise the media strategy accordingly.

Figure 13.2. illustrates how a media strategy consists of two sub-strategies and highlights the crucial relevance of the processes connected to receiving, handling and following up buyer-initiated *as well as* seller-initiated orders and inquiries.

Relevant media characteristics

Two general principles may be noted. The first is that a medium's suitability for communicating appropriate messages to different target groups depends on a number of features. The different media each have their own distinctive and characteristic features. The second principle is that the profitability of a medium as a communication tool depends both on its capacity to create sales volume as well as the cost of using it. Accordingly, a distinction may be drawn between

Figure 13.2. Main elements in a media strategy

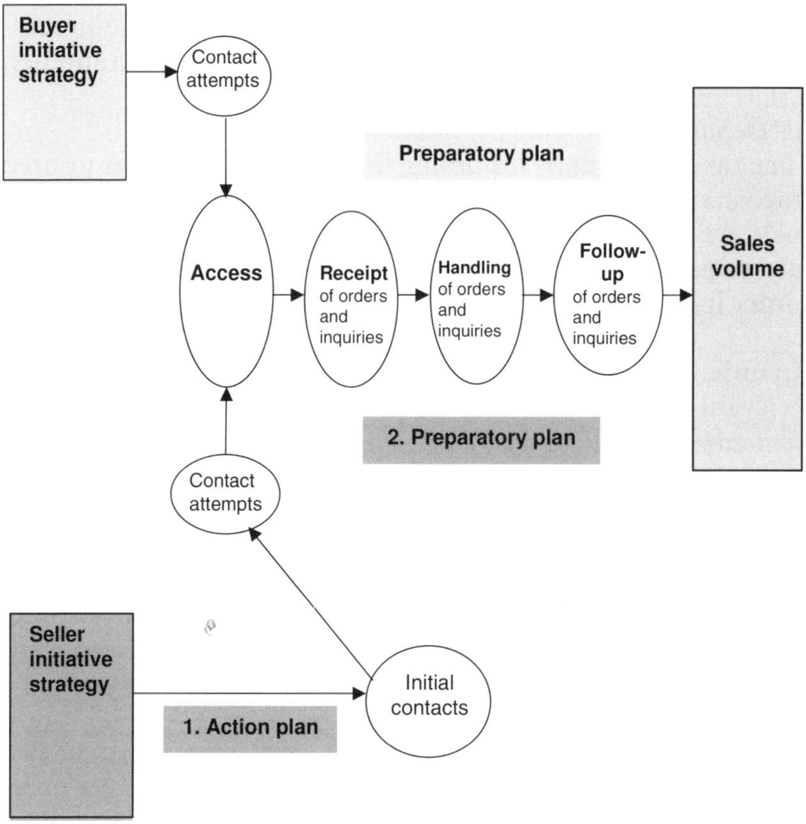

The figure shows how the degree of utilization of buyer initiatives *as well as* the effect of seller initiatives depend totally on the company's accessibility and ability to handle and follow up buyers' attempts to place orders and make inquiries.

- *media sales characteristics, and*
- *media cost characteristics.*

The uncertainty inherent in estimating the sales effect of a potential media strategy is greater than that connected to estimating the media costs incurred. In general, the latter can be calculated fairly accurately, in advance, on the basis of predictable items such as current wage levels, charges for insertions in newspapers and magazines, the cost of ICT equipment etc. The sales characteristics discussed below can help planners find appropriate media and combinations of media that fit their specific sales budget. The cost characteristics discussed here constitute part of the insight needed for making realistic media cost budgets.

The following terms will be used to refer to the sales characteristics dealt with below:

1. Exposure capacity
2. Communication capacity
3. "Intrusiveness"
4. Whether or not competing stimuli are present in the medium itself or in the environment surrounding the medium.
5. Media attitudes and behavior
6. Closeness to point of purchase
7. Timing flexibility

Exposure capacity

The term *"exposure capacity"*, as used here, concerns *the media's basic function of conveying content to and from the market*. In relation to seller initiative aimed at producing initial contacts, exposure capacity refers to the number *buyers* who are exposed to a content symbolization, when this occurs and how frequently. In relation to buyer initiatives and attempts at placing orders or making inquiries resulting from seller-initiated initial contacts, exposure capacity refers to questions such as which appropriate staff members can be reached, when and how often.

It is relatively easy to obtain a general view of the exposure capacity of the various *buyer initiative media* and *controllable seller initiative media*. The options of sending a letter, using an ordinary telephone or making a personal call are open to anyone. Buyers and sellers simply decide who they wish to (try to) contact, how often and when. A precondition for using media such as mobile telephones, telephone meetings, facsimile, and e-mail is, of course, that the relevant equipment and facilities are available to both parties. The accessibility of buyers during the day and week does, of course, vary. The accessibility of the company depends on decisions made about such things as opening hours and capacity as regards personnel, equipment and other facilities.

The exposure capacity of *uncontrollable media* depends on the properties of media as marketing offerings and on the marketing communication activities of media companies. The opportunity to expose consumers and business people to advertisements and commercials in mass media such as trade journals, magazines, newspapers, TV and radio programs is primarily a function of their demand for and actual consumption or use of the editorial content of these media. For example, when reading something on a newspaper page, the consumer/business man is exposed to all the advertisements on that page. Buyers' exposure to posters depends on the location of the billboards carrying them. Quite obviously, surveys regarding reading, listening and viewing habits etc. are needed in order to obtain insight into the exposure capacity of the various media, in short, to find out which buyers can be reached, when and how frequently.

In order to get a proper understanding of the concept of exposure capacity in relation to impersonal mass media, a few related concepts need to be introduced. These concepts are discussed first in relation to specific media such as a particular newspaper, magazine or TV program, and subsequently in relation to broader categories of media.
The related concepts are:

- exposure maximum
- exposure loyalty
- exposure frequency distribution – and
- overlapping and overlapping "speed".

The *"exposure maximum"* of a medium in relation to a target group is defined as *the number of buyers who will be exposed to a given message at least once during the planning period given maxi-*

mum use of the medium. Let, for instance, the planning period be one year, the medium a weekly magazine and the target group: "men between 15 and 30 years of age". The exposure maximum, then, is the number of men between 15 and 30 who are exposed to an advertisement at least once as a result of 52 insertions.

In the same way as some buyers will read specific magazines at least once during a planning period, some will habitually read specific newspapers and trade journals at least once during such a period. Others will habitually go the movies, habitually listen to a particular radio program, view a specific television program, and visit particular shops etc. at least once. Given maximum use of a medium in the planning period, every single buyer who makes use of the medium at all will be exposed to the message at least once.

Each buyer among those making up an exposure maximum will show some degree of *"exposure loyalty"* in relation to the medium in question. The exposure loyalty of someone who reads every issue of a magazine is 100%. For those who read every other issue, it would be 50%. Values would be assigned in a similar way to those who never miss their favorite television program or who regularly miss a proportion of broadcasts, or to people who pass a billboard every day or once a week, or once a month etc.

Exposure loyalty varies widely from one medium to another and even within the same type of medium. For example, readers of morning newspapers, many of whom are subscribers, are more loyal than readers of (tabloid) afternoon papers, most of which are sold singly. Young people go to the movies far more often than do older people. In principle, the exposure loyalty of unaddressed direct mail to a certain postal district is 100%. Every item goes to the same households or companies. The exposure loyalty of shop media depends on the loyalty of the customers, which may vary considerably.

Insight into the exposure maximum and exposure loyalty of a medium makes it possible to get a picture of the exposure frequency distributions produced by alternative uses of the medium. An *"exposure frequency distribution"* in relation to a target group indicates *how many buyers* in the group *are exposed how many times* during the planning period.

The following simplified, hypothetical example should help to illustrate the relationship between exposure maximum, exposure loyalty, exposure frequency distribution and scale of media use. 150 000 buyers in a target group are expected to read Magazine Z at least once during a planning period of one year.

Furthermore:

1. 100 000 of the buyers read every single issue, i.e. they are 100% loyal.

2. 50 000 of the buyers read every other issue, i.e. their loyalty is 50%. This buyer group consists of two sub-groups of equal size, 25 000 (1) and 25 000 (2), each with its own pattern of exposure: 25 000 (1) read odd numbered issues (1, 3, 5, 7 ... etc), while 25 000 (2) read even numbered issues (2, 4, 6, 8 ... etc.).[40]

In the above case, Magazine Z's exposure maximum is 150 000 buyers including two loyalty groups of 25 000 buyers each, the one being 100% and the other one 50% loyal. Box 13.3. demonstrates how the exposure frequency distribution develops as a function of increasing media use, in this case an increasing number of insertions of an advertisement. For instance, if the number of insertions is 4, the 100% loyal buyers are exposed to the advertisement four times, while the 50% loyal buyers are exposed twice. That is, 25 000 (1) are exposed by reading issues no. 1 and 3, while 25 000 (2) are exposed by reading issues no. 2 and 4. The resulting exposure frequency distribution is:

Number of exposures:	Number of buyers:
1	100 000
2	50 000

Relevant media characteristics

If we imagine that the exposure maximum is doubled while the other circumstances remain the same, the result will be a doubling of all the figures in the table in Box 13.3. This shows that the larger the exposure maximum, the higher is the number of buyers exposed 1, 2, 3, 4 and more times. If, on the other hand, all the 150 000 buyers belonging to the exposure maximum are 100% loyal, the result of 4 insertions would be 4 exposures of each one of the 150 000 buyers. Increased loyalty means increased frequency of exposure.

In cases where a combination of media is used the resulting exposure frequency distribution also depends on overlapping and overlapping "speed".

"Overlapping" between two media, A and B, exists to the degree that the buyers belonging to medium A's exposure maximum also belong to B's exposure maximum. Examples of overlapping between media are easy to find. Many buyers read two newspapers and several magazines, watch specific television programs *and* pass by specific street billboards during a planning period. Overlapping also exists between controllable and uncontrollable media, for instance, between the telephone and trade journals. Depending on the number and type of media, there will be cases of double, triple, quadruple or even greater overlapping.

Other things being equal, overlapping means that the overall exposure maximum of several media (when used in combination with each other) is smaller than the sum of their potential exposure maximums, when used on their own. On the other hand, a combined use of overlapping media means high frequencies of exposure. And the higher the loyalty among the "overlapped" buyers, i.e. the higher the *"overlapping speed"*, the higher are the frequencies of exposure produced by any given media use. For example, if an overlapping between two newspapers consists of 50 000 100% loyal buyers only, one insertion in each of the papers is sufficient in order to expose these 50 000 twice. Alternatively, if the loyalty of the 50 000 was 25%, 4 insertions would be needed for these buyers to be exposed at least twice.

Summing up, the exposure frequency distribution produced by a given use of a given combination of media depends on the exposure maximums of the individual media as well as on the degree of overlapping between the media in question. The points of time at which the exposures occur, depends on when the individual media are used. Although strategic planning does not involve deciding which individual media to use, in order to be able to lay down strategic guidelines, it is necessary to have a broad understanding of the actual exposure capacity of various individual media.

As indicated earlier, an overall exposure goal is the point of departure for developing an action plan for producing initial contacts. This goal specifies how many buyers in the various target groups should be exposed to various content symbolizations – how many times and when – in order to produce a sufficient number of orders and inquiries to close the seller initiative gap. An exposure goal may be expressed as *exposure frequency distributions to be aimed at* in relation to actual target groups.

Communication capacity

Exposures do not result in purchases unless the relevant content elements are conveyed. As indicated earlier, media differ with regard to their capacity to convey various kinds of content, partly because they are able to carry different kinds and combinations of symbols. The *"communication capacity"* of a medium includes the following properties:

- Whether the medium is a two-way or one-way communication tool.
- The symbolization capacity of the medium.
- The exposure flexibility of the medium.

Each of these will be explained briefly below.

1. *Whether the medium is a two-way or one-way communication tool:* This property has to do with whether or not a medium can be used in two-way communication processes (dialogues) or for

Box 13.3. Development of an exposure frequency distribution as a function of extent of media use, exemplified here by the number of insertions of an advertisement in a magazine

	Exposure frequency distribution				
	Number of buyers exposed: (in 1000 buyers)				
	0 times	1 time	2 times	3 times	4 times
Number of insertions of an advertisement in a magazine:					
0	100 25 (1) *150* 25 (2)	0	0	0	0
1	25 (2)	100 25 (1) *125*	0	0	0
2	0	25 (1) 25 (2) *50*	100	0	0
3	0	25 (2)	25 (1)	100	0
4	0	0	25 (1) 25 (2) *50*	0	100

Figures are fictitious. Sums in bold italics.

Regarding assumptions and explanations: See text.

one-way communication only. The property has been used above as a criterion for distinguishing between personal and impersonal media.

250 *Developing a media strategy*

2. *Symbolization capacity* refers to four things:

- *whether or not* a medium has the capacity *to convey a course of events*, as have for example cinema and television commercials and homepages on the Internet.

- the *kinds of symbols* and combinations of symbols *a medium can carry:* auditory symbols, visual – or both, color symbols or monochrome symbols only. Newspapers and magazines can carry visual symbols only, and radio solely auditory symbols. Cinema and television are audio-visual media. In a meeting, a person can use speech (auditory symbols) together with visual symbols on a flip-over or an overhead transparency or auditory and visual symbols in a video presentation or any combination of these.

- *the size and number of symbols a medium can carry.*
Depending on type of medium the chief limiting factors are space (magazines, newspapers, posters, e-mail etc.) and time (television, radio, meetings, telephone conversations etc.). Examples of media offering limited space and time are roadside billboards and sponsor advertising on the sports wear of football players or ski jumpers. Meetings and telephone conversations usually have the potential of carrying larger numbers of symbols.

- the *quality of the symbols*
when conveyed in a medium, e.g. the representation of colors and voices.

3. *"Exposure flexibility":*
The concept of exposure flexibility has two different aspects. These are:

- *Whether or not the duration of an initial exposure is flexible* relates to possible behavior on the part of the addressee or recipient (buyer or other member of staff). Examples of flexible media are e-mail and home pages on the Internet. The buyer or staff member decides when to open his mailbox or when to begin searching on the Internet. Examples of inflexible media are television and radio. Commercials are run at certain times during the day. In order to be exposed to the message, the buyer has to be near a television set or a radio on at least one such occasion when the set is actually switched on.

- *Whether or not one can choose to repeat being exposed to a message.* A buyer may decide to reread a newspaper advertisement or a homepage. By way of contrast, it is not normally possible to return to cinema and television commercials.

A general characteristic of all personal media is a high degree of exposure flexibility making these media suited for conveying complex contents.

Obviously, content goals are important premises in media selection. In order to be able to determine the communication capacity required to convey a certain content, some preliminary assumptions regarding content symbolization have to be made. The relevant characteristics cannot be identified unless one has some idea of possible symbolization. One might, for instance, conclude that "concrete demonstrations" are needed to teach buyers correct use of a product. As a consequence, only media with the capacity of conveying a course of events are relevant. Examples of such media would be personal demonstrations and film or video sequences in instructional films for use in meetings and seminars or in cinema or television commercials. Similarly, if the most important properties of a garment to be conveyed are its colors, this would exclude all monochrome media.

"Intrusiveness"

Some media are more "intrusive" than others in the sense that it is difficult for the buyer not to be aware of them. Examples of "intrusive" media are telephone and personal calls, personal letters and e-mails. Cinema commercials are also relatively "intrusive". The same holds true of television and radio commercials especially when these interrupt editorial content. Newspaper and magazine advertisements, shop media, direct mail, posters and exhibitions are less "intrusive" media. While "intrusiveness" enhances the probability of initial awareness, it may also cause irritation.

Competing stimuli

Media differ considerably with regard to the number and nature of other stimuli to which buyers are exposed at the same time as they are exposed to the company's "message". Such competing stimuli may come from within the medium itself, for example, in the form of editorial content or other marketing communication symbols carried by the medium. Other familiar examples are competing newspaper advertisements. Competing stimuli may also be present in the environment *surrounding the medium*. For example, traffic noise may compete with the visual impact of a poster. Children's screaming and laughter may drown the sound message in a television commercial. It is generally assumed that competing stimuli reduce buyers' attention to and awareness of marketing messages.

Messages conveyed through personal and impersonal, individual media are free from competing stimuli from within the media themselves. For example, salesmen focus solely on conveying content regarding their own company's offering. Normally the environment surrounding these media is also favorable, although interruptions such as telephone calls or personal visits are bound to occur from time to time. In general, the environment surrounding mass media is less favorable, although, this too varies. Newspapers, magazines and trade journals contain numerous competing stimuli in the shape of advertisements and editorial copy. The extent and nature of stimuli coming from the surrounding environment will vary according to where and when the reading takes place: at home, at the office, in a restaurant or on public transport. By way of contrast, a cinema commercial has no competition from within the medium, and distraction from the surrounding environment is likely to be minimal.

Media attitudes and behavior

As with any other product, media can be used for various purposes and are subject to individual people's beliefs, preferences and habits. Media beliefs may concern the type of commercial information expected from them, beliefs about their value or relevance, about the reliability and completeness of the information they convey. People may also entertain beliefs about expenditure of money, time and effort involved in looking up and using the information.

A number of media options such as telephone, e-mail, the Internet, facsimile or personal calls may be open to buyers who wish to make inquiries or place orders. However, for various reasons some buyers may prefer to use the telephone or send facsimiles. For example, uncertainty and lack of ICT competence may rule out the Internet option. It is obviously important to bear such preferences in mind when selecting buyer initiative media.

Social factors and direct personal experience combine to form buyers' beliefs about and preferences for seller initiative media as sources of commercial information about such things as shoes or baby carriages. Initial awareness and prolonged attention as well as relevance and probability evaluation will partly follow from attitudes, preferences, and habits relating to media. For example, if a buyer who is actively seeking information calls at a dealer's for a brochure but does not regard the Internet as a suitable source of the information he wants, it is far more probable that he will receive "messages" from the brochure than from the seller's home page. A buyer who does not expect to find advertisements for prefabricated houses in magazine Y will be less likely to become initially aware of advertisements for prefabricated houses in that publication. The fact that dealers cast doubt on the relevance and credibility of trade journal advertisements may cause them to conclude that advertisements in that medium are less relevant to their own requirements or less reliable sources of information. It is much more likely that a buyer will give credence to a salesman's claims where a relationship of trust exists between them. In the absence of other considerations, preference should be given to seller initiative media which are the object of favorable beliefs, attitudes and habits.

Closeness to point of purchase

Closeness to point of purchase has to do with distance in time and space between exposure to a marketing communication message and the point of purchase itself. The closer these are to each other, the less likely the buyer is to forget the content of a message or his response to it *at* the point of purchase. In this respect, shop media are obviously superior to such things as television commercials or magazine advertisements. Accordingly, shop media are likely to be especially well suited to communication tasks related to reminding indifferent buyers of an offering.

Timing flexibility

"Timing flexibility" relates to how quickly a medium can be put to use. A telephone can be picked up immediately and a facsimile or personal computer can be put to use relatively quickly. Conversely, it may take days to arrange a meeting. And it may take weeks before a magazine advertisement can be inserted or a television commercial can be run for the first time. Media such as these are clearly inappropriate for urgent messages.

Cost characteristics

Media costs are costs incurred by media use. As indicated earlier, a distinction may be drawn between production and distribution costs. Media production costs are those connected with producing the selected communication symbols, such as a TV-commercial or video, a homepage, an advertisement or a poster original, overhead charts and handouts, slides etc. Further examples are costs incurred in writing letters, e-mails or facsimiles. Media distribution costs are costs connected with using media in order to establish contacts between buyer and vendor company, e.g. variable costs incurred in inserting advertisements in magazines, in running commercials on TV, in distributing brochures through mail services, etc. Other examples are variable costs in the shape of travel expenses incurred by sales and other personnel, mailing expenses, and telephone, facsimile, and Internet charges. Handling and follow-up activities may involve variable costs connected to such things as individual distribution of brochures and the use of telephones, facsimile transmitters, ordinary mail and e-mail. Typical examples of fixed/stepped distribution costs are wages to managers, sales personnel and other employees who deal with buyers, depreciation on salesmen's cars on telecommunication, ICT, video and printing equipment as well as on showrooms and conference facilities. Distribution costs usually represent the majority of a company's media costs.

Planners may rule out some kinds of media at an early stage in the planning process when the cost of using them is unreasonably high compared with other media. An obvious example is the considerably lower average cost of reaching a buyer through impersonal mass media such as magazines and television commercials than that incurred by using personal media such as telephone (meetings) and impersonal media like letters, facsimile, and e-mail. Clearly, personal media such as videoconferences and face-to-face meetings incur the highest cost per exposure. However, relatively few general statements can be made regarding cost differences. In each specific planning situation a planner must base his final choice of a media strategy on estimates of the total media costs connected to potential media strategies. Such estimates are made on the basis of current wage levels connected to appropriate categories of staff, prevailing charges for inserting advertisements in magazines and running television commercials, current telephone rentals etc.

The following properties of media costs may be useful for planners to bear in mind when budgeting the costs incurred by a specific media strategy:

1. Most media costs fall into two broad categories, i.e. variable and stepped costs.

Stepped media costs are fixed up to a given level of media use and rise as different levels are reached. That is to say that using an item of media equipment may involve some fixed elements such as depreciation, hire charge, interest on capital etc. These costs remain the same as long as the equipment or member of staff can cope with the number and scope of tasks required. Once the capacity of a staff member, a piece of equipment or a facility is exceeded the costs will "jump" to reflect the extra phone line, fax machine or employee that is needed to cope with the excess. For example, if one person can manage to receive, handle and follow up 2000 inquiries per year, and the cost of employing such a person is $ 40 000 per year (including wages, social benefits, etc.) the annual distribution cost of dealing with 2000 inquiries is $ 40 000, while dealing with 2001 inquiries will incur a cost of $ 80 000. That is, in the interval between 2000 and 2001 inquiries, the annual distribution cost "jumps" from $ 40 000 to $ 80 000.

In general, media production costs are variable costs, while media distribution costs have variable as well as stepped elements. Distribution costs connected to impersonal mass media are variable. If magazine Y or television program X is not being used, the distribution cost is zero. The use of other media involves some stepped costs, mostly in the form of wages, depreciation and charges (such as telephone rentals). The ratio between stepped costs and variable costs varies. For example, ICT related media such as e-mail or the Internet, the stepped costs tend to be relatively high, due to such things as capital investment in ICT equipment. The ratio tends to be lower in the case of media such as facsimile and telephone.

2. Staff, equipment and facilities are frequently used for different purposes, so that considerable *interdependence between cost elements* is normal.

Where cost interdependency exists between two cost elements X and Y, X is a function of Y, and vice versa. Let us consider a situation in which a company's telephone equipment is used for receiving, handling and following up buyer initiatives (B) as well as for taking seller initiatives (S). Let us also assume that a planner considers increasing S. Under these conditions the costs incurred for S for the purpose of making initial contacts with buyers are partly a function of B, i.e. of how much of the total capacity that is available for the intended increase in S. If there is no idle capacity, the increase in S gives rise to one or more "jumps" in stepped cost elements (more personnel, a new switchboard, more telephones etc.). Conversely, should there be ample idle capacity, the increase in seller initiatives will incur variable costs only, mostly in the form of call charges. Accordingly, the differential distribution cost incurred for S depends on the costs incurred for B.

The above example illustrates cost interdependency following from uses of the *same medium*. Usually, cost interdependencies also exist between *different media*, owing to the fact that the use of two or more different media draw on the capacity of the same staff, equipment and facilities. For example, the same persons may be involved in meetings and in making telephone calls, sending facsimiles and letters. Cost interdependencies may even arise because certain media are used for other than marketing communication purposes. Telephones, for instance, are used for administrative purposes as well as marketing communication. Sales personnel can be given tasks relating to gathering market information, in-store placement and straightforward order taking. The more the capacity of sales staff is occupied with other tasks, the more probable it is that an intentional increase in their marketing communication activities will give rise to "jumps" in stepped cost elements.

3. Media costs have *direct* as well as *indirect* elements. Production costs are directly traceable, in the sense that they can be attributed directly to the individual medium. The same is true of distribution costs related to impersonal mass media. Using other media incurs direct as well as indirect costs. When letters are used as a medium, postage, paper and envelopes are direct cost elements, while the wages paid to the staff who write and post the letters represent indirect costs, provided the persons in question are involved in other kinds

of work as well. Typically, variable costs are direct, while stepped costs are indirect.

Summing up

The above discussion about media sales and cost characteristics should not be taken to imply that every single characteristic ought to be considered in every planning situation. The discussion should be rather treated as a checklist from which planners may select those characteristics that seem sufficiently relevant at the time. However, exposure capacity and costs provide fundamental guidance to the development of an effective media strategy in every situation. Planners cannot avoid asking the two questions: "Which buyers should we try to reach?" and, "What will it cost?"[41]

14. Developing a media strategy: The process

This chapter goes on to discuss

the process of media strategy development

in markets for standardized products in which the offering is sold directly to the end-buyer. The last two sections of the chapter deal with media strategy development connected to *transformation communication* and markets in which the offering is marketed through *one or more intermediate links*.

The media strategy development process

The process of developing both buyer initiative and seller initiative strategies includes the following five phases:

1. the starting point.
2. preliminary media evaluation.
3. searching for and developing a media strategy.
4. deciding whether or not the intended strategy can be implemented through the existing organizational basis.
5. making a final budget.

1. The starting point:
It has already been pointed out that, the starting point for developing a buyer initiative media strategy is the nature and extent of the expected buyer initiative in the planning period, while the starting point for developing a seller initiative media strategy is the seller initiative gap. Since the seller initiative gap

is equal to the difference between the total budgeted sales volume and the estimated buyer initiative sales volume, it follows that the buyer initiative strategy must be developed before the seller initiative strategy.

The first phase in the strategy development process involves identifying and exploring the respective starting points. Among other things this includes making a number of assessments of such things as the distribution of buyer initiatives between orders and inquiries, the extent of handling and follow-up activities, and the order, inquiry and buyer initiative sales volume.

2. Preliminary media evaluation:
The second phase involves making a rough preliminary evaluation with the purpose of identifying potentially relevant media and *eliminating obviously unsuitable media.* In order to be taken into consideration, the sales and cost characteristics of a medium have to satisfy a number of criteria which will follow from preliminary analyses. These criteria relate to such things as target groups and content goals concretized through preliminary assumptions regarding content symbolization. Media that clearly fail to satisfy one or more of the criteria are left out of further consideration. For example, a seller initiative medium might be rejected because the cost of making an initial contact with a buyer obviously exceeds the expected contribution gained by making a sale. Some media will be left out of consideration because they cannot convey the appropriate symbols. For instance, in cases where the properties and use of a product call for a live demonstration, media such as magazines, newspapers, directly mailed brochures and posters are clearly out of the question. When there are difficult development tasks to be undertaken, some media may be eliminated because they are too easily overlooked or ignored. They are insufficiently "intrusive" in the technical sense used here.

3. Searching for and developing a media strategy:
The third phase involves searching for and developing a media strategy including an *action plan* for seller-initiated initial con-

The media strategy development process 261

tacts and *preparatory plans* for the receipt, handling and follow-up of

- buyer initiatives – and
- orders and inquiries resulting from the intended seller initiative.

This process includes considering, making decisions and laying down guidelines for

- choice of media.
- extent of media use.
- selection of content elements.
- order and timing of media use.

Expected buyer initiative and estimated seller initiative gap constitute important premises in a planner's search for a satisfactory media strategy. The larger the seller initiative gap, the greater the need to use seller initiative media. The capacity of buyer initiative media, such as the telephone or the Internet, is adapted to cope with the number of expected of buyer- and seller-initiated orders and inquiries and timed to coincide with orders and inquiries. The times and periods in which seller initiative media will be used are adjusted to fit in with such things as seasonal variations in demand.

In the process described above, potentially appropriate media are subjected to a more thorough evaluation based on their specific media characteristics. Rough estimates of the media costs connected to potential strategies provide a basis for evaluating cost differences. Variable as well as stepped costs depend on the extent of media use. More media are frequently eliminated during this phase. For example, using a cinema commercial might be preferred to using a television commercial because there will be less competition from other stimuli present in the environment and/or because it will ensure a broader and more selective reach of a highly prioritized target group. (e.g. young people between 15 and 20 years of age.) Similarly, lower distribution costs may bring about a preference for telephone calls and e-mail messages between industrial buyers.

4. Deciding whether or not the intended strategy can be implemented through the existing organizational basis:
In the fourth phase of the strategy development process, a planner will consider whether or not the intended strategy can be implemented through the existing organizational basis. If not, he must set out the necessary changes. These might involve reallocating responsibilities, increasing staff levels and improving their skills. It might also be necessary to invest in such things as new telephone equipment, ICT hardware and software, audio-visual equipment and accommodation.

5. Making a final budget:
The fifth phase of the media strategy development process involves making a final budget, including total media costs, as well as other costs connected to implementing the intended buyer initiative strategy and seller initiative strategy respectively. Fixed/stepped costs are budgeted with due regard to the effects of cost elements on each other (cost interdependency). The developed media strategy and the expected competitiveness of the offering will form a basis on which to make *new estimates of buyer initiative and seller initiative sales volume, turnover and contribution.*

The media cost budget and the new estimates of items such as sales volumes are compared to the corresponding figures in the preliminary operating budget worked out in the planning premises analysis. The revised figures may indicate an operating profit equivalent to, smaller or larger than that which was originally budgeted. If the estimated operating profit is lower, the planner may suggest that the company reduces its profit goal or he may go through the phases of media strategy development once more in search of a more satisfactory solution. On the other hand, if the new estimate of operating profit exceeds the original the company may consider increasing its profit goal.

The development process results in a media strategy consisting of

- a buyer initiative media strategy and
- a seller initiative media strategy.

The media strategy includes the following four elements:

1. *Strategic guidelines regarding media use.* These will cover choice of media, media use, content elements, order and timing of content elements.

2. A description of the *changes that have to be made in the organizational basis* in order to make the media strategy viable. Such changes may include hiring additional staff, investment in equipment and facilities, reorganization of work processes and competence enhancement.

3. A revised media cost budget, specifying production and distribution costs connected to carrying through the buyer initiative media strategy and the seller initiative media strategy, respectively. Two separate sets of costs must be shown: those related to establishing initial contacts with buyers through seller initiative and those connected to receiving, handling and following up orders and inquiries.

4. A *new operating budget*, revised as a result of the planned media strategy. This will combine the new media budget, mentioned in 3 (above), and new estimates of the buyer initiative and seller initiative sales volume, turnover and contribution.

Figure 14.1. sums up the above discussion. The next two paragraphs discuss some important aspects with regard to developing a buyer and a seller initiative strategy, respectively.

Figure 14.1. Developing a media strategy

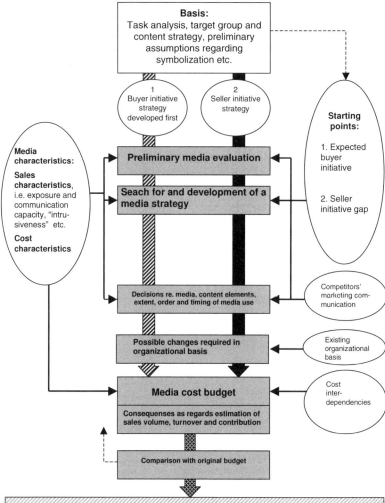

Aspects of buyer initiative media strategy development

Expected buyer initiative as a starting point for strategy development

As has already been emphasized, the extent and nature of the buyer initiative provides the starting point for developing a buyer initiative media strategy. The planning premises analysis, the task analysis and the development of a target group strategy all involve making rough estimates of the likely number of orders and inquiries. Planners can draw directly on these estimates while working on the first phase of strategy development. However, further elaboration and assessments are needed to provide a sufficient basis for developing a preparatory strategic plan that will ensure that buyer initiative sales potential is exploited profitably.

Figure 14.2. illustrates the assessments that need to be made. For the sake of simplicity the illustration is limited to one single target group. Fictitious figures are used for the sake of clarity.

The figure assumes that there are 10 000 buyers in the target group. The average demand per buyer in the planning period is 10 (product) units. The unit price is $ 10 and contribution margin per unit is $ 5. Accordingly, the overall demand, turnover and contribution potentials are 100 000 units, $ 1 000 000 and $ 500 000, respectively. The buyer initiative ratio is estimated at 50/50. Consequently, the maximum buyer initiative sales volume is 50 000 units. The *"order/initiative ratio"* and the *"inquiry/initiative ratio"* are both (25/50=) 0,5, i.e. maximum 2 500 initiatives in the form of inquiries and 2 500 in the form of orders are expected. Hence, the maximum order and inquiry sales volumes are identical, i.e. 25 000 units. The same is, of course, true of the maximum turnovers and contributions, which amount to $ 250 000 and $ 125 000, respectively.

The handling of an inquiry may lead directly to a purchase, or follow-up activity may be required. In Figure 14.2. it is supposed that no more than 2 000 (or 80%) of the 2 500 inquiries will lead directly to purchases, while no more than 500 (or 20%) need follow-up. It is further assumed that the *"purchase/order ratio"* is 0,8 since 2 000 (80%) of the 2 500 orders result in purchases. Similarly the *"purchase/inquiry"* ratio is 0,6 since 1 500 (60%) of the 2 500 inquiries result in purchases. The resulting budgeted order and inquiry sales volumes, turnovers and contributions appears from the table.

The distribution over time of orders and inquiries with regard to days, weeks or months during a planning period may be more or less even, depending, among other things, on seasonal variations in demand. A completely even distribution of the 2 500 inquiries as well as of required further handling (1 500) and follow-up (500) activities amounts to 10 inquiries, 6 handling tasks and 2 follow-up tasks per day for 250 (working) days.

The expected buyer initiative in the planning period provides planners with a number of indicators for strategy development:

Firstly, the estimated maximum figures for buyer initiative sales volume, turnover and contribution determine *cost limits* within which strategic solutions must be sought. In all cases, e.g. irrespective of the actual size of the profit goal, media costs should be kept in a reasonable proportion to the maximum contribution.

Secondly, the expected distribution of buyer-initiated orders and inquiries over time, provides a fairly sophisticated *basis for understanding which media to use, to what extent and when* if the company is to exploit buyer initiative sales potential as profitably as possible. Companies must adapt their media capacity, staff competence, working models and support material (e.g. brochures) to the frequency and nature of buyers' attempts to place orders or make inquiries, as well as to opportunities for performing handling and follow-up activities. These adaptations involve balancing sales contribution against costs. For example, the more accessible a company's staff are, the more sales it is likely to make. However, measures such as increasing the number of telephone lines, introducing beepers and extending opening hours, will always incur additional costs.

Aspects of buyer initiative media strategy development 267

Figure 14.2. Developing a buyer initiative strategy: Some relevant assessments

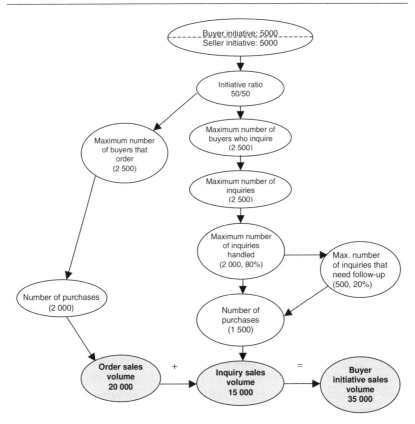

Assumptions:
Number of buyers in target group: 10 000
Expected to show buyer initiative: 5 000
Buyer initiative ratio: 50/50

Average demand per buyer in planning period: 10 product units.
Price per unit: $ 10
Contribution margin per unit: $ 5

Maximum and budgeted sales volume, turnover and contribution:

	Sales volume (units):		Turnover ($):		Contribution ($):	
	Maximum	*Budgeted*	Maximum:	*Budgeted*	Maximum:	*Budgeted*
Orders	25 000	*20 000*	250 000	*200 000*	125 000	*100 000*
Inquiries	25 000	*15 000*	250 000	*150 000*	125 000	*75 000*
Total	50 000	*35 000*	500 000	*350 000*	250 000	*175 000*

In the long run, both the extent of buyer initiative and the relative distribution of initiatives between orders and inquiries will reflect the competitive strength of the company's offering, as well as its marketing communication efforts. Moreover, it seems reasonable to assume that the proportion of inquiries requiring more extensive handling and follow-up activities will depend on factors such as the buyers' advance knowledge of the offering and its competitive strength. The greater the number of inquirers who know about the offering, the smaller the number of those who will require extensive handling and follow-up and the fewer communication tasks there will be. Similarly, the greater the competitive strength of an offering, the less buyers will hesitate, and the higher the proportion of buyers who will require no more than modest handling activity. Since orders generally require less handing and follow-up capacity than inquiries, we may conclude that the proportion of inquiries resulting in direct orders will be inversely proportional to required media capacity. Consequently, in a dynamic perspective, competitive offerings and effective marketing communication will lead to more extensive utilization of buyer initiative sales potentials *as well as* lower media costs.

Thirdly, the maximum estimates relating to order, inquiry and overall buyer initiative sales volume represent a point of departure for *budgeting the buyer initiative sales volume, turnover and contribution*. Rarely if ever can a company receive, handle and follow-up orders and inquiries so perfectly that every buyer who takes an initiative actually goes on to purchase the company's offering. Hence, a planner's task involves assessing the relative proportion of the buyer initiative sales potential that can feasibly be realized.

The following formula indicates one possible way to approach this task. The "*degree of utilization of a buyer initiative sales potential*" (D_{bi}) can be calculated as follows.

Aspects of buyer initiative media strategy development 269

Given that:

N = number of buyer initiatives
P = price per unit
A = average purchase per buyer
O_r = order/initiative ratio
I_r = inquiry/initiative ratio

$I_r + O_r = 1{,}0$ (as initiatives are *either* attempts to place an order *or* to make an inquiry.)

P_{or} = purchase/order ratio (Maximum utilization corresponds to the value 1,0.)
P_{ir} = purchase/inquiry ratio (Maximum utilization corresponds to the value 1,0.)

$$D_{bi} = \frac{\text{Budgeted buyer initiative sales volume}}{\text{Buyer initiative sales potential}} = \frac{N * A * P * (O_r * P_{or} + I_r * P_{ir})}{N * A * P * (O_r * 1{,}0 + I_r * 1{,}0)} =$$

$$\frac{O_r * P_{or} + I_r * P_{ir}}{O_r * 1{,}0 + I_r * 1{,}0} = \frac{O_r * P_{or} + I_r * P_{ir}}{1} = O_r * P_{or} + I_r * P_{ir}$$

That is:

Degree of utilization of buyer initiative sales potential = D_{bi} =

order/initiative ratio * purchase/order ratio + inquiry/initiative ratio * purchase/inquiry ratio

In the example in Figure 14.2.

- the purchase/order ratio is 0,8,
- the purchase/inquiry ratio is 0,6,

- the order/initiative ratio is 0,5, and
- the inquiry/initiative ratio is 0,5.

Accordingly:

Degree of utilization of the buyer initiative sales potential =

$$= 0{,}5 * 0{,}8 + 0{,}5 * 0{,}6 = 0{,}7$$

This means that 70% of the maximum buyer initiative sales volume is realized.

The formula demonstrates clearly how the degree of utilization of the buyer initiative sales potential is a function of

- the relative distribution of initiatives between orders and inquiries, i.e. the order/initiative and the inquiry/initiative ratios – and

- the purchase/order and purchase/inquiry ratios.

These ratios depend on media preparedness and capability in handling and following up orders and inquiries as well as on factors such as the competitiveness of the offering, communication content and content symbolization. Planners can consider and assess the degree of utilization of the buyer initiative sales potential by attempting to estimate the ratios.

Preliminary media evaluation and strategy search

It is a relatively easy task to identify relevant media and media combinations when making a preliminary evaluation of media and searching for a sufficiently effective strategy. The media options are limited to buyer initiative media and personal mass media, such as face-to-face meetings, telephone conversations, and videoconferences. The third option may be relevant for handling and following up inquiries in industrial markets for complex products such as production robots and airplanes. Media and combinations of media should be evaluated in the light of the anticipated buyer initiative potential and content goals discussed earlier, including the preliminary assumptions made about content symbolization. Relevant characteristics of the available media are matched against the requirements arising from expected buyer initiative and content goals. The symbolization capacity of a medium to meet content goals will be assessed in the light of preliminary assumptions regarding content symbolization. As all relevant media are buyer initiative media or controllable seller initiative media, the task of evaluating the relevant media's exposure capacity is relatively easy in most cases.

It involves considering

- which media are at the disposal of which buyers and
- which media buyers tend to use in order to make inquiries and place orders.

The final decision as to which medium or combination of media to select cannot be made without due regard to the intended *extent* of media use. This is because estimates of the required media capacity of the various media included in a possible strategy constitute a necessary basis for estimating media costs. Variable as well as stepped costs will depend on the capacity required. As indicated already, the fact that staff, telephones, ICT equipment and other facilities may be used for different purposes, means that media cost elements are frequently interrelated and cost estimates must be made with due regard to this fact.

Aspects of seller initiative media strategy development

The seller initiative gap as a starting point for strategy development

As has already been pointed out, the starting point for developing a seller initiative media strategy is the seller initiative gap, which is equal to the overall budgeted sales volume minus the estimated buyer initiative sales volume. The aim of the seller initiative is to close the seller initiative gap with an acceptable margin of profit to the company.

272 *Developing a media strategy: The Process*

As emphasized already strategic media planning related to seller initiative involves developing:

1. an *action plan* for producing initial contacts.

2. a *preparatory plan* for receiving, handling and following up resulting orders and inquiries.

The nature of the *preparatory planning process* is identical to that discussed above in relation to buyer initiative and will not be discussed any further here. The only difference is that orders and inquiries are responses to seller initiative in the planning period. In most cases strategy development will be a question of additional use of the media already selected for receiving, handling and following up buyer initiatives. Whether or not some additional use of a medium incurs variable costs only or new "jumps" in stepped cost elements depends on the amount of idle media capacity. As far as timing is concerned, additional use of media will take place after initial contacts produced by the action plan have been made.

Figure 14.3. illustrates the *considerations and assessments* that have to be made when *using the seller initiative gap as a basis for strategy development*. For the sake of simplicity the illustration is limited to one single target group. The figure is based on the example in Figure 14.2.

Given that the (overall) budgeted sales volume is 38 000 (product) units, the seller initiative gap is equal to 3 000, i.e.:

The seller initiative gap =

Budgeted sales volume − order sales volume − inquiry sales volume =

38 000 − 20 000 − 15 000 = *3 000*

The initiative ratio in the target group is 50/50. Accordingly, seller initiative can be directed at no more than 5 000 buyers. It remains to determine the size of the required *"contact ratio"*, or

Aspects of seller initiative media strategy development 273

proportion of the 5000 *buyers who need to be contacted in order to close the seller initiative gap.* A *"buyer contacted"* is here defined as *a buyer exposed to the relevant content symbolization(s) sufficiently often and at appropriate times.*

The answer to these questions depends, in turn, on the answers to the following further questions:

- How many of those contacted may be expected to respond, i.e. attempt to place an order or make an inquiry? In other words, how large is the expected *"response/contact ratio"*?

- How many of the responding buyers may be expected to make a purchase? In other words, how large is the expected *"purchase/response ratio"*?

- How large is (the expected) *average purchase* per buyer (in product units)?

In Figure 14.3. the contact ratio is 60% (of 5 000), i.e. 3 000 buyers need to be exposed to a marketing message. (See middle part of figure.) The size of this ratio corresponds to a response/contact ratio of 0,2 (20% of 3 000 buyers), i.e. 600 buyers. The purchase/response ratio is 0,5, i.e. (600 * 0,5 =) 300 buyers makes a purchase. (See lower part of figure.) The average purchase is 10. Consequently, the seller initiative sales volume is (300 * 10 =) 3 000, which equals the seller initiative gap.

The dotted line illustrates how the contact ratio depends on the response/contact ratio, the purchase/response ratio and average purchase. The relationship may also be expressed as follows:[42]

$$\text{Contact ratio} = \frac{\text{seller initiative gap/average purchase}}{\text{number of buyers in target group} * \text{response/contact ratio} * \text{purchase/response ratio}}$$

Figure 14.3. Developing a seller initiative strategy: Some relevant assessments

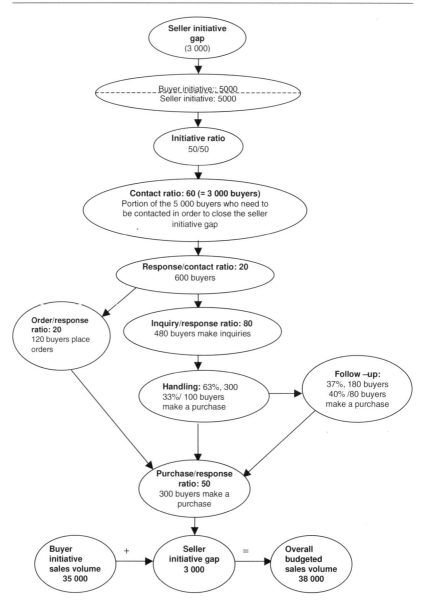

Aspects of seller initiative media strategy development 275

Figure 14.3 cont.

Assumptions:
Average demand per buyer, price per unit etc.: Same as in Figure 14.2.
Overall budgeted buyer initiative sales volume: 35 000 (units).
Budgeted overall sales volume = 38 000 (units).
Seller initiative gap = 38 000 – 35 000 = 3 000 units.

Overall sales budget – sales volume, turnover and contribution:

	Sales volume (units):	Turnover ($):	Contribution ($):
Orders	20 000	200 000	100 000
Inquiries	15 000	150 000	75 000
Seller initiative	3 000	30 000	15 000
Total	38 000	380 000	190 000

Using the numbers in Figure 14.3.:

$$\text{Contact ratio} = \frac{3\,000/10}{5000 * 0{,}2 * 0{,}5} = 0{,}6$$

Given the above assumptions, 60% of the 5 000 buyers need to be exposed to marketing messages in order to close the seller initiative gap. It appears from the formula that the size of the contact ratio is an inverse function of the number of relevant buyers, the response ratio, the purchase ratio, and the average purchase. Conversely, the larger the seller initiative gap, the larger the contact ratio.

The 300 purchases stem from attempts to place orders or inquiries. 20% or 120 of the 600 buyers responding place orders, while 80% or 480 make inquiries. That is, the "*order/response*" ratio is 0,2, and the "*inquiry/response ratio*" is 0,8. The "*purchase/order ratio*" is 1,0, since each of the 120 attempts to place an order result in a purchase. 180 or 37% of the 480 inquiries require follow-up. 80 or 44% of these buyers make a purchase.

276 *Developing a media strategy: The Process*

300 or 63% require handling only. 100 or 33% of these buyers make a purchase. Thus, 480 inquiries result in 180 purchases, i.e. the *"purchase/inquiry ratio"* is 0,375.

The 600 responding buyers represent a *maximum seller initiative sales potential* of (600 * 10 =) 6 000 units. Corresponding to the degree of utilization of the buyer initiative sales potential *"the degree of utilization of the seller initiative sales potential"* (D_{si}) can be calculated as follows.

Given that:

O_r = order/response ratio = 0,2 (20% of 3 000 responding buyers attempt to place orders)

I_r = inquiry/response ratio = 0,8 (80% of the 3 000 responding buyers attempt to make an inquiry.)

$I_r + O_r = 1,0$ (as responses are either attempts to place an order or to make an inquiry.)

P_{or} = purchase/order ratio = 1,0 (Maximum utilization corresponds to the value 1,0.)

P_{ir} = purchase/inquiry ratio = 0,375 (Maximum utilization corresponds to the value 1,0.)

That is:

The degree of utilization of the seller initiative sales potential = D_{si}

= $O_r * P_{or} + I_r * P_{ir}$ = 0,2 * 1,0 + 0,8 * 0,375 = 0,5

This means that 50% of the seller initiative sales potential of 6 000 units, corresponding to 3 000 (= the seller initiative gap) is realized.

The above formula implies that the degree of utilization of the seller initiative sales potential is a function of

Aspects of seller initiative media strategy development

- the relative distribution of responses between orders and inquiries, i.e. the order/response and inquiry/response ratios, as well as of

- the purchase/order and purchase/inquiry ratios.

Both ratios depend on media strategy (media characteristics/preparedness), as well as on factors such as the competitiveness of the offering, communication content and content symbolization. As has been emphasized before, effective receipt, handling and follow-up of orders and inquiries are crucially important both for realizing buyer initiative sales potential and for the effects of seller initiatives.

The seller initiative gap gives planners several significant pointers for strategy development.

First of all it indicates a *limit as to seller initiative costs*. In a short-term perspective, the additional costs incurred by seller initiatives should not exceed the maximum seller initiative contribution potential. This is equal to:

Maximum seller initiative contribution potential =

seller initiative gap $*$ contribution margin per product unit $*$ average purchase per buyer

In a longer-term perspective, seller initiative costs may exceed this limit. However, in all cases, the limit may serve as a pointer in a planner's search for a profitable strategy. Given the assessments made of the average purchase per buyer in the planning period, the contact ratio, the purchase/inquiry ratio etc. in the various target groups, the following questions may be asked:

- Is it possible for the seller initiative gap to be closed at a cost equal to or lower than the limit indicated by the maximum seller initiative contribution potential?

- If this is possible, how can it be achieved?

- If it is not possible, by how much does it exceed the above limit and is that difference acceptable in a longer-term perspective?

Secondly, the seller initiative gap constitutes a starting point for assessing the contact ratio, i.e. the proportion (number) of buyers in the various target groups who need to be contacted in order to close the seller initiative gap. This proportion is a basic element in an overall exposure goal, which, in addition, specifies exposure frequency distributions and timing exposures. Contact ratios are estimated in relation to each target group as elements of the sub-exposure-goals on which the overall exposure goal is built. Exposure goals serve as pointers in a planner's search for media or media combinations that have the potential of matching these goals and producing the required number of responses in the form of attempts to place orders and make inquiries.

Preliminary media evaluation and strategy search

In principle, the search for a strategy includes all controllable and uncontrollable media. Appropriate media or media combinations are identified by comparing media characteristics with exposure and content goals. The latter are taken into account by making preliminary assumptions regarding content symbolization. These assumptions constitute the basis for deciding whether or not more than one medium is required to convey the selected content elements. If two or more media are needed, these assumptions may point to the order in which the selected media should be used to communicate the various content elements. Sufficient exposure capacity should be given highest priority. Only media or media combinations with the capacity of contributing to realizing the overall exposure goal should be taken into consideration.

It should be noted that *costs* connected to using impersonal mass media (uncontrollable media) are easy to estimate. One consideration is that the use of media such as newspapers, television or radio commercials and posters makes few demands on the organizational basis as far as equipment, organization and competence are concerned. However, relationships with media companies, printing works and advertising agencies still have to be handled. Another consideration is that distribution costs are variable and proportional to the extent of use. Cost elements are independent of each other. The distribution costs connected with alternative media plans can be calculated directly on the basis of charges for such items as newspaper and magazine advertisements, and television and radio commercials.

When costs vary in proportion to the extent of use (i.e. marginal costs are constant), the contact price may be used as an indicator of cost effectiveness. Medium X's *"contact price"* in relation to a target group, Y, is defined as:

$$\text{Contact price}_* = \frac{\text{cost incurred by using medium X once}_*)}{\text{number of buyers in target group exposed at least once by using medium X once}}$$

*: Content symbolization given, e.g. if magazines are considered:

Thus, the contact price indicates the cost incurred by exposing one member of the target group to a given content symbolization, e.g. a full-page advertisement in four colors, *once*. If, for example, the price asked for one insertion of a given advertisement in a magazine is $ 10 000 and 500 000 buyers in the target group in question are thereby exposed once, the contact price is:

$$\text{Contact price} = \frac{10\ 000}{500\ 000} = 0{,}02.$$

In tactical media selection, contact prices may be used as a basis for selecting individual media, e.g. newspapers A and B in preference to C and D, magazine X and Y in preference Z and

W etc. In a strategy development context it is the contact price *level* connected to various (kinds of) media that is of interest.

Determining frequency and extent of media use. A theory of response functions

It has been emphasized that sub-exposure-goals connected to each relevant target group provide important pointers in a planner's search for an effective strategy for producing initial contacts. Setting these kinds of sub-goal includes determining

- the contact ratio, i.e. the relative proportion of buyers who need to be contacted in the target group in question.

- an exposure frequency distribution, i.e. a specification of the number of buyers to be exposed once, twice, 3 three times, four times etc.

- the timing of exposures, i.e. when exposures should take place.

While the contact ratio has consequences for the *number* of media that need to be used, the exposure frequency distribution has implications for the *extent* of use of the relevant media. Moreover, the timing of exposures obviously determines the timing of media use. Considerations related to selecting a contact ratio have been discussed already. This section deals with the question of determining the frequency distribution, while the following section discusses the question of timing the exposures.

Basically, the selection of exposure frequency depends on the assumptions made with regard to the effect of repetition. "*Repetition*" is defined here as *repeated exposure of a given buyer with given (i.e. particular and constant) characteristics to a given content symbolization (e.g. a given magazine advertisement or television commercial) in a given media environment.* In the literature the *relationship between* the number of times a buyer is exposed to a marketing message *(repetition)* and his *response* (in a given planning period) is commonly expressed in the form of a "*response function*".

Figure 14.4. shows three examples of such functions where response is defined as the number of purchases of an offering in the planning period. Function (a) is *degressive*. The first exposure produces the largest response. Additional exposures are effective, but response decreases gradually. Function (b) is *S-shaped*. The effects of the first (several) exposures are modest. Additional exposures are increasingly effective up to a point called the "inflection point", beyond which, response decreases gradually. Function (c) is a *threshold function*, i.e. a special kind of S-shaped function where – up to a point (a "threshold") – exposures have no effect whatsoever. Response functions may also be assumed to be *linear*, i.e. response is proportional to the number of exposures.

As stated above the assumptions made with regard to response functions constitute a fundamental premise for determining frequency distributions, which, in turn, determine the extent of media use. This can be understood by observing the direct correspondence that exists between the shape of a *"sales function"* representing the *relationship between sales volume and extent of media use*, and the assumed shape of response functions. For instance, S-shaped response functions obviously imply S-shaped sales functions. Thus, S-shaped, threshold and linear response functions imply higher exposure frequencies and a more extensive media use (and higher media distribution costs) than do degressive ones. In advertising literature as well as in advertising practice it is widely believed that repetition is effective. This is tantamount to supposing that response functions are linear, or even S-shaped or threshold functions.

The assumptions made here regarding response functions are illustrated in Figure 14.5.[43]

Different response functions apply to

- frequently bought non-durable products (offerings), such as groceries, as compared to

282 Developing a media strategy: The Process

Figure 14.4. Various types of response function

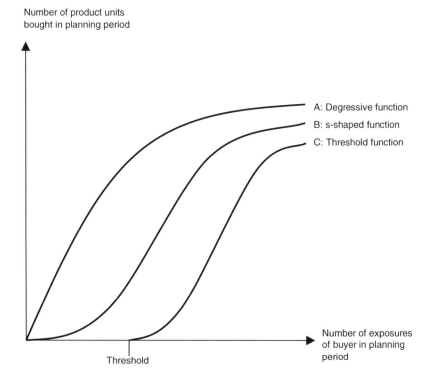

A response function refers to one single buyer.

Underlying assumptions are that:

1. Relevant buyer characteristics *remain unchanged* during the planning period (except for changes brought about by the exposures themselves as a function of e.g. post-purchase experience.)
2. The buyer is exposed repeatedly (1, 2, 3... times) to a *given* symbol structure (e.g. magazine advertisement or television commercial) in a *given* media environment.

- infrequently bought (and typically) durable products (offerings) such as cars, refrigerators, and furniture.

In the case of frequently bought *non-durable products*, three possible types of response to repetition are represented by three

Aspects of seller initiative media strategy development 283

different response functions, depending on whether the buyer reacts to his first (trial) purchase with preference, rejection or indifference, i.e.

1. preference functions,
2. rejection functions, and
3. indifference functions.

Only one type of response function applies to infrequently bought durable products. (See Figure 14.5.)

All the response functions run linearly from origon up to a *"breaking point"*, at which they level off. Furthermore, with the exception of the indifference function, the functions "jump" from origon to the breaking point (its maximum or *"leveling-off value"*) as a result of *one exposure*. *"Response"* is defined as *number of purchases*. This implies that every response to initial contact in the form of an attempt to place an order or make an inquiry leads to a purchase, i.e. orders and inquiries are perfectly received, handled and followed-up. The implication of setting aside this assumption is further discussed below.

The basic hypotheses underlying the above response functions can be outlined as follows:

Buyers who are predisposed to react favorably, with preference or at least indifference, to a specific offering are at the same time favorably predisposed to become aware of, process and remember content related to that offering. This is because initial awareness, attention, interpretation, thinking and remembering are *selective* processes governed by essentially the same buyer characteristics that determine the "match" between buyer and offering. A person is continuously exposed to millions of stimuli. He is not able to process all of these. He is able to cope with this complexity because his sense organs, his ability to think and his memory tend to focus on *significant stimuli*, i.e. stimuli that may contribute to improved problem solving and utilization of opportunities. Examples of such stimuli are advertisements, commercials, brochures etc. that may lead to fewer sacrifices and more rewards connected to purchasing and consuming or using marketing offerings, in short, to enhancing buyer value. Conversely, a person is unlikely to remain aware of stimuli or regard them as relevant when he has identified them as insignificant on first becoming aware of them.

Thus, if a buyer is favorably predisposed to a specific offering at the outset, he is also likely to be receptive and favorably predisposed to content related to that offering. He is more likely to become and remain aware of such content, more willing to consider it carefully, remember it and draw positive conclusions about it. This implies that, all other things being equal, either a buyer responds with a purchase to the first exposure to a given content symbolization, or he does not respond at all. This hypothesis is inconsistent with the belief that buyers must be exposed to marketing messages on a threshold number of occasions before they react. Among other things the latter view implies that people tend to forget about offerings even after they have assessed marketing messages relating to them, concluded that the offerings in question are of interest and decided to buy them or make a trial purchase.

Mere repetition cannot persuade an unfavorably predisposed person to buy an offering even though repetition may make such a person initially aware of an advertisement and perhaps learn something from it. Although, numerous laboratory experiments document the learning effect of repetition, this depends heavily on the existence of a driving force. In the laboratory the researcher or the research method may be the factors that constitute the driving force, motivating the participant to expose himself to, become aware of and interpret the stimulus, and try to remember it. However, in real life situations, content or content symbolization is decisive. If someone responds to an advertisement with indifference or skepticism, no driving force arises. Repeated exposure to the advertisement does not lead someone to interpret it more thoroughly or try to learn more about its content. On the contrary once someone has learned that an advertisement is irrelevant they will tend to respond to additional exposure with diminishing interest and will eventu-

Aspects of seller initiative media strategy development 285

Figure 14.5. Possible types of response functions according to the presented theory

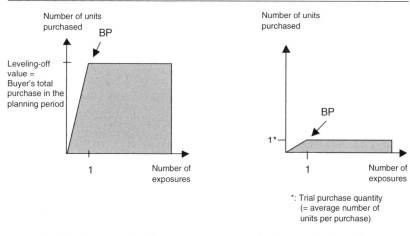

1. Preference function

2. Rejection function

*: Trial purchase quantity (= average number of units per purchase)

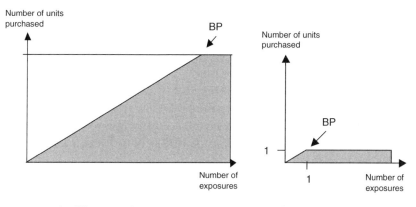

3. Indifference function

4. Response function for an infrequently bought product

Applies to frequently bought non-durable products:

1. Preference functions
2. Rejection functions
3. Indifference functions

BP: Breaking point

Applies to infrequently bought (typically durable) products:

Response function 4. above.

ally cease to pay it any attention. This means that people who are not predisposed to show interest in a particular offering may become initially aware of a marketing message, but will register very little more than such things as a company name or a brand logo. For the reasons stated above, repetition of an advertisement or other content symbolizations has no effect unless these convey a competitive offering. This is the case, regardless of whether the offering itself is not competitive or whether inappropriate content or content symbolization obscures the fact that it is competitive.

The above reasoning provides a basis for understanding the response functions illustrated in Figure 14.5. As a result of one exposure the *response function for a durable product* jumps to a leveling-off value of one (or a few) unit(s), as such products (e.g. refrigerators) are rarely bought in large quantities. The lifetime of durable products exceeds the length of the planning period. Additional exposures will not have additional effects.

In the case of response functions for non-durable products, as a result of one exposure the *"preference function"* jumps to a leveling-off value equal to the buyer's total purchase in the planning period. Preference means that – as a result of pre- and post-purchase experience connected to a trial purchase – the buyer has learnt something relevant, i.e. an enhanced need satisfaction (buyer value), which he is unlikely to forget. Every additional purchase based on the preference serves to reinforce what has been learnt. Additional exposures to content symbolizations will have no effect. Rejection, also, means that through pre- and post-purchase experience the buyer has learnt something relevant, namely, which offering *not* to buy. As a result of one exposure the *"rejection function"* jumps to a leveling-off value of one product unit (the trial purchase quantity). Further exposures will have no effect.

The linear incline of the *"indifference function"* is less steep, running from origon up to a breaking point and leveling-off value corresponding to more than one exposure to a content symbolization. The path of this function is explained by a *reminder effect.* Indifference means that as a result of a trial purchase and post-purchase experience two or more offerings are evaluated as being of equal value. Hence, the buyer is indifferent about which offering to buy. In order to maintain the present level of need satisfaction, it is sufficient to remember only one of the offerings in question. Consequently, a basis exists for reminding the buyer of the company's offering, so that he is or becomes aware of it on further purchasing (shopping) occasions. Provided that exposures are evenly distributed through the planning period, so that the buyer is exposed prior to different purchasing occasions, some degree of linear relationship may be assumed to exist between the number of exposures to content symbolizations and the number of units purchased. Even though indifferent buyers are relatively unsusceptible to communication, the relevant content is so limited (e.g. brand name/logo, company name) that initial awareness may be assumed to be sufficient.

The *leveling-off value* of the indifference function depends on the buyer's total purchasing requirements in respect of the type of product concerned, as well as the number of offerings in relation to which he is indifferent *and* of which he is aware when deciding to make a purchase. Statistically speaking, the buyer is likely to buy an equal number of the offerings in question. For instance, if he is aware of and indifferent to four offerings, the leveling-off value of the indifference function is 25% of his total purchase, which is allocated equally between the four offerings. An increase in the number of relevant offerings involves a decrease in the leveling-off value. Thus, the leveling-off value depends on competitors' marketing offerings as well as on their communication efforts.

The *rate of growth* up to the breaking point is proportionally related to the leveling-off value. In addition it depends on the frequency with which the buyer purchases the product in question. The higher this frequency, the greater the number of occasions on which he needs to be reminded of the company's offering. The duration of the effect of a reminder will also make a difference. The longer the buyer remains aware of a particular offering, the fewer are the occasions on which he needs to be reminded in order to make a purchase. Thus, relatively high purchasing frequency and short-lived effect of a reminder will be reflected in a correspondingly gradual linear incline for the indifference function.

Planners must *consider underlying assumptions* about such things as media environment and buyer characteristics when using the above response functions as a basis for setting exposure goals. The environments surrounding a content symbolization in media such as magazines or television programs will vary from one edition or showing to another, even within relatively short periods of time. Occasional changes in buyer characteristics also occur. Tiredness, for example, varies. A tired person is less apt to become initially aware of a stimulus that a rested one. Thus, tiredness may prevent buyers from becoming aware of advertisements and commercials. Such variations in buyer characteristics and media environments mean that more than one exposure to a media message may be necessary in order to arouse initial awareness. This is not because repetition in itself is effective, but because it will increase the probability of exposing the buyer to the content symbolization in a sufficiently favorable media environment. However, factors such as dominating symbolization (e.g. a full-page advertisement), favorable media attitudes or a high degree of media "intrusiveness" may render repetition unnecessary. One exposure may be enough.

It is impossible to determine an optimal number of exposures. However, the strategically important implication of the assumed response functions is that *exposure frequencies should be moderate*. Resources should not be spent on extensive repetition. Depending on the circumstances, exposure goals for buyers expected to react with preference to trial purchases should be set between 1 to 6.

Purchase frequency and assumed duration of the effect of a reminder may be used as a basis for determining the frequency with which buyers who are expected to react with indifference should be exposed to content symbolizations. The desired exposure may be expressed as follows:

Aspects of seller initiative media strategy development

$$\text{Desired exposure frequency} = \frac{\text{Purchase frequency}}{\text{Duration of reminder effect}}$$

For example, if the planning period is one year and the product is purchased once a fortnight, there are 26 opportunities to remind this category. If the duration of a reminder effect is (close to) 2 weeks, the desired exposure frequency is 26 exposures, one in relation to each purchase. If the duration of a reminder effect is longer than 2 weeks, for example 4 weeks, obviously the desired exposure frequency is halved, i.e. 13.[44]

In the above discussion of response functions and the effect of repetition, "*response*" has been defined as "number of purchases" made by the buyer. In the context of a holistic view of marketing communication, this definition implies that every initial contact leads to a purchase, i.e. that orders and inquiries are perfectly received, handled and followed-up. The sales effect of exposures will obviously be reduced to the extent that this is not the case. In the case of response functions the word response should rather be interpreted as *"number of attempts to place an order or make an inquiry"*. It has, furthermore been implicitly assumed that the entire content goal can be realized through one medium alone. This is often not the case. For example, if some of the selected content elements are to be conveyed by medium A, in the form of an advertisement which invites buyers to find more details (other content elements) by visiting the seller's Internet homepage (medium B), the appropriate response to the advertisement will be *intentional exposure to another medium,* in this particular case, an Internet homepage.[45]

Timing exposures and media use

An exposure goal also states the timing of the exposures. The desired timing of exposures governs the timing of media use.

In markets for *non-durable products* that have reached a high level of product penetration, the buyers "in the market" are the same throughout the entire planning period. In such markets the timing of exposures to content symbolizations that is likely to prompt the greatest sales volume depends on whether the buyers at whom they are aimed are expected to react to the offering with preference or indifference. Potential preference as well as potential indifference should, of course, be realized as early as possible in the planning period in order to obtain the largest possible share of the buyers' overall purchase. However, buyers who may be expected to develop preferences should be exposed to marketing messages at the start of the period, while messages aimed at reminding indifferent buyers of the offering should be distributed evenly through the planning period to coincide with their evenly distributed purchases.

Where the degree of product penetration is low, a growing number of hitherto potential buyers enter the market as actual buyers. Such growth may justify timing messages for later stages in the planning period in order to produce initial contacts with late-entering buyers who may be predisposed to develop preference or who may be indifferent to the offering.

Buyers are constantly entering and leaving markets for *durable products*. Some of those who are on their way in are new actual buyers, while others want to replace previously bought items. Planners will aim to expose these buyers to marketing messages with optimal frequency at the various points of time at which they are "in the market" for the product. Thus, in a market characterized by seasonal variations in demand or by a growing number of potential buyers, media use should be *unevenly* distributed, while the absence of such variations or growth calls for an *even* distribution of media use throughout the planning period.

Markets for durable products with growing numbers of potential buyers or which buyers are continuously leaving and entering call for *relatively extensive media use*. When setting exposure goals the number of exposures should be consistent with exposing buyers with the appropriate frequency *when* they are "in the market". In the following hypothetical example, three insertions of a newspaper advertisement are considered necessary to cause responses from a target group for a durable product where buyers enter and leave the market every month. In order to realize the desired exposure frequency in relation to all buyers, three insertions have to be used to expose those who are "in the market" in January with the desired frequency, three additional insertions to expose those who are "in the market" in February – and so on. Over a period of 12 months 36 insertions would have to be bought in order to expose all the buyers three times.

Summing up

The above discussion leads us to the following conclusions:

1. The purpose of the *action plan* for producing initial contacts is to *close the seller initiative gap*.

2. An *overall exposure goal* indicates a *contact ratio*, an *exposure frequency distribution* and *the timing of exposures* to content symbolizations that need to be realized in order for the seller initiative gap to be closed. The *number of media and the extent and timing of their use is chosen with the aim of realizing the overall exposure goal*.

3. The *contact ratio* indicates the relative *proportion (number) of those buyers who are unlikely to show buyer initiative who must be contacted if the seller initiative gap is to be filled*. The contact ratio is an inverse function of the total number of buyers requiring seller initiative, the response/contact ratio, the purchase/response ratio and the average quantity of the product that each buyer purchases.

4. *Exposure frequencies* should be moderate:

a. in the case of infrequently purchased/*durable products*: 1-6 exposures.

b. in the case of frequently purchased/*non-durable products*:

 - in order to realize potential *preference*: 1-6 exposures.
 - in order to realize potential *indifference*: 1-6 exposures.

- in order to *remind* indifferent buyers: One to several exposures depending on total quantity purchased in the planning period, purchasing frequency etc.

When media characteristics relating to such things as competing stimuli present in the medium itself or in the environment surrounding the medium, "intrusiveness", and media attitudes are favorable and content symbolization is appropriate, correspondingly fewer exposures to marketing messages are needed.

5. Appropriate *timing*

a. in the case of *infrequently* purchased/*durable* products: A more or less *even* distribution of exposures throughout the planning period depending on seasonal variations and the development in the total number of actual buyers.

b. in the case of *frequently* purchased/*non-durable* products

 - buyers who are predisposed to develop *preferences* should be exposed to marketing messages *early* in the planning period. When the number of buyers "in the market" is increasing, more exposures may be allocated to later parts of the planning period.
 - *indifferent* buyers should be exposed to an *even* distribution of exposures throughout the planning period. When the number of buyers "in the market" is increasing, more exposures may be allocated to later parts of the planning period.

6. A strategic action plan should aim at exposing all the buyers indicated by the contact ratio to marketing messages

 - with the desired moderate frequencies
 - from the very beginning of the planning period
 - using as few media as possible
 - as little as possible.

Where *controllable media* are concerned, a planner is in direct control of who is to be exposed to content symbolizations, with

Aspects of seller initiative media strategy development

what frequency and when. In short, he can design a media strategy that perfectly matches the overall exposure goal. In his search for suitable *uncontrollable media* and combinations of such media, the planner should give priority to those that are associated with large exposure maximums and exposure loyalty while avoiding overlapping and overlapping speed. In earlier discussion about the effects of repetition it was noted that overlapping and high overlapping "speed" tend to produce unnecessarily high exposure frequencies. Large exposure maximums mean that fewer media need to be used in order to expose all buyers from the beginning of the planning period. And the higher the exposure loyalties, the less the media need to be used in order to produce the desired exposure frequency distribution.

Low-involvement, response and media use

It should be emphasized that the assumptions regarding the effect of repetition embedded in the three low-involvement hypotheses outlined in Chapter 12 do *not* agree with those underlying the above conclusions. All of the hypotheses – the *brand salience* hypothesis as well as the *elaboration-likelihood hypothesis* and *mere exposure* hypothesis – seem to imply that a considerable number of exposures can prompt slightly involved buyers to make trial purchases. This is tantamount to assuming the existence of *threshold response functions*.

It seems clear that applying the concept of threshold functions to marketing communication planning leads to exposure goals being set with *higher exposure frequencies* than would otherwise be the case – and that correspondingly more resources are spent on advertising as a consequence. In his search for suitable media and media combinations that will obtain sufficiently high exposure frequencies, a planner should prioritize *high exposure loyalty*, *high overlapping* and *high overlapping "speed"*. Exposures and media use should be concentrated in a "burst" at the beginning of the planning period in order to take the largest possible share of the market.

It should be noted that the low-involvement hypotheses do *not* deal with the course of response functions *subsequent to the trial purchase*. As regards the course subsequent to trial purchase and post-purchase experience planner might apply an indifference function.

The following two sections discuss media strategy development in transformation markets and markets with intermediaries, respectively. The discussion focuses on differences relating to strategy content and development.

Media strategy development in transformation markets

Two important characteristics of transformation markets call for *different assumptions* to be made when developing both buyer and seller initiative strategies.

Firstly, there are *several phases in a typical buying process* in transformation markets. Two of these involve making decisions leading to delivery of a customized offering:

- The buyer decides which companies will be considered as potential suppliers and be invited to offer.

- The buyer chooses a supplier and an offering.

Secondly, *all buyer initiatives are inquiries* that may result in invitations to offer. Direct orders do not occur.

These two characteristics indicate that the starting point for developing a buyer initiative media strategy should include estimates of:

1. The (maximum) *number of inquiries* to be *expected* in the planning period.

2. An *"invitation/inquiry ratio"*, i.e. *the proportion of the inquiries that is* expected to result in invitations to propose and develop a customized offering".

Media strategy development in transformation markets 295

3. An *"order/invitation ratio"*, i.e. the *proportion of proposed customized* offerings that is expected to result in orders.

4. The *average purchase per buyer* (having regard to the fact that the price of a customized offering will vary considerably).

The seller initiative gap is calculated as:

Seller initiative gap = Budgeted sales volume – inquiry sales volume

And the contact ratio can be expressed as follows:

$$\text{Contact ratio} = \frac{\text{seller initiative gap/average purchase}}{\text{number of buyers in target group requiring seller initiative} * \text{inquiry / contact ratio} * \text{invited / inquiry ratio} * \text{order / invited ratio}}$$

It is clear that:

Order/inquiry ratio = order/offering ratio * offering / inquiry ratio

Furthermore, action planning aimed at producing initial contacts must take into account the fact that customized offerings are bought only once, and that buyers are continuously entering and leaving the market place. *Preference* means *supplier* preference, or being on a buyer's "bidders' list". Supplier *indifference* may be assumed to exist, but as repurchasing does not occur, indifference response functions are not an issue. Response to repeated exposures may, therefore, be represented by response functions similar to those relating to durable products, i.e. functions running from origon to 1 as a result of 1-6 exposures. The relevant definition of *"response"* is *"opportunity to obtain an invitation to offer"*. Consequently, resources should not be spent on repetition. Since buyers are continuously entering and leaving the market, exposures to marketing messages – and media use – should be distributed evenly throughout the planning period.

Preparatory planning involves selecting media and estimating such things as the necessary media capacity and costs connected to receiving, handling and following up both seller-initiated and buyer-initiated inquiries and invitations to offer. Each inquiry needs to be received, handled and (perhaps) followed-up with the purpose of obtaining an invitation to offer. It must also be borne in mind that every invitation to offer involves a *dialogue* in the course of which a customized offering is specified and developed. Such transformation communication processes may involve handling as well as follow-up activities, using appropriate individual media and personal mass media, such as face-to-face meetings, e-mail, letters, facsimile, telephone conversations and telephone and video conferences. In general, the media characteristics that are most important where negotiations are concerned are two-way-communication capacity and timing flexibility. Other important media characteristics are symbolization capacity (to communicate graphic material, working drawings and photographs) and exposure flexibility. Since there are many different kinds of inquiries and invitations to offer, communication tasks are largely unpredictable. It is therefore almost impossible to make sufficiently realistic assumptions about such matters as the time and space needed for content symbolization. Capacity and cost estimates are correspondingly difficult to make.

Media strategy development in markets with intermediaries

Two main "strategies" were prominent in the discussion in Chapter 11 about how to coordinate the selection of end-buyer and dealer target groups. Depending on dealer "strength" the choice lies between:

a. a "push-strategy", and
b. a (combined) "push-and-pull strategy",

If a "*push-strategy*" is appropriate, the strategy development process is quite similar to that applying to markets without in-

Media strategy development in markets with intermediaries 297

termediaries. This is because all target groups consist of dealers and, consequently, there are only two relevant market "links". The lines of thought and the arguments that apply to end-buyers are equally valid for dealers.

However, the concept of "infrequently bought products" makes little sense in markets with intermediaries. Dealers buy products for the purpose of resale. A dealer's purchase of say 20 refrigerators at the beginning of a planning period does not necessarily mean that he is "out of the market" for the rest of the time. On the contrary, he will be interested in selling more. In the absence of other considerations, the number of products units a dealer wants to (or is able to) stock will determine the frequency with which he purchases them and the number he purchases at any one time. Thus, preference and indifference response functions corresponding to those discussed above are sufficient to account for all possible types of response to seller initiative aimed at producing initial contacts. Generally speaking, a preferential relationship between a supplier and a large dealer (e.g. a supermarket chain) is supported by contracts of supply.

A *"push-and-pull strategy"* implies that a planner has to define and prioritize target groups among dealers as well as end-buyers. Buyer initiative may be expected from dealers only. Figure 14.6. illustrates how a "push-and-pull" strategy consists of three sub-strategies:

- a dealer-related *buyer initiative media strategy,*
- a seller initiative strategy relating to dealers, i.e. a *dealer-related seller initiative media strategy,* and
- a seller initiative strategy relating to end-buyers, i.e. an *end-buyer-related media strategy.*

In addition, the figure illustrates that seller initiatives directed at end-buyers may affect a vendor company's sales volume in two ways:

1. They may *increase the extent of buyer initiative on the part of the dealers.* When this happens, seller initiatives directed at

end-buyers influence the basis for developing the company's buyer initiative strategy.

2. They may *enhance the effect of the company's seller initiatives directed at the dealers,* e.g. by increasing the response/contact ratio, the order/response ratio and/or the inquiry/response ratio.

The buyer initiative strategy and the dealer-related seller initiative strategy cannot be determined without taking the effects of the end-buyer-related seller initiative strategy into account. In other words, the sub-strategies are interdependent and cannot be developed separately.

Figure 14.6. The "push-and-pull" case: Seller/buyer initiative and sub-strategies

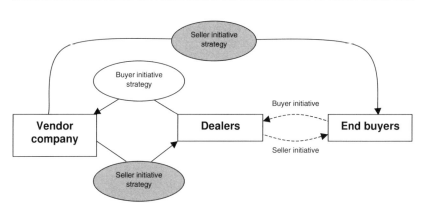

Figure 14.7. demonstrates how an *integrated dealer/end-buyer media strategy* might be developed by working in two steps, indicated by the figures 1 and 2:

- Step 1 involves outlining a buyer initiative strategy and a dealer-related, seller initiative strategy while ignoring the possible effects of a seller initiative strategy directed at end-buyers. Given the premise that both "push" and "pull" *are*

Media strategy development in markets with intermediaries 299

needed, the result of the two sub-strategies will not close the seller initiative gap.

- Since a seller initiative gap remains, step 2, entails outlining a seller initiative strategy related to end-buyers. Account must be taken of the influence of that strategy on

  - the extent of dealers' buyer initiative and on

  - the sales effect of the vendor company's dealer-related seller initiatives.

The question to be answered is: How much needs to be spent on closing the seller initiative gap by an enhanced buyer initiative one the part of dealers and a more effective dealer-related seller initiative?

300 Developing a media strategy: The Process

Figure 14.7. A two-step strategy development process

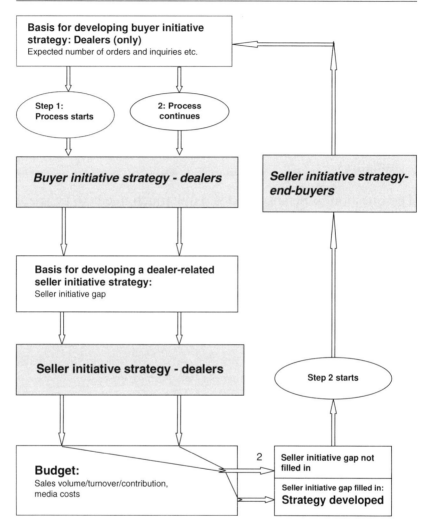

15. Developing a symbolization strategy

The final step in the planning process involves

developing a (content) symbolization strategy.

A company's content and media strategies provide a foundation for its symbolization strategy. This lays down guidelines for ensuring initial awareness as well as the continuous awareness that is necessary to fulfill its content goals.[46]

Symbolization as a communication tool

Figure 15.1. (which is a section of Figure 12.1. with some elements added) provides a basis for outlining the elements of a symbolization strategy in the following three ways:

It
- illustrates the role of symbolization in a communication process.
- demonstrates the role of symbolization as a communication tool.
- shows how initial awareness as well as interpretation is determined partly by properties of the symbol structure, and partly by buyer characteristics.

Firstly, the figure illustrates the *role of symbolization in a communication process.* Communication relies on exposure to symbols. As a communication tool, symbolization consists of an infinite choice of symbol structures. The term "symbol structure" has already been defined as a specific, mutually independent set of symbols that are related to each other in a unique way in time

302 *Developing a media strategy: The Process*

Figure 15.1. Relevance of "alphabet" and symbol structure properties for content symbolization

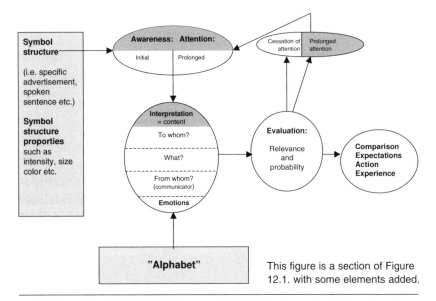

and/or space. Every single advertisement, brochure, poster, letter, facsimile, Internet home page and e-mail message may be regarded as a unique example of a symbol structure. Television commercials, radio spots, spoken sentences and gestures are examples of symbol structures arranged in chronological sequence.

Secondly, Figure 15.1. demonstrates the *crucial role of symbolization as a communication tool*. It is hardly an overstatement to say that appropriate symbolization is a *precondition* for a sales effect to occur. No matter how effective the task analysis, or how appropriate the target group strategy, content strategy and media strategy: all the effort that has been spent on these will be wasted if the content is not actually conveyed to the buyer. Every time a buyer is exposed to any kind of symbol structure represents "a moment of truth" which can have only two possible outcomes. Either the buyer actually becomes initially aware of the symbol structure, remains attentive long enough to interpret the communication symbols, experiences the appropriate emotions, etc. – or he does not. Only two kinds of solutions exist: effective and ineffective. Partial success at this stage is not an option. In every communication episode, the selection of the symbol structure is decisive.

Finally, Figure 15.1. illustrates that *initial awareness* as well as *interpretation* is *determined* partly by certain *properties* of the symbol structure, and partly by certain *buyer characteristics*. Examples of symbol structure properties that are likely to influence initial awareness are the size of an advertisement and color contrast. The factors that influence interpretation of symbols and symbol structures are referred to by the rather wide term "alphabet". For the purposes of this book, *"alphabet"* is defined as *the meanings and emotions that a buyer is predisposed to attach to particular symbols and symbol structures.* A person's "alphabet" is a result of social/cultural learning processes (socialization).

The scope and elements of a symbolization strategy

A symbolization strategy entails drawing up two sets of guidelines. These are designed:

1. to apply in connection with the preparation and selection of all symbol structures that are determined in advance.

2. to ensure that staff have sufficient symbolization competence.

Symbolization guidelines must be designed for the *preparation and selection of all symbol structures that are determined in advance*, as in the case of impersonal mass media such as advertisements, commercials, Internet home pages and support materials like brochures.

Guidelines in this group take the form of specifications or recommendations regarding certain symbol structure properties. They constitute a basis for in-house production of communication materials such as price lists and presentations, for "briefing" or "instructing" company staff and for developing symbolization solutions in the form of such things as specific advertisements, brochures, commercials or home pages, in cooperation with external suppliers like advertising agencies and printers.

The second group of guidelines consists of those that are designed to ensure sufficient *symbolization competence* on the part of the staff. When personal media and impersonal individual media are used, the important characteristics of each of the many contact episodes that occur during a planning period cannot be foreseen. In addition, each such communication episode represents an opportunity to *learn more about the buyer*. Consequently, symbolization cannot be determined ahead of time. Content elements and symbolization solutions are developed, selected and implemented on the spot, step by step and based on what are the results of a continuous learning process. In each such episode, selection and production of an appropriate symbolization structure depend entirely on the symbolization competence of the member of staff involved.

The guidelines for symbolization competence are concerned mainly with competence development and maintenance programs and with the development and use of working models indicating what should be done in various typical situations. A high level of symbolization competence includes awareness of the crucial role of symbolization and communication abilities. Such abilities comprise, among other things, knowledge about factors that determine initial awareness and interpretation (e.g. the buyer's "alphabet") as well as empathy, the ability to listen and oral communication skills. Symbolization competence also includes a thorough knowledge of existing symbolization guidelines, as well as the ability to use available working models.

The question of possible guidelines for symbol structures that are determined in advance will not be discussed in any detail here. Relatively few general statements can be made about appropriate symbol structure properties. Appropriate solutions are largely context-specific. However, a few examples relating to print mass media such as newspapers and magazines may serve to illustrate the nature of symbolization guidelines:

The scope and elements of a symbolization strategy 305

1. A degressive relationship between the size/the number of colors (i.e. 1, 2 or 4 colors) in an advertisement and the degree of awareness is an empirically well documented relationship.[47] That is, the percentage of a target group who notice an advertisement does not increase in proportion to increases in its size or to the number of colors used in it. In addition, the increase in awareness through larger sizes or more colors is most likely to be achieved with moderately or non-motivated buyers. If, as is normally the case, the cost of inserting an advertisement is proportional to its size or to the number of colors used, the relationship between size or number of colors and effect might suggest the following symbolization guideline:

"An advertisement should never be larger or have more colors than is considered necessary to convey its content. Only rarely will buying more space prove profitable."

2. A number of experience-based "rules of thumb" exist regarding how to ensure the readability of texts, including advertisements. These rules might serve as a basis for laying down certain guidelines such as:

   - Only use Roman fonts.
   - Avoid italics if at all possible (at most, they should only be used to accentuate one or two words).
   - Column breadth should be 8-12 cm.
   - Words should never be written with capital letters only.
   - White letters should not be used on a black or colored background.
   - Sentences should consist of no more than ten words.
   - Whenever possible, illustrations or photographs should be used to convey product properties.

The primary function of a symbolization strategy is to ensure that the *priority assigned to this communication tool reflects the far-reaching effect of symbolization decisions on the overall success of a marketing communication strategy.* One of its key aims must be to ensure that sufficient resources are spent on developing and maintaining the symbolization competence of company staff.

Competence enhancement will lead to improvements in two areas:

- communication processes between buyers and company managers/employees.

- the ability and skill of company staff to communicate with and make appropriate demands on external suppliers such as advertising agencies, printers and media companies.

Developing a symbolization strategy also involves considering possible implications for the organizational basis. Furthermore it entails estimating the symbolization costs, including costs incurred by internal symbolization competence development and maintenance efforts, fees to advertising agencies etc.

Working with the symbolization strategy a planner may come to realize that some (or all) of the preliminary assumptions made at earlier stages of the planning process regarding content symbolization are unrealistic. To the extent that this is the case it may be appropriate to make changes in the media strategy as well as in the estimates of media costs and sales volume/turnover/contribution.

16. Holistic strategic marketing communication planning: Some further issues

This chapter deals with some further issues relating to holistic strategic marketing communication planning. Firstly, five assumptions, made in the preceding chapters for the sake of simplicity, are set aside. Secondly, taking a multi-period perspective we discuss the question of adapting communication strategy to changes in the planning premises that normally occur from one planning period to another. Chapters 9-15 have discussed holistic, strategic planning merely in relation to one single planning period. Thirdly, the question of learning and control, which also arises in a multi-period perspective, is raised. Finally, the chapter touches upon the question of information sources and information use in strategic marketing communication planning.

Setting aside five simplifying assumptions

Vendor company is newly formed

So far we have assumed that the companies under consideration are established businesses, even though the strategic planning process outlined above also applies to *new* ones. However, there are some rather obvious differences in the general context in which planning takes place. The fact that a company has no "history" means that the market is completely unaware of its existence, of its offerings and of the "way to" its offerings. This means that new companies face varied and extensive communication tasks.

Heterogeneous relevance/supplier criteria

It has been assumed also that buyers within a business area will have the same relevance criteria and supplier criteria. *Heterogeneous criteria* make the *task analysis* more complex. Most importantly, in order to identify the communication tasks facing the vendor company buyers in a business area have to be segmented according to the nature and importance of relevance criteria, and the competitiveness of an offering has to be assessed in relation to each of the resulting segments. The identification of communication tasks is affected to the extent that the competitiveness of an offering varies from one segment to another. For example, there may be segments where competitiveness is so poor that no communication tasks exist. The results of the task analysis influence *how target groups are defined and prioritized* as well as subsequent decisions regarding *content, media* and *symbolization*.

Decision units have more than one member

The above discussion has treated *buyers* and *decision units* as if they were identical. However, it has also been emphasized that in many – if not most – markets, two or more persons influence the decision-making process leading to the purchase of products which they may then share. This is the case where several family members are involved in purchasing a video machine and where both purchasing manager and office staff are involved in buying office furniture. Usually the members of a decision unit will have different *roles* when it comes to introducing relevance criteria, providing information about offerings, discussing the pros and cons of offerings and making the final decision. These members may also have different relevance criteria and may attach different degrees of importance to various criteria.

Planning tasks are *more complex* when decision units include several persons. This is because planners cannot assume that they can communicate all relevant information about their offerings or companies to all members of decision units through single members of such units. In cases where relevance criteria and their relative importance vary between various categories of decision unit members (e.g. fathers and sons), tasks will include assessing the competitive strength of an offering in relation to each category. In order to identify communication tasks, planners must obtain a picture of the knowledge and beliefs that each category of member has about the offering. It is also important to obtain some insight into those categories of decision unit members, who, by virtue of their role in the unit, may be expected to show buyer initiative. Mothers carry out the *act* of purchasing many products on behalf of other family members. In an industrial market a purchasing manager may make inquiries on behalf of a group consisting of a CEO, a production manager, and a marketing manager.

The outcome of the task analysis affects how target groups are defined and prioritized and – consequently – which content elements are selected and how these are symbolized. The impact on media selection and use may be substantial. Different media may have to be used in order to reach different types of decision unit members. Purchasing managers and assistants may read journal X, while users do not. Similarly, mothers, fathers and teen-agers generally read different print media and are likely to make different uses of the Internet. A further complicating factor arises when inquiries made through one medium by one type of decision unit member have to be handled and followed-up by relating to other categories of unit member through other media. For example, production managers may tend to make inquiries about a new production management system over the telephone or Internet, while effective handling and follow-up require personal meetings with the company's production manager, CEO and marketing manager. Since a company's communication costs depend on how many individuals it has to communicate with, the size of units involved in purchasing decisions is also reflected in the costs.

The company offers a range of offerings: "Cross-communication", "separate communication" and "co-communication"

To conclude this discussion, we have treated holistic strategic planning on the assumption that the company in question markets one offering only. The implications for the planning process of setting this assumption aside depend on the circumstances.

The fact that a company offers *several varieties* of a product to a *given set of target groups* has minor implications. None of the planning tasks are substantially more complex. Increasing the number of varieties may, in fact, be regarded as tantamount to strengthening the offering insofar as buyers are given a wider range of options relating to properties such as size, color, price, etc. Of course, sales volume, turnover, contribution and costs have to be budgeted with these varieties in mind.

For companies that offer *different products* to *different target groups* the planning process becomes somewhat more complex. Sub-strategies for the various products are developed, not, however, without taking possible interdependencies into account. Each product makes its demands on the seller's organizational basis as far as staff, equipment and division of work are concerned, and cost interdependencies arise from the fact that communication activities for two or more products partly draw on the *same* staff (capacity, competence) and equipment. This means that the overall marketing communication strategy must be developed with these interdependencies in mind. Changes in the organizational basis must be coordinated. In the operating budget sales volume, turnover, contribution and communication costs must be allocated to the various products.

However, many companies offer two or more *different products* to more or less the *same* target groups. In such cases, additional favorable properties of the company's offerings arise from the fact that a buyer can purchase two or more products on the same occasion and thus save time, effort and, perhaps, money. However, the complexity of the planning process increases with each such interdependency. A sub-strategy applying to any one product can only be developed with due regard to the sub-strategies for the other products in the company's range of offerings. One reason for this is that when two or more products are offered to the same target group, the possibility arises for cross-communication. "*Cross-communication*" is similar to "cross-selling" and denotes the practice of *utilizing buyer or seller-initiated orders and inquiries related to one offering as opportunities for communication about other offerings*. For example, an incident where a purchasing assistant makes an inquiry about office chairs might be used as an opportunity to bring up questions about a possible need for new desks and/or shelves. Opportunities for carrying through this kind of cross-communication arise in connection with individual buyer initiative media only. In most cases, personal two-way communication media such as meetings and telephone are especially well suited for cross-communication. Assessing *"cross-communication sales potential"* is important because exploiting it can save costs and enhance sales. In most cases, cross-communication is far a more cost effective way of conveying knowledge about offerings than initially exposing buyers to marketing messages through seller initiatives which may result in inquiries, which in turn will have to be handled and followed up. The probability of making a sale may be enhanced when the buyer considers that it is more efficient to purchase one or more additional products on the same occasion.

Where there are opportunities to cross-communicate the marketing communication strategy for a product should be extended to include *a "cross-communication strategy"*. Developing such a strategy involves preparing the organization to make use of orders and inquiries related to one offering to communicate about other offerings. In addition, the task of budgeting entails estimating a cross-communication sales volume, a cross-communication turnover, a cross-communication contribution, and cross-communication costs. Among other things, handling orders and inquiries resulting from cross-communication initiatives may require additional personnel and technical capacity.

"Co-communication" takes place when *two or more offerings are communicated together to the same target group on the seller's initiative*. Such communication takes place when brochures or advertisements provide information about several different products, or when salesmen introduce potential customers to the complete range of his company's products. Co-communication

represents a further reason for developing sub-strategies coherently. Co-communication may be contrasted with "*separate communication*", where *each single offering is communicated separately.*

When developing a seller initiative strategy planners must decide to what extent and in what ways offerings should be communicated together or separately. Co-communication can often be justified on the grounds of lower communication costs. For example, a single telephone conversation which conveys three different offerings, A, B and C, is likely to take less time than three conversations conveying the three offerings separately. Similarly, one advertisement about two different offerings, A and B, is likely to cost less to make and distribute than two separate advertisements. The seller is more likely to make a sale when the buyer is given more efficient access to information. It is easier for the latter to acquire and study one brochure dealing with three products than three brochures, each dealing with one product.

The potential for co-communication depends on *"target group overlap"*. In this context, "overlap" refers to *the degree to which the company's target groups are potential buyers of two or more of the seller's offerings*. All other things being equal, the greater the degree of overlap, the greater the potential for co-communication. However, decisions regarding co-communication must also be taken with due regard to the communication capacity of the proposed medium or media. Conveying content relating to two or more offerings requires additional media time/space, which may not be available. "Getting the messages through" is, of course, a necessary condition for adopting co-communication solutions.

Planning cross-communication and co-communication.
The concept of a "locomotive offering"

The consequences of lifting the assumption about one single offering for the strategic planning process can be demonstrated by the following hypothetical example:

A company's range of products includes two offerings, A and B. The budgeted sales volume with regard to A is 10 000 prod-

Setting aside five simplifying assumptions 313

uct units. Starting the planning process with A, we estimate the buyer initiative sales potential to be 5 000 units. Consequently, the seller initiative gap for A is (10 000 – 5 000 =) 5 000 units. However, instead of turning directly to the question of developing a seller initiative strategy for A, we estimate how far the seller initiative gap might be closed by utilizing buyer-initiated orders and inquiries for B as opportunities for cross-communicating A.

This cross-communication sales potential depends on the degree of overlap relating to the target group for A and the target group for B. Furthermore, it depends on the communication capacity of the relevant buyer initiative media, i.e. the degree to which suitable opportunities for cross-communication arise (e.g. with regard to time available).

After having considered how to handle these opportunities effectively we conclude that 2 000 additional A-units can be sold through cross-communication. That is, the seller initiative gap for A is reduced to (10 000 – 5 000 – 2 000 =) 3 000 product units. Since possible seller initiatives for B may result in orders that represent additional opportunities for cross-communicating A, our next step now is to estimate how many additional A-units can be sold in this way *rather than* proceeding immediately to develop a seller initiative strategy for A, aimed at closing the gap of 3 000 units. As a result of this work we may conclude that an additional 1 000 A-units can be sold in this way, thus reducing the seller initiative gap for A to (3 000 – 1000 =) 2 000 units.

We could end the planning process by developing a seller initiative strategy for selling these 2 000 A-units. However, since we have started the planning process with A, we do not yet know whether any seller initiatives should be taken for B. If we had started the planning process with B, we would not have decided to take any seller initiatives for B without first having considered the cross-communication sales potential connected to utilizing buyer- and seller-initiated orders and inquiries directed at A. We cannot know that any seller initiatives should be taken for A without considering whether utilizing a seller initiatives for B would be more profitable. We are, in a sense, back where we started.

No matter which product in a product range we use to start a planning process, we are in a *dilemma*. It is impossible to take all possible alternatives into consideration simultaneously. Nor is it a viable option to compare all possible offerings and combinations of offerings as potential starting points, since the number of alternatives would be practically infinite and the process of considering them correspondingly interminable. The only practicable method is to start by choosing no more than two or three products and running through the whole planning process for these, including the development of one or more seller initiative strategies. Using the resulting sub-strategies as a premise, we proceed to estimate buyer initiative and cross-communication sales potentials for other company offerings in order to assess the extent to which we can expect to achieve our profit goal. If the strategy first developed is not considered satisfactory, the search for a satisfactory solution continues until one is found.

The offering used as a starting point should be suitable for creating an ample number of opportunities for cross-communicating other offerings in a company's range of products. The following characteristics may be used to identify such a *"locomotive offering"*:

1. Its *target groups overlap* to a *large degree* with the target groups for other offerings.

2. It is very *probable that seller initiatives will result in a relatively large number of orders and inquiries at relatively low communication cost*. That is, the company is able to take seller initiatives with a fairly large number of buyers, and is likely to achieve relatively large response/contact ratios, large purchase/response ratios and a high average purchase per buyer as a result of the competitive strength of the offering.

    More than one locomotive offering may be needed in order to fulfill a sales budget. However, the *stronger a locomotive offering is, the fewer such additional offerings are needed*. This means that the costs of communicating the offerings in a company's range of products may be substantially reduced

Setting aside five simplifying assumptions 315

as an effect of one (or a few) strong offering(s). Target group overlap and the communication capacity of appropriate seller initiative media will determine whether or not it will pay to co-communicate locomotive offerings.

We can sum up the above argument as follows. The fact that a company offers a range of products has the following major implications for the development of its media strategy. This development entails:

- ensuring that the organization is prepared to make full use of opportunities for cross-communication stemming from both buyer initiatives and seller initiatives.

- identifying possible locomotive offerings, and considering the relative advantages and disadvantages of co-communication and separate communication of offerings.

A task analysis thus includes identifying suitable locomotive offerings. Analyses made in connection with selecting and prioritizing target groups will indicate the extent of target group overlap. Changes in a company's organizational basis will be made with due regard to the fact that two or more offerings may make extra demands on such things as competence, and on personnel and equipment capacity. Communication activities for several offerings drawing on the same staff and equipment may lead to cost interdependency. Cross-communication and co-communication through personal and individual, impersonal media may, however, be limited in cases where different offerings require specialized competencies. Sub-budgets with estimated sales volume, turnover, contribution and marketing communication costs will have to be made for each of the offerings.

Adapting communication strategy to changed planning premises

Chapters 9-16 discussed holistic, strategic planning in relation to one single planning period. However, in a *multi-period perspective* the question arises of how to *monitor* and *adapt* the company's marketing communication *strategy to changes in the planning premises* occurring from one planning period to the next. It is obviously vital for a company to monitor and, if necessary, adapt its strategy if its marketing communication strategy is to remain profitable.

Broadly speaking, plans must take the following matters into account:

1. *Factors completely controlled by the company*, such as business areas, properties of the marketing offering(s), characteristics of the organizational basis, and profit goals.

2. *External conditions influenced by the company's marketing communication* activities, such as awareness of and beliefs about the company, its offerings, "ways to" the offerings and the extent of buyer initiative.

3. External conditions, which are entirely or largely unaffected by the company's *actions*. Examples are the number of buyers in various business areas or segments, the degree of product penetration and buyers' purchasing competence, the number of competitors and their offerings and communication activities, the exposure capacity of the various media and the costs incurred in using them.

It has already been pointed out how, in present day market conditions, considerable changes from one planning period to another can affect the premises that underlie a planning process. In holistic strategic planning, the planning premises analysis made in relation to each subsequent planning period monitors relevant changes in factors controlled by the company such as business areas and properties of the offering. The task analysis monitors and considers the implications of changes in external factors such as actual and potential demand, important relevance and supplier criteria, and competitive strength of offerings in various business areas, segments and target groups. Moreover, the company uses task analysis to keep track of the effects of its earlier marketing communication efforts. These effects can take the form of enhanced buyer competence, increased awareness and knowledge on the part of buyers about offerings and "the way to" offerings and larger buyer initiative ratios. Thus, in holistic strategic planning of marketing communication, one of the most *important functions* of the *planning premises analysis* and the *task analysis* is to monitor changes in *strategic premises*. In a multi-period perspective, the function of the task analysis is to *keep* the company's marketing communication planning *task oriented*, and so, potentially profitable. Most importantly, resources should only be spent on communication tasks actually facing the company. It has already been pointed out that the extent and nature of communication tasks may vary considerably over time as a result of such things as changes in the competitive strength of offerings and of the company's own marketing communication activities. For example, the greater the effects of the communication strategy that a company implements in one planning period, the more changes there will be in the planning premises that apply to its communication tasks in the following period.

By manifesting changes in the extent and nature of communication tasks over time, task analysis helps to ensure that decisions concerning amounts and allocation of resources are based on an understanding of the tasks that actually face the company, rather than on *past behavior*. This contrasts sharply with common practice, which often amounts to little more than "patching up" what has been done in the preceding period. Such practice is reflected in the literature, which pays scant attention to task orientation of resource use in marketing communication planning.

Some comments on pre- and post-control

The *question of learning* also arises in a multi-period perspective. Planners may be expected to become more efficient as they carry out and gain general experience from holistic strategic planning activities. The process itself is likely to help them to master concepts, models and methods, identify relevant circumstances, make sufficiently accurate estimates and draw reasoned and appropriate conclusions. However, learning may be considerably enhanced through systematic use of control procedures.

A distinction may be drawn between the following two types of control procedure, i.e. pre-control and post-control procedures:

1. *Pre-control* procedures are integrated into the planning process. Possible solutions are first identified at different stages of the process and then tested by comparing the effects that the company sets out to achieve with those that it actually realizes. Attempts to explain any discrepancy will often lead to ideas for improvements.

2. *Post-control* procedures are taken after a strategy has been implemented. Control and learning depend on company's having explicit expectations relating to such things as sales volumes, costs, extent of buyer initiative, purchase/order ratios and purchase/inquiry ratios. Comparing expectations with reality, and analyzing and explaining discrepancies stimulates learning.

There are numerous opportunities for taking *post-control* procedures. For example, advertisement texts and layouts may be tested using a representative sample or a focus group selected from one or more given target groups. Small-scale trials can be run to estimate the effects of seller initiatives such as those taken in the course of telephone or direct mail campaigns. It is similarly possible to evaluate the company's organizational preparedness to receive, handle and follow-up orders and inquiries. In some instances a company's entire strategy might even be evaluated on the basis of a controlled experiment. In that case the strategy is implemented and various effects assessed within a restricted geographical area that is representative of the total market, such as a town and its suburban and rural surroundings.

Some attention has been given in the literature to the possibility of using what are referred to *"communication goals"* in post-control procedures.[48] Communication goals are set in relation to factors that are supposed to be "clean" in the sense that they are mainly a function of the company's marketing communication activities. That is, the influence of other factors is relatively small.

Examples of such supposedly "clean" factors are

- the proportion of buyers in a given target group who are aware of the existence of a certain offering or

- the percentage of the buyers in the group who (correctly) believe that the price of the offering is $ 355.

Examples of communication goals are:

- "among buyers exposed to an advertisement in a medium, knowledge of the important properties A, B and C of the offering should increase from 30 to 50%."

- "the proportion of those exposed to a marketing message who intend to buy the offering should increase from 5 to 15 %."

While communication goals can be used as standards of comparison for checking the effects of any kind of communication activity, most discussion about them is to be found in the literature on advertising, in which hierarchies of effect are recommended as the primary basis for setting goals. A *"hierarchy of effect"* is a *hypothetical step-by-step progression in the effects of mass communication.* Two examples of such hierarchies are:[49]

1. High-involvement hierarchy (i.e. conviction before action):

> Lack of awareness → awareness → comprehension → conviction → action

2. Low-involvement hierarchy (i.e. action before conviction):

> Lack of awareness → awareness → action → comprehension → conviction

Factors that are "clean" in the sense explained above may not be easy to find. It has been argued that the effect of communication is heavily dependent on the competitive strength of the offering in question. This means that even the percentage of buyers in a business area who are aware of an offering is a function not only of communication activities, but also of the properties of the offering itself. Nevertheless, the main idea underlying the concept of a "communication goal" is, no doubt, useful. In principle, the "cleaner" an unfulfilled goal (i.e. the greater the degree to which it is a function of a company's marketing communication activities), the easier it is to decide whether its failure is due to ways in which communication tools have been used. For example, it may be possible to trace unsatisfactory results back to inappropriate decisions regarding content, symbolization and/or media use.

It should, however, be emphasized that communication goals can be used *only* as *complements* to – and *not* as *substitutes* for – the company's profit goal. That is, planners should be able to make at least reasonable assumptions regarding the relationship between communication goals and financial factors such as sales volume and costs. If this is not the case, communication goals are meaningless. For example, it is impossible to argue sensibly in favor of a communication goal aimed at increasing awareness of an offering among buyers in a target group, without referring to sales/turnover, contribution, and costs.

A holistic approach to planning strategic marketing communication creates *favorable conditions for using communication goals*. To a large extent, the planning process itself takes care of the problem of relating potential communication goals to relevant financial factors such as sales volumes and costs. The task analysis, in particular, entails a number of options. Existing communication tasks provide the starting point for planning how to use communication tools. The aim of the company's communication activities is to perform some of these tasks. That is, the process of identifying which communication tasks to carry out constitutes a substantial part of setting the communication goals themselves.

Information sources and information use

As in all planning and decision-making processes a holistic approach to planning strategic marketing communication calls on planners to describe, consider, estimate and predict – in short, decide what to assume about a considerable number of circumstances in relation to the forthcoming planning period. Among the relevant ones are:

- important relevance and supplier criteria in various target groups,
- the number of actual and potential buyers in a target group,
- the extent and nature of buyer initiative to expect from buyers in a target group,
- the relationship between the degree of awareness of an offering in a target group and sales volume,
- the degree of awareness of an offering in a target group, and:
- costs incurred by using the various media.

In carrying through the planning process a planner bases his understanding, beliefs, estimates, judgments etc. on information about *past* events or – at best – updated information about the present. Several sources offer information about relevant considerations and circumstances. A distinction may be drawn between:

1. the planner's experience as a source of informed judgments,

2. the planner's everyday observations derived from contact with his own organization and with the business environment outside it.

3. various kinds of systematic analyses based on primary and secondary sources involving the organization (internal analyses) or the business environment (external analyses).

Informed judgments are based on experience and consideration of the marketing tasks. Thus, reasoning based on knowledge about how product penetration has developed up to the present time may lead to insights about future development. Alternatively, planners may draw on experience in other kinds of markets. For example, experience gained in transformation markets for various kinds of large constructions may indicate that ability to deliver on time and complaint settling are very important relevance criteria in the market for steel constructions.

The second type of information comes from *ordinary internal and external observation and communication.* This includes anything of relevance that can be learned through daily observation and contact with company staff, dealers, end-buyers and members of and experts attached to relevant trade organizations. Information may also be obtained from such media as newspapers, magazines, trade journals, broadcasting and the Internet. This kind of intelligence is not confined to what may be acquired through purposeful research. Planners may simply be selectively perceptive to relevant information that happens to come their way in the course of everyday routines, shared activities, reading newspapers, listening to the radio etc. On the other hand, it will sometimes be appropriate or necessary to take active steps to seek information in sources such as books, trade journals and the Internet. In order to obtain insight into relevant market conditions, planners may intentionally initiate dialogues with salesmen, other staff members or dealers who may be useful sources of information about such matters as compe-

Information sources and information use 323

titors' offerings and important relevance and supplier criteria. There are two types of *systematic analysis*. These are:

- secondary (desk research) or
- primary.

Secondary analyses are based on information already available from various internal and external sources. Examples of internal sources are

- various kinds of documents and reports such as copies of customer correspondence (letters, e-mails and facsimiles),
- market analysis reports,
- written strategic and operative plans,
- customer indexes,
- statistics of orders, inquiries, follow-ups and sales, accounts/ accounts analyses, and budgets.

Examples of external sources are

- trade indexes and analyses and various kinds of statistics in the public domain, such as population, production and trade statistics taken by national or regional public institutions,
- surveys published by media companies, trade organizations or research institutes regarding buyers' behavior and attitudes media (e.g. newspaper and magazine reading, television viewing, radio listening), and
- competitors' annual reports, price lists, catalogs and other advertising material.

Primary analyses provide new information based on direct observation, interviews or some technical method of measurement. For example, methods exist for measuring

- the number of unsuccessful telephone calls to a company (number occupied),
- the number of rings that occur before the telephone is answered,

- the number of unanswered calls,
- the number of calls where the buyer did not get in contact with the right person etc.
- Home page traffic is registered automatically.

Some aspects of buyers' in-store behavior can be observed directly. Buyers can be asked questions about such things as

- relevance criteria,
- awareness of and beliefs about offerings,
- whether an offering is the subject of preference, indifference or rejection,
- awareness, reading and comprehension of advertisements, and viewing and comprehension of television commercials etc.
- a company's accessibility. Its handling and follow-up of orders and inquiries.

A distinction may be drawn between quantitative and qualitative analyses according to whether or not the relevant factors can be quantified. One type of quantitative analysis is a survey based on a representative sample of a relevant "population", e.g. a target group, in which the respondents are interviewed on the basis of a multiple-choice questionnaire. In general, smaller, but not necessarily representative, samples are used in qualitative analyses, which may take the form of individual, indepth interviews and group discussions (e.g. focus groups) based on "open" interview guides. Qualitative analyses may be used to identify such things as important relevance and supplier criteria, incorrect product beliefs, and competitive weaknesses and strengths of the company's offerings and those of its competitors.

In some cases it may be appropriate to follow-up with a quantitative survey charting the spread of e.g. a relevance criterion or a certain product belief.

For further insight into forms and methods of analysis the reader is referred to the market analysis literature.[50]

Information sources and information use 325

Obtaining valid and reliable information about every relevant circumstance is, of course, *impossible*. When making decisions regarding use of information sources there are several factors to consider:

- Information about some *"critical" factors* may be more useful than information about others.

- Some decisions may be *less dependent* than others on planners obtaining *exact information*. For example, a content element regarding a certain property X of an offering may be given top priority regardless of whether 90% or 60% of the members of a target group are aware of X.

- While certain sources of information may be theoretically relevant, tight *time limits* often make it impossible to utilize them in practice. Theoretically useful information is often out of date before practical use can be made of it.

- The *costs* of obtaining information, in terms of time and money, may be prohibitive.

- There may be insoluble *methodological problems*.

It is easier to advocate a balance between information utility and information cost than it is to achieve it. Information utility is particularly difficult to assess. Nevertheless, attempts to maintain such a balance may help to keep resources spent on information collection at an appropriate level. It may also ensure that those resources are focused on important questions and on decisions that depend on access to accurate information. The view held here is that, in practice, the various kinds of information sources should be utilized in the following order of priority:

1. Informed judgments.
2. Ordinary *internal* observation and communication.
3. Ordinary *external* observation and communication.
4. Secondary analyses based on *internal* sources.

5. Secondary analyses based on *external* sources.
6. Primary *internal* analyses.
7. Primary *external* analyses.

The above list of priorities should not be taken to mean that external primary analyses should only be used on rare occasions. Rather, the order of priority suggested above should be taken as a guide to ensuring that the benefits of informed judgment, everyday observation and personal contacts are put to good use. The experience of planners and other staff represents a wealth of valuable knowledge about markets, customers, competitors, suppliers and the company 's organizational basis. In the author's view, *companies frequently underestimate the value of their employees' informed judgment and knowledge acquired in the course of everyday contact with customers and other business associates*. One possible explanation for this may be the prevalence of positivist approaches in the literature and in university courses dealing with market analysis, where the pursuit of scientific rigor has favored "objective," inter-subjective, representative and, preferably, quantitative information. Writers have largely ignored the potential importance and appropriate use of staff acumen derived from experience, everyday observation and communication in the marketplace. Many would not even regard these as valid sources of information in practical planning and problem solving.

Despite the failure of theorists to recognize the above kind of staff knowledge as a resource, it is, nevertheless, widely used in practice. Indeed, business life would be brought to a halt without it. However, when a company undervalues this resource by failing to give its staff sufficient credit for using their knowledge and experience of market conditions, their organization's potential as a knowledge base will be insufficiently utilized or developed. It is futile for a company's staff to be alert and receptive to relevant information if no one seems to want to hear about it. They cannot be expected to interpret, remember and disseminate that information unless employers show interest and willingness to learn from it and apply it for the benefit of the company.

Attitudes and practices such as those described above place unreasonable and inappropriate restrictions on the use of informal, modest, small-scale and low-cost inquiries of the following kinds:

- conversations or group discussions with a few dealers and/or end-buyers,
- copy tests (e.g. of text readability) based on a few representatives of a target group,
- tests of accessibility and order/inquiry handling – and
- follow-up based on a calls to a few customers.

The present author's view is that decisions should be made on the basis of all relevant circumstances. If material considerations are ignored because they cannot be supported by "scientifically valid" data, decision-making will suffer from a dysfunctional "data-dependency". Paradoxically, lack of "scientifically incontrovertible" information will lead to fewer circumstances being considered and so, to a more superficial process of decision-making.

Planning, like all problem solving, involves the exercise of human judgment. Information should never be dismissed as "unworthy of consideration" without first being considered, however cursorily. Since the rejection of any source of information is itself a matter of judgment, all sources of information must, in principle, be taken into account at some stage of a planning and problem solving process. This means that planners cannot shirk responsibility for their own decisions by insisting that some relevant information was not worth considering and that those decisions were *determined* exclusively by scientifically valid data. They can never claim that they "had no choice".

17. Summing up a holistic approach to strategic marketing communication planning

This chapter rounds off our discussion of holistic strategic marketing communication planning. It contains summaries of the concept of marketing communication, the planning process and the elements of a holistic marketing communication strategy. In this connection some aspects connected to the task of budgeting will be dealt with more fully. Discussion will include ways of using the concepts, models and procedures suggested earlier. It will be emphasized that what has been presented is meant to serve mainly as a framework for continuous *real-time* monitoring and development of a company's marketing communication strategy. Reasons will be given for having ignored long-term communication effects and long-range planning in this book. The chapter concludes with some comments and suggestions relating to adopting holistic approaches to strategic planning in an organization.

A holistic approach to strategic marketing communication planning: A summary

Figure 17.1. outlines a holistic concept of marketing communication introduced in this book. The figure indicates the crucial relevance of buyer initiative, cross-communication, and accessibility and highlights the processes connected to receiving, handling and following up buyer-initiated as well as seller-initiated orders and inquiries as *core* elements of a marketing communication strategy. Box 17.2. lists the elements of a holistic marketing communication strategy.

330 *Summing up a holistic approach*

Figure 17.1. A holistic view of marketing communication compared to the prevailing, narrower view

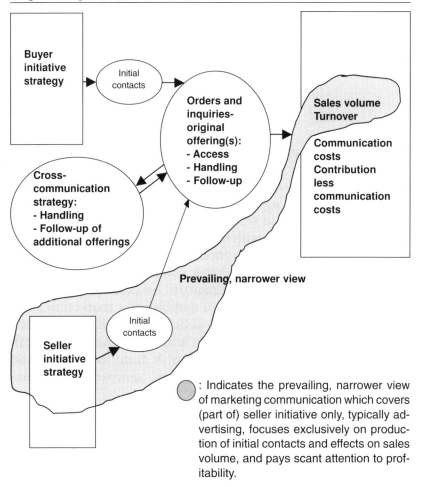

At this stage, it may be appropriate to add a few points regarding the budget and the underlying budgeting process.

Box 17.3. illustrates a *marketing communication cost budget*, while Box 17.4. shows an *operating budget*. For the sake of simplicity, both illustrations are based on the assumption that the company in question offers a range of standardized products. However, sub-budgets for the various products are not shown. As appears from Box 17.3., costs are specified according to type of communication, i.e. medium, in marketing communication cost budgets. Furthermore, a distinction is drawn between media and symbolization costs, as well as between costs incurred as a result of buyer initiative and seller initiative, respectively. Box 17.4. outlines an operating budget that shows the extent to which sales, turnover, contribution, and contribution less marketing communication costs can be expected to stem from buyer initiatives and seller initiatives respectively.

The "structure" of these budgets is clearly consistent with the main ideas underlying a holistic, strategic planning process, discussed in Chapters 9-15. Most importantly, first priority is given to appropriate handling and follow-up of buyer-initiated orders and inquiries, in the interests of achieving the highest possible sales/cost ratio. Second priority is given to cross-communication, while seller initiative takes third place. In the process, estimates are made of sales volumes and costs connected to buyer initiative, cross-communication and seller initiative, using preliminary budgets prepared in the planning premises analysis as starting points. The cost budget specifies costs incurred in connection with each of the media selected. It also identifies costs attributable to media and symbolization, handling and following up buyer initiatives, cross-communication activities and seller initiatives, respectively. Similarly, operating budgets summarize the result of estimates made during the process so as to reflect how planners expect buyer initiative, cross-communication, and seller initiative, respectively, contribute to the operating profit. The operational accounts are itemized accordingly, making it possible to compare estimates and actual results.

A framework for describing, monitoring and developing a company's marketing communication strategy

The present author's view of who should be regarded as a planner, of planners' working conditions and of the planning process itself was presented in Chapter 1. It was emphasized that:

Box 17.2. Elements of a holistic marketing communication strategy

I. Guidelines with regard to the use of marketing communication tools: Media and content symbolization

A. Buyer initiative strategy

1. **Preparatory plan for receiving handling and following up orders and inquiries, and for cross-communication.**

a. Target groups (end-buyers, dealers), sub-target-groups (in case of for example heterogeneity among buyers with regard to relevance or supplier criteria). Target group overlap related to various offerings.

b. Task analysis: Expected actual and potential demand, turnover and contribution potential in business areas/target groups. Extent and nature of communication tasks. Initiative ratio. Expected buyer initiative (extent and nature of orders and inquiries), number of initiatives requiring follow-up etc. Cross-communication opportunities: Number and nature.

c. Media to be used for receiving, handling and following up orders and inquiries, and for cross-communication.

d. Required degree of accessibility.

e. Estimated order/initiative ratios, inquiry/initiative ratios, purchase/order ratios etc.

f. Required capacity (staff, ICT equipment etc.) and competencies/skills (staff).

g. Content platform(s).

h. Content symbolization guidelines.

i. Support material (brochures, catalogs, overhead projector etc.).

j. Working models (regarding handling/follow-up of orders/inquiries, and cross-communication, among other things concerning media use, use of support material and work organization).

B. Seller initiative strategy

2. **Action plan for producing initial contacts**

a. Target groups (end users, dealers) and sub-target-groups (where such things as heterogeneous relevance or supplier criteria are present). Target group overlap related to various offerings.

b. Task analysis: Extent and nature of communication tasks.

c. Seller initiative gap. Estimated response/contact ratios, purchase/response ratios, average purchase per buyer, required contact ratio etc. Overall exposure goal and sub-exposure-goals.

d. Media to be used : Extent, order, and timing.

e. Required capacity (staff, ICT equipment etc.) and competencies/skills (staff): Controllable media, personal and impersonal.

f. Content platform(s).

g. Content symbolization guidelines.

A framework for describing, monitoring and developing 333

h. Support material (brochures, catalogs, overhead projector etc.) and working models: Personal media.

3. **Preparatory plan for receiving handling and following up resulting orders and inquiries, and for cross-communication.**
   a. Target groups (end-buyers, dealers), sub-target-groups (for example, where buyers have different relevance or supplier criteria). Target group overlap related to various offerings.
   b. Task analysis: Extent and nature of communication tasks. Expected extent and nature of resulting orders and inquiries, expected number of orders and inquiries requiring follow-up etc. Cross-communication opportunities: Number and nature.
   c. Media to be used for receiving, handling and following up order and inquiries, and for cross-communication.
   d. Required degree of accessibility.
   e. Estimated order/initiative ratios, inquiry/initiative ratios, purchase/order ratios etc.
   f. Required capacity (staff, ICT equipment etc.) and competencies/skills (staff).
   g. Content platform(s).
   h. Content symbolization guidelines.
   i. Support material (brochures, catalogs, overhead projector etc.).
   j. Working models (regarding handling/follow-up of orders/inquiries, and cross-communication, among other things concerning media use, use of support material and work organization).

II. Required changes in other sub-strategies

In
a. business areas.
b. offering(s).
c. organizational basis, relating to e.g. 1. equipment (type, capacity), 2.staff (number/capacity, type, attitudes, competence), 3. organization (distribution of tasks and responsibilities, management, interaction between staff and equipment), and 4. competence development (with regard to content competence/preparedness, media competence/preparedness, symbolization competence etc.)

III. Operating and marketing communication budgets

Overall operating budget and overall marketing communication budget as well as sub-budgets (related to e.g. business areas, target groups, and offerings).

The budgets specify sales volumes, turnover, contribution and marketing communication costs (media and symbolization costs) attributable to buyer and seller initiatives and cross-communication, respectively, as well as contribution less marketing communication costs.*

*: See also Box 17.4. and Box 17.5.

1. Any manager or employee involved in describing, monitoring or developing a company's marketing communication strategy is considered a "planner". Thus, a "planner" is not just a specialist who is in charge of developing a company's marketing communication strategy.

2. Marketing communication planning involves complex problem solving in a fast-changing environment, which is characterized by uncertainty. A realistic aim for planners can, at best, be to develop and maintain a *satisfactory* – rather than an optimal – strategy.

3. Strategic management is not a clear-cut, two-step process of making a comprehensive written strategic plan which is subsequently implemented and followed-up. While planning and subsequent implementation *may* consist of two major, distinct events, generally it takes place *incrementally, in a continuous, step-by-step process of searching, experimenting and learning*. In this process, planning and implementation are often interwoven activities. This is the case when, for example, suggestions for improved handling of inquiries may be prompted in the process of implementing a recently agreed plan. How much should be put down in writing will depend on circumstances. In an ever-changing and complex environment, written plans tend to date rather quickly.

The perspective, views, concepts, hypotheses, procedures, and models put forward in this book should accordingly be taken as a *framework for describing, monitoring, developing and implementing changes in a company's marketing communication strategy* – no more and no less. The fact that the framework is holistic does not imply considering and working with all elements of the strategy simultaneously and on all occasions. Nor does it mean that all the concepts and hypotheses suggested here should be taken into consideration in every planning situation – or that every part of every one of the models suggested should be used, or that all the procedural steps suggested should be taken. Consequently, the summary in Box 17.2. should be taken as *aides mémoire* only.

A framework for describing, monitoring and developing 335

Box 17.3. Illustration of a possible way of itemizing a marketing communication cost budget

	Media costs attributable to:			Symbolization costs:	Overall communication costs:
	Buyer initiative: Receipt, handling and follow-up of orders and inquiries	Seller initiative			
		Production of initial contacts	Receipt, handling and follow-up of resulting orders and inquiries		
Media:					
Individual/personal:					
Telephone	350	20	15	-	385
Personal calls	-	60	20	-	80
In-house meetings*					
....	20	15	5	2	42
Individual/impersonal:					
Facsimile/E-mail	110	-	25	-	135
Letters*	20	-	10	2	32
....	5	-	-	-	5
Mass/personal:					
In house meetings*	10	-	5	2	17
Mass/impersonal:					
Addressed direct mail	-	10	5	10	25
Trade journal advertising	-	30	5	4	39
....	-	10	5	-	15
Total	515	145	95	20	775

*: Support material included (e.g. brochures or other advertising material)

The figures (in $ 1000) relate to a vendor company operating in an industrial market. They are purely fictitious and presented for illustrative purposes only. Please note that fixed, stepped as well as variable costs are included. For the sake of simplicity costs attributable to cross-communication are not specified separately.

The framework presented here may be used to obtain insights into a company's total strategic "pattern", and to prepare major *strategic turnarounds*. It may also be used in *a piecemeal process of continuous, incremental strategy development* to identify, evaluate and develop one or more strategic elements that have the potential for improvement. The concepts, models, and hypotheses presented here may be found useful in isolation from each other. In their search for better advertising media or improved accessibility, inquiry handling or cross-communication, planners may consider and apply the particular ones that seem most applicable to their own needs. However, *whenever planners attempt to develop part of a strategy, they must recognize the interplay between strategic elements and not lose sight of their company's overall marketing communication strategy*. There are no recipes for how to use a framework. Planners themselves must accept responsibility for such decisions as selecting how many and which strategic elements to work with, which models to use, and which premises to consider.

The question of sources and use of information was discussed above. It was emphasized that decisions should be made on grounds of relevance, independently of whether or not "scientifically valid" information about a condition is available. In other words: *Good questions are more important than exact and certain answers*. The suggested framework may serve as a useful source of "good" questions.

Many of the questions arising from attempts to apply the framework will be unfamiliar to planners and may be impossible or, at least, difficult to answer precisely and with certainty. This is likely to be the case when a question is raised for the first time, and there is little or no experience on which to draw. For example, estimating a buyer initiative and cross-communication potential for the first time may require some effort. The same may hold true of ratios such as buyer initiative ratios, purchase/inquiry ratios, and response/contact ratios. Communication cost budgeting may also be daunting, partly because no existing charts of account are itemized in a way that corresponds to the cost elements in a marketing communication cost budget. A further complication arises from the fact that estimating fixed and stepped costs, such as wages, calls for some insight into how personnel are assigned to various administrative tasks and tasks connected to marketing communication. Evaluating and developing buyer initiative and cross-communication strategies involves estimating such things as the number of expected buyer-initiated orders and inquiries and the number of cross-communication opportunities these initiatives represent. However, the view taken here is that *any answer to a relevant question is preferable to not posing the question at all. In the absence of such questions, learning cannot occur.*

Chapter 16 concluded with the view that planners cannot escape responsibility for selection and interpretation of whatever information underlies their decisions, and that they should therefore treat all sources of information as deserving of equal attention. A corollary of this is that where limited time or resources prevent a planner from obtaining some desired information, he should resort to making an informed judgment. The moment such a judgment appears to be erroneous, learning occurs.

Comments on long-term effects and long-range planning

The *framework* suggested in this book is specifically intended to facilitate *continuous monitoring* and *development* of a company's marketing communication strategy *in real time*, based on *real-time* information. Neither long-term communication effects nor long-range planning have been emphasized. In discussions and examples we have assumed a planning period of one year or less. The aim has been to obtain and maintain short-term profitability.

Reasons for this deliberate lack of emphasis on long-term effects and long-range planning are given below. However, the concept of "long-term effect" is rather ambiguous and needs to be clarified before discussing it further. A distinction may be drawn between three types of long-term effects of communication:[51]

338 Summing up a holistic approach

Box 17.4. *Illustration of a possible itemization of a summary operating budget specifying marketing communication costs and contribution less marketing communication costs*

attributable to:	Sales volume (Units)	Turnover*	Contribution**	Marketing communication costs	Contribution less marketing communication costs
		(All figures in $ 1 000)			
Buyer initiative: Receipt, handling and follow-up of orders and inquiries	3 500	35 000	17 500	5 000	12 500
Seller initiative: Production of initial contacts and receipt, handling and follow-up of resulting orders and inquiries	300	3 000	1 500	1 000	500
Total	3 800	38 000	19 000	6 000	13 000
Media costs connected to administrative work etc.					1 000
All other costs***					8 000
Operating profit					**4 000**

The figures relate to a vendor company operating in an industrial market. They are purely fictitious and presented for illustrative purposes only. Please note that fixed, stepped as well as variable costs are included. For the sake of simplicity sales volume, turnover, contribution and costs attributable to cross-communication are not specified separately.

Assumptions:
*: Price per product unit: $ 10 000.
**: Variable production cost per product unit = $ 5 000. Contribution per product unit = $ 5 000.
***: Fixed costs connected to production, administrative functions etc.

The budget reflects a company operating in business areas where product penetration is relatively high. The degree of penetration of the company's offerings is also relatively high. The extent of buyer initiative is relatively high as 96% of the sales volume is attributable to buyer initiative. On the other hand, the prospects of profitable seller initiatives are relatively modest.

"Duration effects": A duration effect is an effect *that lasts from one planning period into one or more subsequent periods.* That is, it is created in one period and persists in the following period(s), in which it may remain constant, increase or decrease. For example, preferences created in one planning period may endure and bring about buyer-initiated purchases in a following period. As a result of favorable word-of-mouth or product visibility, the effect of the preferences created may even increase over time.

"Delayed effects": A delayed effect is an effect *that comes about at some point in time after the planning period,* e.g. in the following planning period. For instance, a buyer who is not in the market for cars in one planning period may nevertheless learn enough about a specific model to initiate an inquiry in the following period.

"Cumulative effects": These *build up over time as a result of communication activities carried through in a number of consecutive planning periods.* A buyer's beliefs about a company, for instance, may be created piecemeal over several planning periods. At some point in time, the accumulated image may bring about a purchase.

None of these three types of effect have been considered directly in the pages of this book. However, the framework *indirectly* serves to ensure that potential duration effects are properly taken care of and exploited by focusing on the importance of good accessibility and appropriate handling and follow-up of buyer initiatives. Delayed and accumulative effects have been ignored and the focus has been on responding to buyer initiatives and on short-term effects of seller initiatives. This focus is felt to be justified because the modern world of business is too volatile and complex to be predicted with any reasonable degree of completeness and certainty more than, at most, a year or so ahead. In a relatively short time, most companies are likely to have different ranges of products – and new competitors, with new competing products, are likely to enter the market. These competitors will sometimes employ presently unforeseeable communication channels and methods. What kind of beliefs any company would like buyers to have about its offerings and itself over the next two, three or four years can only be a matter for idle speculation.

A further argument in favor of adopting a short-term focus is that communication *activities whose profitability rested on delayed or cumulative effects would always be directed at buyers who were not "in the market" for the product in question.* This is the modern equivalent of "sowing on stony ground" since such buyers are rarely likely to take notice of, interpret or remember communication messages. In most cases, it pays to wait until buyers enter the market and become more receptive to marketing communication. Given a holistic approach to planning strategic marketing communication, *one of the important functions of task diagnosis is precisely that of continuously monitoring the entry of buyers into the market.* It is possible to carry out the process of identifying and communicating with buyers at this point at relatively low cost. Consequently, it makes no sense to consider costly communication activities aimed at creating delayed or cumulative effects.

Despite the point made above, some stable and predictable situations may arise in which planners should consider the possibility of exploiting delayed or cumulative effects. In such cases the planning horizon could be extended to include two or more successive planning periods. However, the view held here is that such conditions very rarely arise.

Introducing holistic strategic planning in an organization

In general, a manager who wishes to introduce a holistic approach to planning strategic marketing communication in his company should be prepared to undertake the following tasks:

1. *Developing staff competence:* Managers must take steps to ensure that all staff members involved are able to contribute to

the planning process by developing sufficient understanding of the framework and by acquiring appropriate skills in using the various tools (concepts, models etc.) required for this purpose.

2. *Reorganizing :* A company's transition to holistic strategic planning is likely to call for at least some changes in its distribution of tasks and responsibilities, lines of communication, and budgeting routines in order to obtain the necessary degree of coordination, horizontal communication, and flexibility in resource allocation. Appointing a marketing communication manager might facilitate the process of transition.

3. *Motivating and dealing with resistance:* Managers and employees should develop the necessary determination to contribute to the planning process. In most organizations some resistance will need to be overcome and replaced with positive attitudes. Such resistance may be due to professional disagreements or to fear of failure to master new tasks. Generally speaking, sectional attitudes to marketing communication, planning and implementation are deeply rooted in functional organizations with separate departments for advertising, sales, information and so on. In such environments, fear of losing resources, status or prestige may easily bolster resistance to change. Other barriers to innovation include aversion to doing things in unfamiliar and perhaps more demanding ways, hostility towards changing priorities concerning time and effort allocated to various tasks and reluctance to consider changes in the relationship between one's company and its advertising agency.

The three *strategic development tasks* outlined above may be approached by a manager in many different ways, the most effective of which depends, among other things, on the degree of resistance to innovation:

In cases where there is no *resistance, or where resistance is moderate*, there may be a basis for concentrating on a *formally planned,*

342 *Summing up a holistic approach*

open development program in which all appropriate staff members participate. In such a program, the tasks of building competence, reorganizing and dealing with resistance may be solved in a relatively short time through a coherent set of smaller development projects carried out by groups of staff. Each project focuses on explicitly formulated tasks and learning goals suited to the participants. Real planning tasks facing the company might be incorporated in the projects, so that a holistic strategic planning process is initiated through the program.

In cases where there is *considerable resistance* to change, tasks may have to be approached in a more circumspect manner, taking and building on opportunities for innovation as they arise. A holistic approach to strategic marketing communication planning may provide managers with a *framework for developing their own personal "agendas"*, listing *areas where there is room for improvement* in the company's planning process and marketing communication strategy. For instance, a company manager may conclude that:

- no one has compiled a sufficiently comprehensive inventory of the important elements in the company's offerings.
- no attempt has been made to assess the competitive strength of the company's offerings.
- the extent and nature of buyer initiative has never been identified or even estimated.
- the company lacks insight into the nature and extent of the communication tasks that it should be carrying out.
- there is little or no focus on accessibility or on how orders and inquiries should be handled and followed up.
- advertising budgets are based on past practice, without any attention to whether these resources have been spent effectively or profitably.
- nothing resembling a content platform has ever been worked out.
- no attempt has been made to make a marketing communication budget.

On the basis of such an agenda, a manager may *exploit favorable*

Introducing holistic strategic planning in an organization 343

opportunities of moving the organization in the desired direction, for example:

- by raising questions and following up answers to these.

"What do we really know about the extent to which buyers are aware of our offerings and about what beliefs those buyers hold about them?"
"How can we justify such a large advertising budget?"

- by asking to have something looked into and analyzed.

"I would like to know how many buyer-initiated orders and inquiries we received last year, and what sales volume they represent."
"Would you please work out a suggestion as to how we can evaluate our accessibility."

- by asking for something to be done/initiating small-scale projects.

"I suggest that we ask "Tele-X" to make technical measurements regarding our accessibility. Please include the switchboard, the order, production, marketing and sales departments as well as all top and middle managers."
"I think it would be a good idea to get a grip on our overall communication costs. We could form a group and have it report back in, say, two weeks' time."

- by taking piecemeal initiatives to raise staff understanding and acceptance of a holistic approach to marketing communication planning.

"There is much more to an offering than the price and the product. I know of a way to find out all there is to it."
"Let's not forget that buyers themselves make a considerable number of inquiries and place a lot of orders on their own initiative. And we must bear in mind that these are low-cost orders and inquiries."

- by recruiting staff who are familiar with – and well disposed towards – a holistic approach to strategic marketing communication planning.

As a result of such initiatives, an organization may gradually adopt a holistic view of marketing communication.

The hypothetical scenarios discussed in these pages are intentionally somewhat extreme. Most situations in the real world will be less so. They will also vary considerably. There may be considerable opposition to some ideas or procedures. Others may attract less resistance or none at all. Attitudes in some parts of an organization may be very hostile, while staff in other parts may be more favorably disposed to change – and even enthusiastic. In such cases managers may choose a strategy which combines relatively open and formally planned development projects with more modest initiatives that grasp and build on opportunities for innovation as they arise.

References

Aaker, D. A., Batra, R. & Myers, J. G.: *Advertising Management.* Upper Saddle River, N.J. 1992.
Aaker, D. A. & Biel, A. L. (eds.): *Brand equity and advertising. Advertising's role in building strong brands.* Hillsdale, New Jersey 1993.
Allen, C. T. & Madden, J.: *A closer look at classical conditioning.* J. of Consumer Research, 12, 1985.
Anderson, J. C. & Narus, J. A.: *Business market management – Understanding, creating, and delivering value.* New York 1999.
Assael, H.: *Consumer behavior and marketing action.* Cincinnati, Ohio 1992.
Batra, R., Myers, J. G. & Aaker, D.: *Advertising management.* Upper Saddle River, N.J. 1995.
Berry, D.: *Marketing mix for the 90's adds an S and 2 C's to the four P's.* Marketing News, Dec., 1990.
Berry, L. L. & Parasuraman, A.: *Marketing services. Competition through quality.* Lexington, Mass. 1991.
Blackwell, R. D.: *Integrated marketing communications.* I Frazier, G. L. & Sheth J. N. (eds.): «Contemporary views on marketing practice», Lexington, Mass. 1987.
Bradley, F.: *Marketing management. Providing, communicating and delivering value.* London 1995.
Brownlie, D. T. & Saren, D.: *The four P's of the marketing concept: Prescriptive, polemical, permanent and problematic.* European Journal of Marketing, 4, 1992.
Chaffey, D., Mayer, R., Johnston, K. & Ellis-Chadwick, F.: *Internet Marketing.* Harlow 2000.
Churchill, G. A.: *Marketing research.* Hindale, Ill. 1994.
Clabaugh Jr., M. G. & Forbes, J. L.: *Professional selling: A relationship approach.* St. Paul 1992.
Colley, R. H.: *Defining advertising goals for measured advertising results.* New York 1961.
Comer, J. M.: *Sales management: People and profit.* Boston 1991.
Deighton, J.: *The interaction of advertising and evidence.* J. of Consumer Research, 11, Dec., 1984.
DeLozier, M. W.: *The marketing communication process.* New York 1976.
Fill, C.: *Marketing communications. Contexts, contents and strategies.* London 1999.
Gross, A. C., Banting, P. M., Meredith, L. N. & Ford I. D.: *Business marketing.* Houghton Mifflin, Boston 1993.
Grönroos, C.: *Service management and marketing.* Lexington, Mass. 1990. (New ed. New York 2000)

Gummesson, E.: *The part-time marketer.* Center for Service Research, Karlstad, Sweden 1990.
Hutt, M. D. & Speh, T. W.: *Business marketing management: A strategic view of industrial and organizational markets.* New York 1995.
Jackson, B.: *Winning and Keeping Industrial Customers. The Dynamics of Customer Relationships.* Lexington Mass. 1985.
Keeley, A.: *The "New Marketing" has it's own set of P's.* Marketing News, 6, Nov. 1987.
Keller, K. L.: *Brand management.* London 1998.
Kent, R. A.: *Faith in the Four P's: An alternative.* J. of Marketing Management, 2, 1986.
Kotler, P., Armstrong, G., Saunders, J. & Wong, V.: *Principles of Marketing.* Second European Edition. London 1999.
Krugman, H. E.: *The impact of television advertising: Learning without involvement.* Public Opinion Quarterly, 29, 1965.
Leenders, M. R. & Blenkhorn D. L.: *Reverse marketing.* The new buyer-seller relationship. New York 1988.
Lovelock, C. H.: *Services marketing – A European perspective.* Englewood Cliffs, NJ 1991. London 1999.
McCarthy, E. J. & Perrault, W. D. Jr.: *Basic marketing.* Homewood, Ill. 1990.
McDaniels Jr., C. & Gates, R.: *Contemporary marketing research.* Minneapolis/St. Paul 1998.
McKenna, R.: *Marketing is everything.* J. of Marketing, Jan./Feb. 1991.
Nash, E. L.: *Direct marketing strategy: Planning, execution.* New York 1999.
Ottesen, O.: *Noen bemerkninger om bedriftens kontaktparametre.* ("Some comments on a company's contact parameters") Markedskommunikasjon,1,1964.
Ottesen, O. & Kværk, A.: *Segmentering og mediavalg for dagligvarer på basis av merkekjennskap, merkeerfaring og merkeinntrykk.* ("Segmenting buyers and selecting media on the basis of brand awareness, brand experience and brand beliefs".) Markedsføring, 2, (Oslo) 1972.
Ottesen, O.: *Studier i virksomhedens mediabeslutninger.* ("Studies in mass media decisions".) Copenhagen 1973.
Ottesen, O.: *Innføring i markedskommunikasjon.* ("Introduction to marketing communication".) Copenhagen 1977.
Ottesen, O.: *Views of man and research into the primary and secondary effects of advertising.* Copenhagen 1980.
Ottesen, O.: *Long run effects of advertising: A conceptual discussion.* European Research, April 1981(1).
Ottesen, O.: *A theory of short-run response to advertising.* I J. Sheth (ed.): "Research in Marketing", 1981(2).
Ottesen, O.: *Buyer initiative: Ignored, but imperative for marketing management.* Tidvise Skrifter nr. 15, Department for Business, Cultural and Social Studies, Stavanger. University College, Stavanger 1996.
Ottesen, O.: *Markedskommunikasjon – Strategisk helhetsplanlegging for økt lønnsomhet.* ("Marketing communication – Strategic planning for increased profitability"). 1. ed. 1992, 2. ed. Copenhagen 1997.

References

Peter, J. P., Olson, J. C. and Grunert, K. G.: *Consumer behavior and marketing strategy.* European Edition. London 1999.
Petty, R. E. & Cacioppo J. T.: *Central and peripheral routes to persuasion:* Application to advertising. I Percy L. & Woodside A. G. (eds.): "Advertising and consumer psychology", Lexington Books, Lexington, Mass. 1983.
Ries, A. & Trout, J.: *Positioning. The battle of your mind.* New York 1993.
Rotchild, M. L.: *Marketing communications.* Lexington, Mass. 1987.
Russel, S. T. & Lane, W. R.: *Kleppner's advertising procedure.* New York 1990.
Schreiber, A. L.: *Life-style and event marketing: Building the new customer partnership.* New York 1994.
Smith, R. E. & Swinyard, W. R.: *Cognitive responses to advertising and trials: Belief strength, belief confidence and product curiosity.* Journal of Advertising, 17, 1988.
Shimp, T. A.: *Advertising, promotion, and supplemental aspects of integrated marketing communication.* New York 1997.
Schultz, D. E., Tannenbaum, S. I. & Lauterborn, R. F.: *Integrated marketing communications.* Lincolnwood, Ill. 1993.
Spekman, R. E., Kamauff J. W. & Salmond D. J.: *At last purchasing is becoming strategic.* Long Range Planning, 2, 1994.
Starch, D.: *Measuring advertising readership and results.* New York 1966.
Stevens, M.: *Telemarketing in action: A handbook of marketing and sales applications.* London 1995.
Still, R. R., Cundiff, E. W. & Govoni, N. A. P.: *Sales management. Decisions, strategies and cases.* Englewood Cliffs, NJ 1988.
Stobart, P. (ed.): *Brand power.* MacMillan, London 1994.
Trout, J. & Ries, A.: *Positioning cuts through chaos in the marketplace.* I Enis B. M. & Cox K.H. (eds.): "Marketing classics", Boston 1991.
Wells, W. D.: *Brand equities, elephants and birds.* I Aaker D. A. & Biel A. L. (eds.): «Brand equity and advertising. Advertising's role in building strong brands» Erlbaum, Hillsdale, New Jersey 1993.
Webster, F. E.: *Marketing communication.* New York 1971.
Webster, F. E.: *Industrial marketing strategy.* New York 1991.
Webster, F. E.: *The changing role of marketing in the corporation.* Journal of Marketing, Oct., 1992.
Wilton, P. C. & Tse, D. K.: *A model of consumer response to communication and product experience.* I Percy L. & Woodside A. G. (eds.): "Advertising and consumer psychology", Lexington Books, Lexington, Mass. 1983.
Zajonc, R. B.: *Attitudinal effects of mere exposure.* J. of Personality and Social Psychology, 9, 1, 1968.

Subject index

4P paradigm 64

accessibility, handling and follow-up of buyer-initiated orders and inquiries 236
action plan 148, 239, 260, 272, 291
action planning 149, 295
action-encouraging facilitative content 227
actual buyer 112, 166
actual contribution 166
actual demand 166
actual turnover 166
addressee-indicating content 225
advance transformation 93
alphabet 303
areas of use 111
association hypothesis 135

brand building 136
brand salience hypothesis 229, 293
breaking point of response function 283, 286
business areas 54, 63
buyer competence 33, 75, 103, 111, 134, 207
buyer contacted 273
buyer initiative 36, 115, 119, 120, 121, 177, 201, 204, 205, 265, 297
buyer initiative media 148, 234
buyer initiative media strategy 233, 259, 265, 294
buyer initiative proportion 178
buyer initiative ratio 177, 265
buyer initiative sales potential 115, 233, 265, 268

buyer initiative sales volume 115, 155, 180
buyer initiative strategy 39
buyer value 23, 31, 62, 87, 129, 135
buyer-seller relationship 100
buyer's contribution 35, 134
buyer's expectations 133
buyer's route 87
buyer's total experience 31, 41, 70

choice criteria 83
classical conditioning 136
closeness to point of purchase 254
co-communication 311
co-communicator 226
cognitive content 212
communication capacity 45, 248
communication goals 319
communication symbol 43, 45, 302
communication task matrix 125
communicator 226
company reputation 117
competence transformation 40, 95, 96
competing stimuli 252
competitive strength 169, 182, 309
conditioned stimulus 136
contact price 279
contact ratio 272, 278
content 41, 45, 96, 210, 212, 229
content competence 218, 230, 237
content goals 217, 251, 278, 301
content groups 232
content platform 147, 217, 230, 231
content preparedness 218, 230
content strategy 146, 209, 210, 215, 230

Subject index 349

content symbolization 45, 149, 209, 273, 280, 284, 290
contribution less marketing communication costs 158, 331
controllable media 235
core content 146, 215, 221, 223
correspondence between buyer and vendor language 82
cost interdependency 257, 262, 310, 315
credibility-enhancing content 226
cross-communication 310
cross-communication contribution 311
cross-communication costs 311
cross-communication sales potential 311
cross-communication sales volume 311
cross-communication strategy 311
cross-communication turnover 311
cumulative effects 339
customized offering 40, 63, 100, 174, 294, 295

dealer target groups 205
dealer-related buyer initiative media strategy 297
dealer-related seller initiative media strategy 297
dealers 32, 55, 72, 145, 165, 205, 297
dealers offering and communication 32
decision unit 84, 161, 308
degree of (market) penetration of an offering 112
degree of market penetration of an offering 115
degree of utilization of the buyer initiative sales potential 270, 276
delayed effects 339
derived experiences 75
development communication 103
development task 103
direct experiences 75
duration effects 339

elaboration-likelihood hypothesis 229, 293
emotional content 212, 221
emotional core content 215
emotional facilitative content 216, 225
end-buyer target groups 205
end-buyer-related media strategy 297
end-buyers 32, 55, 145, 165, 205, 297
expectations 213, 219
exposure 44, 210
exposure capacity 243
exposure flexibility 250
exposure frequency distribution 246
exposure loyalty 245
exposure maximum 244
extent and nature of buyer initiative 164
extent of communication tasks 163
external organization 56

facilitative content 147, 216
fixed costs 121
framework for describing, monitoring and developing a companys marketing communication strategy 334

guidelines for symbolization competence 304

hard contacts 62, 73
harvesting case 124
hierarchy of effect 319
holistic marketing communication strategy 50, 61, 329
holistic strategic marketing communication planning 21, 39, 59, 143, 151, 152
holistic view of marketing communication 21, 53, 129, 130, 289

image building 136
imperceptible or unverifiable properties of an offering 131
impersonal and personal individual media 44

Subject index

impersonal and personal mass media 44
impersonal communication 43
impersonal individual communication 43
impersonal mass communication 43
in-contacts 62, 73
indifference 114, 116, 174, 295
indifference function 283, 286, 294
individual communication 43
individual content platforms 231, 233, 259, 265
information sources 321, 323, 325, 327
informed judgments 322
inherent properties of an offering 129, 137
initial awareness 210, 224, 303
initial contact 36, 214, 239, 243, 248, 272
initial marketing communication cost budget 156, 158
inquiries 36
inquiry proportion 180
inquiry/initiative ratio 265
inquiry/response ratio 275
intangible products 27
integrated dealer/end-buyer media strategy 298
integrated marketing communications 18
internal organization 56
interpretation 212, 303
intrusive media 210
intrusiveness 251
invitation/inquiry ratio 294

leveling-off value of response function 283
locomotive offering 314
long-range planning 337
long-term effects 337
low-involvement hypotheses 229, 293

main elements of a holistic marketing communication strategy 150

market development 112, 119, 224
Market Map 170, 174
market utilization 112, 119
marketing communication 17, 35, 88
marketing communication budget 50, 151
marketing communication cost budget 20, 158, 330
marketing communication costs 155
marketing communication strategy 55, 57, 59
marketing communication tools 31
marketing offering 31, 32, 34, 40, 41, 69, 88, 95, 100, 169
marketing offering tools 31
marketing strategy 55, 63
marketing tool 27, 31, 61
mass communication 43, 57, 319
media 44
media attitudes and behavior 253
media characteristics 234, 241, 243, 245, 247, 249, 251, 253, 255, 257
media competence 237
media cost budget 149, 243, 263
media cost characteristics 242
media costs 48, 157, 256, 268
media distribution costs 157, 255, 256, 281
media preparedness 236
media production costs 157, 254, 256
media sales characteristics 242
media strategy 44, 148, 233, 259, 262, 294, 295, 297, 299, 306, 315
mere exposure hypothesis 230, 293
multi-period perspective 316, 318
multi-step communication effects 114

nature of communication tasks 163
necessary insight into a marketing offering 87

offering strategy 55, 57
operating budget 156, 263, 310, 330
operative planning 25
order proportion 180

Subject index 351

order sales volume/turnover 156
order/initiative ratio 265
order/invitation ratio 295
order/response ratio 275
orders 36
ordinary internal and external observation and communication 322
organizational basis 55, 63, 71, 169, 263
out-contacts 62, 73
overall contribution 167
overall demand 166
overall exposure goal 239, 248, 291
overall sales volume/turnover 156
overall turnover 167
overlapping 247
overlapping speed 247

penetration rate of an offering 114
personal communication 43
personal individual communication 43
personal mass communication 43
physical product 27
pioneering case 124
planner 26, 331
planning premises analysis 143, 153, 316, 331
points of contact between buyers and the companys organizational basis 61, 70
positioning 136
post-control 318
post-purchase experience 294
potential buyer 112, 166
potential demand 166
pre- and post-purchase experience 41, 114, 137
pre-control 318
preference 114, 116, 173, 295
preference function 283, 286
preliminary assumptions regarding content symbolization 237, 241, 251, 260, 271, 278
preparatory plan 148, 239, 261, 272
preparatory planning 236, 239, 272, 296

primary analyses 323
Prioritization Path 201, 203, 207
probability evaluation 213
problem solving role 92
process transformation 94
product 27
product penetration 110
product visibility 115
product/market matrix 54
product/market strategy 54
profitability criteria 190, 194
prolonged attention 213, 224
pull-strategy 206
purchase/inquiry ratio 266
purchase/order ratio 265
purchase/response ratio 273
purchasing or user/consumer role 34, 76, 103, 134
push-and-pull strategy 297
push-strategy 206, 296

qualitative analyses 324
quantitative analysis 324

real-time information 337
receipt, handling and follow-up of orders and inquiries 51
receipt, handling and follow-up of resulting orders and inquiries 148, 239
rejection 114, 116
rejection function 283, 286
relevance criteria 82, 84, 96, 308
relevance criteria segments 85
relevance evaluation 212
reminder effect 287
repetition 280
response 283, 289, 295
response function 281, 295
response function for a durable product 286
response functions for non-durable products 286
response/contact ratio 273

sacrifices and rewards 31, 70, 73, 75, 132

sales function 281
saturation level 109
secondary analyses 323
selective processes 283
seller initiative 19, 36, 120, 201, 205
seller initiative contribution potential 277
seller initiative gap 155, 156, 179, 233, 236, 271, 277
seller initiative media 148, 235, 253
seller initiative strategy 39, 312
separate communication 312
services 27
soft contacts 62, 73
standard communication 40, 91, 95
standard market 39, 40, 221
standardized offering 39, 112, 116, 119
stepped costs 121
stepped media costs 256
strategic management 26
strategic media plan 148, 291
strategic planning 25, 26
strategy 19, 53
strategy development 26
strategy in real time 337
sub-exposure-goals 239, 278, 280
sub-strategies 54, 57
sub-target groups 191, 231
sufficient knowledge 171, 214
supplier criteria 95, 96, 308
surrogate effect 131
switching costs 100
symbol structure 45, 209, 301
symbolization capacity 45, 147, 209, 250, 271, 296
symbolization competence 304
symbolization cost budget 149
symbolization costs 48, 157, 306, 331
symbolization guidelines 303
symbolization strategy 149, 301, 303

tangible products 27
target buyer 192
target group 145, 190, 192
target group overlap 312
target group strategy 145, 189, 192, 205
task analysis 126, 145, 163, 165, 185, 308, 315, 316
task profile 177, 185
task structure 170, 172, 174, 175, 178, 180
tasks of marketing communication 35, 49, 106, 129, 135
tendering role 92
"the buyer's route" 71, 72, 75, 98
threshold response functions 293
timing flexibility 254
total business strategy 54
transformation communication 40, 92, 95, 97, 119, 230, 296
transformation market 40, 63, 91, 100, 120, 173, 180, 221, 294
types of systematic analysis 323

unconditioned stimulus 135
uncontrollable media 235
use of information sources 325

value adding through marketing communication 138
variable costs 121, 256
vendor roles 91, 93
viability criteria 189

word-of-mouth 41, 114
working models 237, 266, 304

Notes

1   See for example Webster 1971, DeLozier 1976, Rotchild 1987, Fill 1995, and Shimp 1997.

2   See for example Blackwell 1987, Schultz, Tannenbaum & Lauterborn 1993, Fill 1999, Shimp 1997, and Kotler, Armstrong, Saunders & Wong 1999.

3   See for example Comer 1991 and Clabaugh & Forbes 1992 (personal selling), Batra, Myers & Aker 1995 and Russel & Lane 1990 (advertising), Stevens 1995 (telemarketing), Nash 1999 (direct mail), Schreiber 1994 (event marketing) and Chaffey, Mayer, Johnston & Ellis-Chadwick 2000 (Internet marketing).

4   Examples of textbooks within various sub-fields are: Bradley 1995 and Kotler, Armstrong, Saunders & Wong 1999 (consumer marketing/mass produced consumer products), Webster 1991, Gross, Banting & Ford 1993, Hutt & Speh 1995 (industrial marketing), and Grönroos 2000, Lovelock 1999 and Berry & Parasuraman 1991 (service marketing/consumer markets).

5   Related terms/concepts are "consumer value" and "customer value". The wider term/concept "buyer value" is preferred here to cover all kinds of buyer. Buyers need not necessarily be "consumers" or "customers". They may be e.g. "industrial buyers" and "potential customers".

6   See for example Peter, Olson & Grunert 1999 (consumer behavior) and Anderson & Narus 1999 (chapters on industrial buyer behavior).

7   See for example DeLozier 1976, pp. 91-95.

8   The "optimal" is used here to denote the solution a planner – or the offering a buyer – would choose provided he had perfect knowledge of all relevant circumstances.

9   The present writer presented the following terms/concepts and hypotheses together with a discussion of strategic implications of buyer initiative in Ottesen 1996. The marketing literature only scant attention has been paid to the existence and strategic relevance of buyer initiative. However, hypotheses regarding "active information seeking" can be found in any textbook on consumer behavior. Leenders & Blenkhorn 1988 ("reverse marketing") and

Spekman & Kanuff 1994 ("strategic purchasing") are examples of writers emphasizing active purchasing behavior on the part of industrial buyers.

10   A "symbol" is (often) defined as "a stimulus *representing* (for a person) something different from itself".

11   In the following the terms "segment" and "category" are used interchangeably.

12   See for example Kotler, Armstrong, Saunders & Wong 1999 (the augmented product) and Grönroos 1990 (the augmented service offering).

13   Although the perspective on marketing presented here is wider and more general, it is in accordance with views held by writers on industrial and service marketing. The terms "front stage" and "back stage" are, for example, widely used within the service management/marketing literature. Grönroos 1990 uses the term "line of visibility" to denote relevant contacts between buyers and the organization. Webster 1992 and Gummesson 1990 puts strong emphasis on the relevance of the whole organization in marketing.

For discussions of the 4P paradigm, see for example Kent 1986, Keeley 1987, Berry 1990, McKenna 1991 and Browlie & Saren 1992.

14   Several different terms are used in the literature to denote concepts similar to those which is termed here as "sacrifices and rewards", "total experience", and "(net) buyer value". Lovelock 1991, for instance, applies terms such as "customer value", "gross value", "costs" and "net value". He defines "costs" (p. 237) as the sum of monetary prices, time, physical efforts, sensory costs, and psychic costs. He defines "customer net value" as: "The sum of all benefits (gross value) minus the sum of all perceived costs". (See note 5.)

15   The concept of "service blueprinting" (Grönroos 1990, chapter 15) may be understood as a way of "traveling along the buyer's route" in service markets.

16   Buyer behavior literature offers several hypotheses regarding the relationship between what is termed here as properties of an offering, relevance criteria and sacrifices/rewards. One example is the "means-end-chain" hypothesis which assumes that that relevance criteria are formed in chains starting with concrete "product attributes" and ending with "terminal values". See for example Peter, Olson & Grunert 1999.

17   It should be noted that the term "job production" is widely used in connection with customized products (offerings). However, the author finds this term to be too narrow (and focused on "production") to connote the various types of vendor roles, customization processes, communication tasks etc.

18 Regarding buyer-seller relationships, see for example Jackson 1985 and Webster 1992.

19 The relationship between communication tasks and product penetration/ degree of penetration of the offering has received only scant attention in the literature. It should, however, be mentioned that as much as 60 years ago Otto Kleppner introduced a theory termed "the advertising spiral" in which he operates with three different stages, i.e. "the pioneering stage", "the competitive stage" and "the retentive stage". According to Kleppner, at the pioneering stage advertising content should focus on properties of the (generic) product, at the competitive stage on properties of the brand, and at the retentive stage on reminding of the existence of the brand. (See Russel & Lane 1990.)

20 This point of view is further elaborated in Ottesen 1980.

21 Hypotheses regarding the importance of meeting buyer expectations have been discussed especially within the service marketing literature. See for example Berry & Parasuraman 1991, chapter 4: "Managing and exceeding customer expectations".

22 See for example Aaker, Batra & Myers 1992 and Assael 1992.

23 See Aaker, Batra & Myers 1992, p. 70.
Advertising by which experience of using a brand is *transformed* or changed into something quite different, is termed "redefinition advertising" by some writers: The advertising "redefines" the product (offering). Some authors use the term "transformational advertising". See Wells 1993.

24 See for example Ries & Trout 1993, Trout & Ries 1991, Stobart 1994 and Keller 1998.

25 Regarding the Marlboro example, see for example Assael 1992, Batra, Myers & Aaker 1995 and Peter, Olson & Grunert 1999.

26 Regarding the concept of "badge value", see for instance Assael 1992, pp. 32-33.

27 Regarding "classical conditioning", see for instance Aaker & Biel 1993, Assael 1992, Batra, Myers & Aaker 1995 and Peter, Olson & Grunert 1999.

28 Among the very few contributions are Deighton 1984, Wilton & Tse 1983 and Smith & Swinyard 1988.

29 See for example Allen & Madden 1985, Trout & Ries 1991, Aaker & Biel 1993, Stobart 1994, and Keller 1998.

30 The variable unit costs are assumed here to be constant (proportional). Examples of costs that may be included in variable unit costs are costs connected to discounts, wages, (raw) materials, complaint handling and guarantee and service. Variable unit costs may also include communication costs such as costs connected to a set of printed directions for use accompanying each product unit. For the sake of simplicity such costs are left out of account here.

The concept of constant variable unit costs does not make sense in transformation markets. Each individual customized offering will incur a certain amount of direct costs and bring a certain contribution.

31 When assessing competitive strength a planner should, of cause, consider the possibility and probability of counter-actions on the part of competitors to (changed/improved) properties of the offering.

32 The Market Map model was introduced by the present author in Ottesen & Kværk 1972, based upon the advertising response theory published in Ottesen 1973 (doctorial thesis). The model was further elaborated in Ottesen 1977. The response theory as well as the Market Map was presented and discussed in English in Ottesen 1981 (2).

33 Strictly speaking, 1 (one) should be added to the denominator to prevent the ratio from converging towards infinity as the minimum seller initiative proportion approaches 0 (zero). If 1 is added to the minimum seller initiative proportion, the buyer initiative ratio will approach 100.

34 Any textbook on buyer behavior discusses the relevance of motivation and various types of problem solving. See for example Assael 1992 and Peter, Olson & Grunert 1999.

35 Most textbooks – especially those on advertising – touches on the issue of content selection ("message strategy"). See for example DeLozier 1976, Rotchild 1987 and Batra, Myers & Aaker 1995. Terms such as "creative approaches" and "creative appeals" are widely used to characterize various types of content. Emotional content is often termed "emotional appeals". In the literature on personal selling discussions of content selection may be found under headings such as "theories of selling", "selling approaches", "presentation structures" and "handling objections". See for example Still, Cundiff & Govoni 1988 and Comer 1991.

36 This hypothesis originates from Krugman 1965.

37 This hypothesis originates from Petty & Cacioppo 1983.

38 This hypothesis originates from Zajonc 1968.

Notes 357

39 Aaker, Batra & Myers 1992 and Assael 1992 offer good summaries of various low-involvement hypotheses.

40 The media (magazine reading) habits assumed this highly simplified example are, of course, not found in reality. However, in practice it makes sense to work with groups of buyers reading (approximately) every issue (being 100% loyal), reading *on the average* every second issue (being 50% loyal), reading every third issue etc.

41 The issue of media selection is dealt with explicitly in the advertising literature only under headings such as "media strategy" and "media selection". See for example Rotchild 1987, Russel & Lane 1990, Batra, Myers & Aaker 1995 and Shimp 1997. The literature on personal selling deals with related questions such as "how to "optimize salesmen's calling frequency (related to the question of exposure frequency) and timing of calls (related to the question of timing of exposures). The literature within the other sub-fields of marketing communication contributes scantly to the issue of developing a media strategy. In general within all sub-fields the issue is dealt with on a tactical – not a strategic – level. See for example Still, Cundiff & Govoni 1988 and Comer 1991.

42 This formula is derived from the expression:

   seller initiative gap = number of buyers in the target group requiring seller initiative * response/contact ratio * purchase/response ratio * average purchase

43 The following is based on a theory developed by the author in Ottesen 1973, further developed in Ottesen 1997 and published in English in Ottesen 1981 (2). Most textbooks in advertising deals with response functions. See for example Batra, Myers & Aaker 1955.

44 Obviously, the desired exposure frequency corresponds to the breaking point in an indifference function.

45 Our discussion of response functions has not considered possible implications of multi-step communication effects, i.e. word-of-mouth and product visibility. Quite obviously the leveling-off value of a buyer's response function increases to the extent that he influences others to purchase an offering.

46 The issue of symbolization is dealt with in the advertising literature under headings such as "advertising copy", "copy writing" and "advertising layout". See for example Rotchild 1987, Batra, Myers & Aaker 1995, and Shimp 1997.

47 See for example Starch 1966 and Batra, Myers & Aaker 1995.

48 The idea of using "advertising goals" was introduced in Colley 1961. See also Batra, Myers & Aaker 1995. The term used here, "communication goal", is general and relates to any kind of marketing communication.

49 See for example Batra, Myers & Aaker 1995 and Shimp 1997.

50 See for example Churchill 1994 and McDaniels & Gates 1998.

51 Hitherto the issue of long-term effects has received scant attention in the literature. See Ottesen 1980 and 1981 (1).